Alabama's Mitcham Wars

Essaying Mortal Wounds

With best wishes,

Jerry Brown

Alabama's Mitcham Wars

Essaying Mortal Wounds

Jerry Elijah Brown

LOOKING GLASS BOOKS

Alabama's Mitcham Wars: *Essaying Mortal Wounds*

Published by Looking Glass Books, Inc.
Decatur, Georgia

The cover image is believed, based on a photograph of the elderly Elijah Brown, to be the same man (see p. 262). Elijah Brown (1840-1920) was the younger brother of Peter Irvine Brown, and the author of this book was named for him. The tintype (c. 1875) was found in the papers of the late Nora Brown Huggins, a granddaughter of Peter Brown.

ISBN: 978-1-929619-44-3

Book and cover design by Burtch Hunter Design

For John Coley and Alliene Etheredge Brown,
Who from their labors rest,
And for their descendants . . .

These are the researches of Herodotus of Halicarnassus, which he publishes, in the hope of thereby preserving from decay the remembrance of what men have done . . . and to put on record what were their grounds of feud.

—

THE HISTORY OF HERODOTUS, C. 450 BC

CONTENTS

Alabama's Mitcham Wars

Essaying Mortal Wounds

INTRODUCTION

SUGGESTIVE FACTS

Death is always a suggestive fact . . .

—

THE REV. TIMOTHY H. BALL
*A Glimpse into the Great South-East, or Clarke County, Alabama
and Its Surroundings* (1879)

A wise old friend, also an Alabamian, put it to me direct not long
ago. "Peter Brown has lain in his grave more than a hundred years waiting for a descendant to tell the Mitcham Beat story from a Mitcham
perspective," he wrote, "and if you don't he's going to rise up from that
gully dirt and beat you to death with his wooden leg."

Straightway, I set out, searching. The resultant book, I hasten to
say, is less a response to a call from the grave by my great-grandfather
and more than the history of a forgotten, bloody, and beleaguered district of lower Alabama. In the process of trying to write a family history, I found myself musing on a ligature fundamental to life in a
democracy, or, for that matter, civic accord anywhere. To be sure, it's
an abstract linkage. I refer to that joining of the private person or
family with the body politic, or the commonweal, or the republic, or

whatever label is put on representative government. Upon that ancient though oft-overlooked isthmus, my attention came to dwell.

This old theme has lain in the clay longer than Peter Brown's bones, but it arose from his particular grave only after I'd begun to explore an incident in the early life of one of his sons, Lee Brown, my grandfather. In the current family's collective memory, his life looms above all others. Lee Brown, named for the general his father wished he'd fought under, was born in 1871, when the state was still occupied, and Federal (meaning, Civil War, Yankee) soldiers were posted at both Selma and Mobile. He died in 1960, as the Civil Rights Movement was raging across the latest of New Souths. In retrospect, his life frames a century, and, though he lived six decades in the twentieth century, he was very much a man of the nineteenth. He was distinct in his manners; he carried himself formally, cane and moustache; he was merry by temperament but not to be trifled with. Given his enthralling stories of life in Mitcham Beat, all of us grandchildren thought we knew him well.

Yet, as I learned long after his death, in his early twenties Lee Brown had been arrested, tried in a coroner's court and then in a county court, and jailed for a killing called a murder. Lee Brown was not convicted, but the incident was reported widely in Alabama papers, in stories rife with errors; one even said he had been lynched. As children, we heard nothing about it, from him or our parents or other people who knew about that killing. In a community in which lively talk, enlargements, and embroideries were commonplace, the story of that one slaying lay hidden. All I knew was that at the end of a bloody episode called the Mitcham War in the early 1890s, a man named Pink or Pinkerton, vaguely described as a bully, had been killed, but nothing in those accounts linked my grandfather to the killing or even to the main story of what came to be called the Mitcham War.

The killing happened in late November of 1894, more than fifty years before I was born. The circumstances were simple and complex, as I will strive to explain. That slaying, or execution, appears to me as more than an act of vengeance or a sensational climax to a bloody feud between yeoman farmers and town merchants. Now it seems to me as one community's achievement of justice and as a political watershed.

In the last days of the genocidal twentieth century, the obscure story of a feud in a remote backwoods section in Alabama that left ten people dead in the last decade of the nineteenth century would have struck most readers as inconsequential. Now, as we enter the second decade of the even more threatening twenty-first, the story strikes me, basically a reporter, as, for want of a better word, *newsworthy*.

The public angles are manifold—terrorism, a collapsing economy driven by greed and corruption, Wall Street manipulation, free trade, rich vs. poor, ethnic cleansing, sensational media, and hapless, oblivious people. Just like us. In another sense, this story is not newsworthy at all. It's merely another variation on the theme of a marginalized people working their way into the muddy mainstream. *Rags to riches* it is not. If one measures magnitude by body count, it is not worth public attention. I obviously think otherwise, else I wouldn't have written this book, for in the boldest outline, the story I have to tell and the community I describe are universal. The blood, terror, and trial herein reported all tell of pioneers becoming full-fledged citizens, engaged in the public arena, moving from troublous clan into turbulent commonwealth.

The private story that merges with the public is another matter: Could the grandfather I knew in the 1950s have been the young killer of the 1890s? Given the evidence I discovered long after Lee Brown's death, I wonder how he could have lived a life so merrily, apparently without remorse, after his name had been spread across daily papers and he identified as a "murderer" from "Clarke County's Criminal Colony"? And I have entertained the counter thought, "Why the hell *not* merrily?"

I can't reconcile images of Lee Brown as a younger man, gleaned from newspaper accounts and stories told about him, and memories of the real man I knew for the final fifteen years of his life; however, I can see a little clearer through the darkling glass by placing his actions against the backdrop of Mitcham Beat history. More than curiosity about one family has kept me going. I've been after a better understanding of that small place where I was born, where, within a short span, versions of injustice and justice stood in stark contrast. And I've wanted to examine whatever roles my private and public grandfather played in both.

The essence of Mitcham Beat is part and parcel of every word in this book. I wish there were less essence and more exactitude, but as successive generations lived and died, they left few public records, even fewer private records. All that is left within our family are fragments of handed-down stories and random details. The documents and news reports I have found do help to clarify the events. Still and all, what I have in the main is a rag box for making quilt covers of many patterns. This patchwork is mine. I can't tell the whole truth, because no truth is whole, no matter what people swear to in court. Inasmuch as I claim to be a journalist, I have tried not to make up anything, yet I acknowledge that imagination is at play; nevertheless, I hope that facts are accurate and opinions evident.

Whatever this book may be called, it is not a work of fiction, a novel. I don't intend to make those ancestors, who were once flesh and blood, into heroic or, at worst, pitiable characters, for many good reasons. For one, I am afraid of their judgment. They weren't, by and large, extraordinary, nor were they the crude characters that make for conventional grotesquerie. Moreover, many mysteries inform me that I may someday see them, face-to-face, across Jordan's stormy banks.

I have attempted to *essay*, using the term in the old sense, as the trying of a subject, the way a case at the bar is tried. The aim is to illuminate the subject, or, put another way, to expose it. Though, as Mark Twain said, much information is spewed, this is not a scholarly book, or, for that matter, a simplistic history. The logic—or lack thereof—is entirely my own, and my writing is intended to inform and to spark as much as to convince.

About the language and the ordering of this book: I was raised around many very old country people, most of them more intelligent, brave, and resilient than I ever will be, though with minimal formal education, who talked in an old-timey vernacular. Their manner of speech comes most readily to me. They liked taking up subjects, at home or in the field, and, without knowing the word, essaying them, with many voices chiming in, with facts undocumented or obscured by speculation, but with comments rich in details. I expect most of us raised in insular communities hear similar voices, never dead. The antique voices I hear tell long, often ambiguous, stories, and leave off tidy conclusions. Old words crop up, old cadences take over: "It's got to where here lately I can't get about like I use to. . ." That sort of turn.

Though I have ventured far from Mitcham Beat, those voices have never been educated out of my system. At times, I've been ashamed enough of my own background, which I do not intend to romanticize, to wish the voices could have been silenced by an act of will, but I'm now glad they kept speaking. For me their stories, cross-hatched with digressions, provide the context, or, to use an old figure, thicken the gravy. Such rambling and revealing discourse is no longer in fashion, I regret to say, but that slow-paced talk, so antithetical to this world of superficial, chatterbox electronics, brings its own cheer. This circular exploration seems natural, though it is not. Nature is a more singular force.

My father, graver of temperament than his father and chary of the public airing of private matters, knew more of the Mitcham details than I ever will. He carried that history around in his head, turning it the way he used to turn his snuffbox or his pocket knife on his rocking-chair arm, ruminating. He's been dead for forty years, but if he were here he'd try to warn me off writing about murders and what he called The Old Place. He'd say something along the lines of, "Let the matter rest, for our hands are not clean either." A subtle fellow, he'd know that such a show of repression would be all the spur I needed.

When I was twelve years old, my father was sixty, and he had come to meditate on history—not simply that of Mitcham Beat and Clarke County but also of the country generally and especially of early Alabama. For one example: Not long before he died, when I was a graduate student at Vanderbilt, my father and I were off hunting in the Clarke County woods. We stopped and sat on a log to eat biscuits filled with tenderloin pork, home-churned butter, and pear preserves, a meal my mother had made, and he turned to me, as if expecting a response, and said, "I dreamed about Sam Dale last night." (For those unversed in frontier history, Dale was the Daniel Boone of Alabama and the county to which our ancestors came from South Carolina was named for him.)

In another age, my dad would have been a first-rate historian or an editor. Newspapers and magazines were his university, and he relished the reading, the finding of mistakes of fact, the typographical errors—all this from a man who basically followed a plow and with my mother raised a passel of chirren. If he were around to read this book, he'd find many nuances lost on me. He is, more or less, my major source for the scant details and the large attitudes that inform this writing, and I'd be happiest if I thought my report would please him. He was generally good natured, but he was born with a critical compulsion. Every compliment he ever gave me concluded with a qualifier: Whatever I had succeeded at as a student was fine, *but*. . . . Still, he meant to be encouraging: I had not quite measured up to the brightest of the town boys, but I was on my way.

John Coley Brown, my father, was born in August 1897 and was the first child of Lee and Mattie Mott Brown. He was his father's alter ego. The two men, Lee and Coley, were different in almost every obvious way: the father thin and sinewy and living in the present; the son as broad-shouldered as his maternal grandfather, Jack Mott, and prone to brood on the past; the elder bold and linear, the younger cautious and lateral; the old man always active, his son a born contemplative. I wonder if any boy could have grown up around two men so connected by blood and affection who personified greater contrast. As these habits of mind suggest, each had his own kind of strength and his own weakness, but they complemented each other in notable ways. They had the same values, the same immense physical strength, and the same personal resolve, or, if you will, stubbornness, a refusal to be bossed. However different, they epitomized a middle class in our part of the South; they were subsistence farmers and loggers, free-holding peasants, yeomen, living in an enclave of sorts.

I do believe that my father and I would agree on the essential questions: How did that "war" happen? Was there a right and a wrong, and if so to what degree? And what about that last killing, in which his own father was either triggerman or accomplice? And that larger question— what combination of motives and opportunities propelled us from a remote, provincial society into one in which larger, public engagement was considered essential to survival? Put bluntly, why should we have given a damn about the general public? Why could we not be secure, confident, peaceful?

Large forces were afoot in the outward mobility of most of our family—better education, more options, more money, social shifts, fortunate outcrossings—yet I believe that something particular in that Mitcham Beat experience was the prime mover. Though more than a few of our bunch have continued to live in quiet rustication, resistant, waiting for the world to pass us by and not wanting to get engaged with forces that would do us in, what seems to me an uncommon number have opted for risky, public lives. Citizens who had held to the notion they could exist forever in isolation without establishing connections to a wider world were educated in a hot crucible. And the scorching lesson stuck.

Like other groups who've attracted ridicule and persecution, we became the sort of folks who'd venture into areas in which we were outclassed, if temporarily, take on the consequences, endure the embarrassments, and, generally, take delight in the conflict. The central question for me, as I am in the homestretch of my life, is why would we, the most backwoods of people, have ventured into such danger? Is our audacity driven by fear, or anger, or ambition? Or is it simply that we love a good fight? And will future generations be so smug or uneducated and encapsulated in their own ways that they'll eventually face the same Mitcham Beat dilemma? Or are all of these merely rhetorical questions?

As outcast as Mitcham War survivors were, we were somehow, by hook or crook, or action of the Almighty, not to be outlasted or outsmarted. And much that I have learned in this history of one family supports that surmise. Though this story reflects a general American experience, in which ethnic groups struggle with the tension between group think and assimilation, in its particulars this account of Mitcham Beat stands alone.

Even if they'd wanted to, my grandfather and father could not have told me the story about those Mitcham Beat killings and how they related to the sorry way of life in Clarke County, Alabama, of the 1890s, at least in a way I could understand as a boy. That is probably because they didn't understand it themselves. Nettling enigmas and old grudges kept the talk going. The digressive, fascinating sidebars further concealed any central narrative. In the hearing of history, told in this way, laced with its confusions and contradictions, I absorbed what other children of Mitcham Beat in the middle twentieth century did: Hushed but dramatic accounts, told around firesides, usually, about night riders and murders and people hiding in wells and chimneys and women forced to cook for a mob of vigilantes, with way too many mysterious ellipses for a youngster to follow.

That fear meshed neatly with others of that time: the fear that we would be blown away by an atomic bomb (our teachers said Brookley Field in Mobile was a prime target for the Communists) and all that talk of the Last Days, the End Time, prophesied from pulpits and from Garner Ted Armstrong, on "The World Tomorrow," ironically titled because that radio ranter and certifiable charlatan predicted the Second Coming and a hearse backed up to every front door. And then there were the horror movies, in which atomically infused mutant monster insects, or creatures from black lagoons, terrified helpless citizens. Mostly, from these several sources, what I picked up was a legacy of fear, and its counterpart, a rising in the blood, a striking out, against all forces that use fear as a bludgeon. But it is more than a simple knee jerk reaction to fear that has put me to thinking. I may be making too fine a point when I say that there's a difference between reflexively responding to fear and working one's way deliberatively away from the hateful self-centeredness that ordinary fear engenders.

Granted, this subtle distinction may be lost on some, but to me the difference is substantial.

One injustice motivating my journalism is that little good has been spoken or written of Mitcham Beat. That backwoods community never got fair press coverage during the Mitcham War, and even that conflict has been largely ignored by Southern historians with no ties to the county. John Simpson Graham, editor of *The South Alabamian* in Jackson, a town on the lower Tombigbee run by men with a cold meanness in their hearts, during and long after the Mitcham War, endorsed the mob's unlawful acts to stamp out lawlessness. Graham's feeble attempt to rationalize a vigilante raid that merely concealed a feckless and corrupt government rings more and more hollow as the years pass. Isaac Grant, publisher of *The Clarke County Democrat*, venerated though he might be as a pioneer journalist, was a pragmatic man, connected by blood and business to the mob. The Mobile papers were even worse. Sloppy reporting, tabloid-hysteria, and broadside stereotyping were accepted as fact. But, as even Mitcham people knew, there were enough bad characters that settlement to make any idealistic defense absurd.

The greatest injustice, which further impels me to write, remains a lingering indictment of those people in Mitcham caught in the crossfire between killing forces, with no ready escape and no recourse in law.

Though Grandpa Peter Brown may still come at me with that wooden leg, I will try my best to answer his call. The mysteries I will approach are more than any one person can fully describe, much less resolve. To borrow that great word from Brother Timothy Ball's famous 1879 history of Clarke County, published more than a decade before the Mitcham War, all I can offer is a "glimpse" and that from only one vantage.

To express this bind in yet another rural-route metaphor: I can't shuck this ear of corn and shell it clean all by my lonesome. When I'm done there'll be a-plenty of kernels left on the cob for somebody else. With just that kind of countrified imagery, an old man whose ways I learned by heart, who apparently considered himself neither quaint nor curious—nor, I believe, a murderer—would have started out.

NIGHT THOUGHTS, APRIL 29, 2010

The bedroom is dark. It has been a memorable day, one I have kept to myself. Fifty years ago this afternoon, my grandfather died. But I am thinking less of him than of this moment, when I am alive. My wife is asleep beside me, and my head rests on a pillow my mother made from cotton my father had brought home from the gin, lord knows how many decades ago. The pillow is stuffed with the samples taken after our one or two bales had been banded in burlap. The first ginning I remember was at Whatley, across Clarke County, Alabama, from Mitcham Beat, nearer the Alabama River and on the Southern Railway. It was 1949, and I'd just turned four. We had one of the few pickup trucks lined up among the mule-drawn wagons. Later, we went to a gin in Grove Hill, the county seat. After the baling, a narrow, long knife would be used to excise a strip for grading—usually fair-to-middling. Then my father would be given an object, that sampling of our labor, with the clean cotton fluffed out on each end of brown-paper binding, like a big dog bone.

From some of those samples, my mother made my pillow, and many others. My wife is disgusted by the lumpy thing, with its coarse-woven, blue-lined ticking. She wonders why I would prefer it to feather or foam, but she tolerates it and puts it in double cases, the outer trimmed in eyelet to refine the rawness underneath. It has been with me from Alabama, through Tennessee, Virginia, New Hampshire, back to Alabama, to Montana, now to the mountains of North Carolina. Like many from the old place, I fled far across the muddy Mississippi. Now that my work in the West is done, I am lying awake, rusticated in the Blue Ridge, ruminating and reflecting, like other prodigals and exiles. Over all my travels, I have always thought of returning to some hallowed place, but where?

All that I have is the talisman I curl under my head. Back and forth, my mind moves: abstract to concrete, general to particular, a loom of thought. I've invested much history in the comforting old cotton pillow—the reasons for our people coming from Germany, Scotland, England, Ireland, Wales, and Switzerland, seeking a fresh chance in church and commerce; the knowledge gained from mountaineer whites, Indians, and Africans, our fellow Americans; the blending of many cultures and manners; the restlessness and hopes for prosperity; the resistance to authority; the failures of the Jeffersonian notion of yeomanry; the fiber plant that drove the Southern economy to greed, pretense, and catastrophe; my grandfather's insistence that my father was not planting enough cotton; my childhood in our hardscrabble cotton patch; my dad and his dealings with bankers and bollweevils, fire ants and nutgrass; my energy-charged mother and her remarkable make-do creativity; remembrances of aching backs and Watkins

Liniment; the smell of a cottonhouse; and, thanks to the good Lord and the U.S. government, the coming of the Soil Bank plan, which paid us not to plant cotton. Unwittingly, I witnessed the end of an era.

The pillow connects me to a particular place and time in southwest Alabama and to a blood feud that involved my family and changed a way of life forever. How that cotton-driven economy related to an episode of terror inspires leaps of logic that only one of my background, at this time of night, can make with irrational ease. Without having felt the hope, fear, disappointment, defeat, and resilience handed down from the old people, such night thoughts as mine would not exist, much less be recorded.

Now, as sleep approaches, a disjunctive ritual begins. The racket of an ordinary day fades. Everyday worries and topical musings are displaced by feelings and images planted deep. As tempests depart and my mind lists where it will, I envision scenes and hear the voices of Mitcham Beat. They speak, unbidden, in the old idioms, unconscious or uncaring of currently proper speech. Faces of wrinkled and musing talkers appear, active, even urgent. At this dark hour, they are not dead. They are a complicated bunch of people, each person a set of paradoxes, about whom no simplistic, linear narrative would suit.

The graveyards in Mitcham Beat that I know well—Oak Grove, New Prospect, and Bell-Brewer—are full of life. On tombstones in Oak Grove, I see the names of Jack Brown and the memorial to Eula Ann, lying elsewhere in her lonely grave, and those of Peter and Winnie Truett Brown, Lee and Mattie Mott Brown, John Coley and Alliene Etheredge Brown, and my brother Charles LeRoy—five generations, two centuries, one cemetery.

But for a few of us, these folks would be forever forgotten. The most financially fortunate of their descendants are well-educated and living in the best neighborhoods in Mobile, Atlanta, and Nashville, as well as in inconsequential Northern and Western cities. The least financially fortunate, but probably the happiest, are school dropouts living in tidy double-wides with 60-inch flat-screen TVs and cheering for the Crimson Tide. But wherever we've come to perch precariously on the social scale, most of us know, generally, how much is owed to ancestors. I doubt that many wonder about a specific period in which was shattered the illusion that seclusion offers safety. And many wouldn't agree with me regarding the role of the Mitcham conflict in propelling us into another political arena. Yet what seems to me a disproportionate number of descendants have become elected officials, managers, lawyers, public servants, journalists, and teachers. What would otherwise seem to be ordinary American upward mobility obscures the driving violence and fear which came to a head in the early 1890s.

Which is not to say this family was a monolith. It was probably never as united as it was in 1894. A permanent monument to internal strife is evident in Oak Grove graveyard, where the families of two brothers are buried as far apart as possible. The spat between the brothers was over religion and was resolved only after some members of their families had died while they were on the outs. So, the brothers remain at some eternal distance. But the old blood proved thick in the crisis that I will describe. At a critical point in their later lives more than three decades after they had left together for to be soldiers, the two brothers and their individual families stood together, on home ground, against an enemy more threatening than Yankee soldiers or a vigilante mob.

Try as I might to isolate one story from others, brothers' quarrels are subsumed in family connections and related to their setting aside of intrafamily squabbling to counter an imminent threat to their families and land. Unlike Confederates in the national conflict, in Mitcham

Beat they could call upon a ready reserve, neighbor-and-kin allies whom they could trust for support. The interlacings of bloodlines are typically tangled. There, in Oak Grove and at the other two family cemeteries, these Brown brothers' dead lie amongst the neighbors and kin of several generations—Brunsons, Truetts, Huttos, Hugginses, Bedsoles, Brewers, Otts, Smiths, Etheredges, Woodhams, Geigers, Norrises, Hares, Goodmans, Hutchinsons, Mauldins, and Urquharts. Over more than six decades, I have wandered amongst various tombstones, in these three cemeteries, each with its story. Narratives have accrued, as if, in bankers' lingo, each tombstone is gaining interest. Every one of these now-dead people had, over the years, mingled by blood and other bondings with the others. And now their offspring have scattered and spread, seeds in the breezes of time.

Rather than catalogs of the dead, as sleep approaches, the names on the gravestones come back to me as connected people, alive and passionate, still caught up in survival and raging to have their public lives illuminated. But names taken alone tell no stories, have no life.

In the wide spaces left by time and change, these interlinking dead form a chorus, keening the lay of the last survivors: Too much, the world has too much room. The ghosts wander about, begging someone to tell them the stories of their lives. My old friend's admonition comes back to haunt me: Peter Brown has lain in his grave, with his wooden leg, waiting for the Mitcham side of history to be told. An absurd thought that is. In whatever rational mind I have left, particularly at this time of night, a sensible voice tells me that I can't do it: I'm too ignorant, too trapped in my own time. And why should I presume to speak for them? And who gives a damn anyway? In one rebellious quarter of my brain, I say, as I have so many times, to hell with that place, and everything backward and despicable about it. There's no epic tale here, much less a set of fully realized characters. Yet, as my mind circles back to rationalizing, there's enough evidence from five or six generations to humble the proud and to raise up the humble. As one fortunate enough to have been born where and when I was, and to have had the right parents, I want to feel a smattering of smugness: I'm glad to be amongst those lucky enough to've escaped that backwoods borderland, those provincial, proud, poor, and prickly people. Let the dead bury the dead.

Would that such a notion would bring me peace of mind and swift sleep. Yet the thoughts race on. Those lively dead won't let me rest.

As these obsessings begin to wear themselves out, I hear an unmistakable sound, setting a ground tone like the drone of a bagpipe. It is the voice of my grandfather, Lee Brown, Papa. The sound begins as a mumble, cadenced and steady, taking me back to the fireplace room in our house, our old dogtrot house, in Antioch, in the McLeod's Beat, the house where my memory was kindled, before he died across the hall. And after the sound, come the images. Memory, accurate or not, for how can I tell, takes over.

As my disjointed thoughts wander, it is 1956 in the winter after Grandma Brown has died. I am going on eleven, in the fifth grade, Miss Kathleen Davis's class, at Jackson School. It is night in our big fireplace room, with chairs drawn round the limerock hearth and red oak splitwood glowing between the firedogs. It is said that to save money we don't burn the electric lights. Shadows lap around the walls, pine boards, aged brown with smoke. Resting on the forks of tree limbs nailed near the fireplace are three guns—a double-barrel 12-gauge Fox; another 12 gauge, a single barrel/one-shot Harrington & Richardson; and a .22 rifle, Winchester, model 62A, a pump with an exposed hammer. All are ready to take down and fire, immediately. My dad says, "I don't want a gun in this house that is not loaded." And I knew then he did not mean loaded only for varmints. Those guns were dangerous and to be respected. You could kill somebody. And yet he would usually pronounce before bedtime that the door latches should not be thumb-bolted. "You never know when somebody might be passing by without a place to stay," he'd say.

My parents are there, and my sisters are down the hall, in the kitchen, listening to the Truetone and, over and over, to the latest radio hit—and an old melody wafts by: "Memories Are Made of This." My sisters are mysterious creatures, living in another world, theirs, a close-present where hearts dwell on love and longing. They don't want me around, and I can't stand their silly ways.

I am half-hearing what is being said by my grandfather and not understanding. I am trying to read by the firelight one of the orange-bound Bobbs-Merrill hero biographies, with the colonized titles, the big-serif, sweet-smelling type and the silhouette illustrations, from the school library. I can usually read one in two nights. *Andrew Jackson: Young Hickory* I have read twice. But my attention drifts to a voice that does not offer up such an exemplary American icon. The stories that voice tells are too complicated and circular, no real heroes, no pitiful victims. Fire, yes, but not much light.

One name is spoken with a strange passion:

Babe Burke. In Mobile. On Govmit Street. And he was wearing a derby hat.

Sowing fragments like the broadcasting of seedoats, the voice moves along. My parents seem to be in a deep study, their eyes on the fire. They know all of these stories by heart. Do they wonder, as I do, what each tale means, or how the details connect? I have heard many of the stories myself in his house, around his own hearth, and on the porch of the house in which Grandma had died. Now that house is gone, razed by the timber company he sold out to, and I am hearing him telling the stories in our house. And still I don't understand.

I sense that whatever Papa is saying is important, and I know it is grave and ominous. The stories are never clear, but no questions are asked. I look back at my parents for comfort or connection. Something secret, something bad, something shameful, is the air. If I raise my questions in public, or even to them, I will be in for it, told to hush. Their faces are lost largely in the shadows. I see the fire reflecting in my mother's glasses, glistening on my father's broad face with the stubble of beard. He is musing and brooding. They both seem to know how to fill in the ellipses. They say nothing, add nothing.

I am alone. I hear my grandfather's voice rise an octave, a shrill lift above the drone, then it drops back, takes on a new beat and rhythm. He says flat out:

So, they took down Tooch Bedsole not a mile from Bedsole Store.

At the rests, silence prevails. My father pokes the fire. My mother's rocking chair creaks. Their breathing is slow and deep. I can hear the hissing of the green wood and the slow tock-tick of the mantel clock, gaudy and grotesque with its ornamented glass face and topknot façade and Roman numerals. As our bedtime nears, I hear it clear its throat at five minutes before the short hand gets to VII, when the tinny chime will strike seven times. And then his voice begins again.

Papa's right index finger is beating the measure. He talks with his hands, as if he were addressing a public crowd. The bone felon at the knuckle bends the nail into a claw. He pauses, leans forward to light his pipe from a splinter thrust into the fire and brought carefully to the bowl. The flame turns upside down, and he breathes out the mellow Half & Half smoke and throws the splinter back into the fire. And that is it, that is all I have left—a gap, a sudden stop, an incomplete sentence finished in somebody else's mind.

As Papa is dressing in his nightshirt, which drapes across his bony body, and putting on his old-timey night cap, and pissing into the chamber pot with his back turned, I am already in bed and waiting: I expect to hear again, repetition being the way of old people, about .38-caliber Winchester rifles, and something garbled about somebody telling him to shoot, but he appears to be talking less to me than to himself. What he says makes no sense to me. Surely he will tell me one story he seems fond of, about his father, Pa, who was in some war I don't know a thing about:

When Pa thought all was lost, they saved his life and set him free.

Then I knew nothing of Pa, or of Yankees, or of rifles. I only knew that this old man, whom I loved, and who loved me, was talking, and it had a meter to it. It lulled me, as it must have him. There was a conflict and a drama in it. I listened to his voice rise and fall until sleep overtook us.

Now, five decades after Lee Brown's death, as my sleep awaits, I try to remember and to put fancy and speculation aside and to challenge memory. Some matter troubles me: He was holding something back. There was some passion in him as we prepared for sleep. He was not a praying man, but each night he seemed to be settling something in his own mind. Then I see, on a knoll in New Prospect Cemetery, a shattered tombstone, bearing the name *John R. Pinkerton, 1842–1894.*

PART I
KILLING PINK

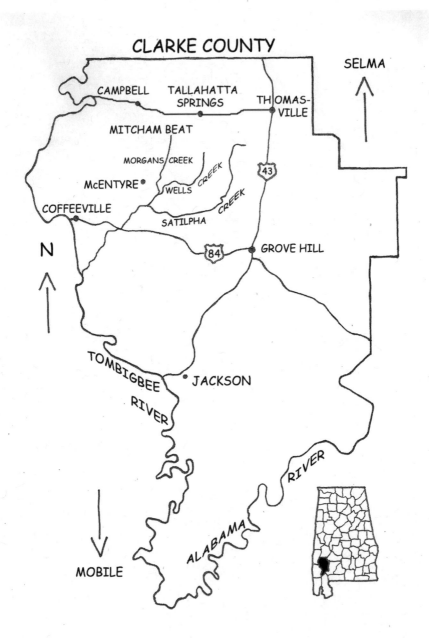

CLARKE COUNTY

SELMA

CAMPBELL
TALLAHATTA SPRINGS
THOMAS-VILLE

MITCHAM BEAT

MORGANS CREEK

CREEK

McENTYRE

WELLS

CREEK

COFFEEVILLE

SATILPHA

CREEK

43

N

84
GROVE HILL

TOMBIGBEE

RIVER

JACKSON

ALABAMA
RIVER

MOBILE

(MAP BY AUSTIN RHODES)

O THEY TELL ME OF A HOME

The hamlet in which the murderous actions I ponder took place is no longer officially called Mitcham Beat, but it was once a real settlement. It's gone now, but the name is still used amongst us natives for that most infamous and remote section of Clarke County, Alabama, about eighty miles north of Mobile, one county away from the Mississippi line, with the Tombigbee River for its west boundary and the Alabama River for part of its east. Located in the northwest of the county, the hundred or so square miles of this micro-world lay along the watershed of Satilpha Creek, a long winding stream, growing bigger as it approaches the Tombigbee, which joins the Alabama at the southern tip of the county. The two rivers make a *V*, pointing to the Mobile-Tensaw delta. Satilpha or Satilpa, in Choctaw, means something like "stream where the pumpkins grow." As a borderland protected by

Choctaws from the more bellicose Creeks, that country was violent even before the whites brought their own version of killing.

Once the bottomlands by Satilpha Creek were lined with loamy fields. The soil was easy to work, and the cotton and corn flourished without commercial fertilizer. In the blue holes in the creek bends, some as deep as twenty feet, people caught channel catfish, punkinseed and war-mouth perch, green trout, drum, buffalo, grinnel, eels, gars, and other Southern fishes. Oxbow ponds in the lowgrounds were surrounded by cypress trees, and ducks and snipe (our name for woodcock) could be shot around them. Amongst the fencerows of adjoining fields were coveys of bob-white quail, or, as they were called in Mitcham, "pottidges." In the creek flats, Spanish moss trailed from tall and spreading hardwoods—oaks, hickories, beech, sycamore, ash, tupelo gum, and the huge-leafed cowcumber magnolia. In those woods, squirrels, canecutter rabbits, and various varmints—raccoon, otter, mink, fox, polecats, possums, wildcats, and weasels—were plentiful.

By my father's time, the wolves and panthers were gone, and by my time the turkeys had been steadily diminishing—they were shot in all seasons without respect for age or gender—and the white-tailed deer had virtually disappeared. But not the snakes. From swamp to high ground, you had to be on the lookout for cottonmouths, timber rattlers, diamondbacks, rattlesnake pilots (which highlanders call copperheads), and the rare, beautiful, but deadly coral snake. Even the nonpoisonous coiling creatures could bite you or upset your henhouse—chicken snakes, corn snakes, king snakes, rat snakes, puff adders, and bull snakes as long as seven feet. Most fearsome of all were the unseen serpents—the hoop snake that could take its tail in its mouth and roll down a hill, the glass or joint snake that would break into pieces when you hit it and then rejoin when the sun went down, the stinging snake that would kill a human or a tree with a barb in its tail, and the dreaded coach whip that first would charm you and then frail the tar out of you.

The ancestors, direct and collateral, lived in that part of the county, between Coffeeville and Thomasville, for most of two centuries. There, as the historians of old said, they "stayed," though, as in all matters terrestrial, nothing forever stays. In fact, many of the pioneers were passers-through, leaving their names on landmarks before moving on west. No matter what their bloodlines—a mix of Scots, Germans, English, Irish, Welsh, French, maybe Indian, and I don't know what all else—by the early 1800s the residents were a Deep Southern–American clan, intermarried, tetchous, quarrelsome, mirthful, standoffish, formal, hardworking, and, most obviously, charged with energy.

The habit of hewing to the borderlands, politically, socially, and geographically, had long been dominant, and its roots run clearly to the European experience, when our sort was persecuted and cut off from advancement. Gradually, the pioneers who settled the frontier moved to the back of society, from hero to hick. Like other country folk, they were easy to caricature, even amongst themselves, as rubes and backwoods people, but they were heterogeneous, rich in their variety, and evidence points to a high level of social and political intelligence, to sheer doggedness, and, when pressed, not a little courage. They were, by and large, literate and religious. Land-holding farmers, they were driven by a relentless work ethic. Except for that one horrible episode, the violence and trashiness evident in their settlement probably did not exceed that in any of the towns, but the country folks didn't write the newspaper stories about themselves or set down a defense of their way of life in writing.

The earliest arrived in what was to become Mitcham Beat in the Mississippi Territory about 1805, seven years before Clarke became a county and fourteen before Alabama became a state. They came in the early nineteenth century to *claim*—a verb the Creeks and Choctaws would view as ironically exact—land in the rich creekbottoms of the Tombigbee watershed. Others settled before the territory was opened by Andrew Jackson's military campaign against both the Indians and the British in the southwestern theater of the War of 1812. They came for reasons common to the frontier, but one pull was prominent in Mitcham: the desire to make money on cotton.

These settlers never intended to become planters of the Black Belt stripe. They wanted to combine their style of subsistence farming, the Jeffersonian ideal of yeomanry, with capitalistic cotton farming—to make money and still be independent. It was a crazy notion, preposterous, the American dream recapitulated in the swamps and ridges of Clarke County: fertile dirt turned into dollars, and freedom from the political tyrannies of Europe rewarded, after much sweat, by safe homesteads and bountiful harvests. As history would prove, the ideal never could be fully realized, human beings being what we are, and time and chance being the lot of all humanity. All they wanted was to be as self-sufficient and independent as possible, free from oppressive government, and still have folding money—a quest which is still right common.

The Brown emigrants from Kershaw County, South Carolina, to Dale County, Alabama, consisted of five brothers. According to one brother's statement in the 1880 census, their father had been born in Prussia. Their mother was Miss (probably short for Melissa, since one granddaughter bore that name) Brooks, probably of English or Scotch-Irish stock. In the family records, the first known male progenitor is listed in family records as John Brown, but I can't find these Browns in the scant official documents kept in South Carolina at the end of the 1700s. If his sons were born in the late eighteenth and early nineteenth centuries, that original Brown, Braun, von Braun, Bronstein—or none of these—was probably either a soldier of the Revolution or one among many Jews or Germans living near Charlestown, or Charles Town; the city didn't become Charleston until 1783. Jack Brown's grandson, my grandfather, said we were Germans. Lee Brown heard that from old Jack himself. Like just about everything my grandfather remembered about names and dates and general history, the link to Germany was confirmed in a written record he never saw.

The five brothers departed the rice country above Charleston in the 1830s. Their names were Peter, Jack, Louis (or Lewis), Jacob, and Henry. The five brothers lived as neighbors for about twenty years in hardscrabble southeast Alabama, in what became Dale County. Then, about 1858, my great-great grandfather Jack Brown (1802-1885) and his wife, Eula Ann Ansley (1804-1864), and three of their four sons and three daughters split off and moved. The migrant group was sizable. Land claims indicate that various Truetts and Huttos in our line were also amongst those moving to the wider, blacker soils in southwest Alabama, to Mitcham Beat. Like others of that time, they probably came in a group, in covered wagons, with sheep and cows and hogs and first-rate dogs that would run and tree and protect.

Records at the St. Stephens land office, down on the Tombigbee, reveal the hundreds of acres various Browns and Truetts claimed in the Satilpha watershed. Cattle were allowed to range freely, so the settlers had use of more land than they owned. They built homes, first of logs and later board-and-batten, on ridges, with the floodplain of the Satilpha before them and the piney woods barrens behind them. Once settling in the beat, they fenced off the fields, to keep the cattle out, not in, and they tried a little rice farming, for stockfeed and human sustenance. Eventually, they switched entirely to corn for grain, and, of course, they grew the full span of table vegetables, though cotton brought the money and thus held the throne. In forming a community, they brought with them attitudes associated with their colonial roots and especially the mindset of South Carolina ancestors. They quarreled and compromised amongst themselves and then united against the county establishment and soon became part of the formation of a society so distinct in its ethos that it has left its mark on all of us who were begotten by those pioneers.

———•◦•———

A green wilderness has long enfolded most of that old Mitcham Beat settlement. In places, the third generation of planted pines now stands thirty feet. Hunting club signs warn that the sandy hills and alluvial lowlands are posted, reflecting the power of rich men, mostly doctors, bankers, and lawyers, from Mobile and Birmingham. Because of cutovers by big paper companies and the subsequent erosion, the branches and creeks that coil toward the Tombigbee are silted beyond my recognition by coastal plain sand. Their banks are a tangle of rank underbrush.

Deer and turkey, unneeded now for meat, have returned and multiplied. Where wolves once howled, coyotes sing. And that Texican newcomer, the armadillo, waddles where possums once were common. Except for a few houses built in suburban styles and the occasional double-wide notched into a thicket, the old places are gone. The dogtrot houses, with water buckets and dippers and rocking chairs on broad porches, which were shaded by live oaks and fenced in palings, exist only in memory or old photographs. Their cow lots, hogpens, and cribs, their smokehouses, wagon sheds, and privies, and their roads, all leading to fields, each road and field named, in the Satilpha creekbottom—all are gone, with nothing even to signify where the old homeplaces stood. No cowbells are heard, or children playing in schoolyards. No voices are telling of witches, horsemen in the night, mysterious deaths, miraculous recoveries. No tales of hilarious or harrowing hunts and of mythical beasts and dogs are heard around hearths on winter nights. No rolling stores pass through. No four-part harmony is sung from the old Stamps-Baxter brownback hymnal. No liniment is rubbed on backs aching from picking cotton or peas or hauling out logs. To speeding travelers, that ribbon of road between Chilton to near Coffeeville—ironically, those purple bands of asphalt are still called "farm-to-market"—is largely a mute expanse.

Though the emptiness and ugliness of that landscape might engender nostalgia in the few old natives who remember the last days of Mitcham Beat, I don't grieve for the settlement and would not want to bring it back. Viewed from one perspective, the place merely suffered a fate common to communities all over the United States, as change laps change, economies and habits vary, and nothing new grows up to embrace the old. From the vantage of Mitcham people, however, the death of our community was different. The distinctive mark, or scar, of the place had to do with that feud between backcountry farmers and town merchants in the early 1890s that came to be called the Mitcham War, which I regard as the beat's mortal wound. After that violent episode, the old district bled to death slowly, over a fifty-year period. It was finally finished off by the outmigrations associated with the Great Depression and World War II.

———•·•·•———

I am the last child of the old set, the youngest of fourteen children of two parents and part of a vast, extended family, to have been born there. Our family moved nearer to a town when I was a year old, but

I was brought up in the Mitcham Beat ways, even as I was also becoming part of what might charitably be called the modern world of Clarke County. My parents, who were old when I was born, left Mitcham Beat in 1946, but that place was the center of their universe, their point of reference. Now even their earthly remains are in a churchyard there.

I left Clarke County for good more than forty years ago. There was nothing in that place for me, none of the hundreds of acres of land my ancestors had homesteaded and bought and then their descendants had sold or lost. This I knew: Whatever estate I had was above my shoulders and to be established by luck or by faith in forces beyond my knowing. Even if there had been enough land for me to survive on as a farmer, the town set, counterparts or descendants of 1890s merchants, lawyers, sawmill owners, and bankers, was still in firm control. A few clung to power and never gave up their attitude toward Mitcham Beat people, who, in turn, did not believe for a minute they would be accepted in town circles—or care to be. After I left, paper mills and chemical plants came in and employed scores of relatives, who have prospered and whose children have leapfrogged or bypassed the various town cliques and moved into many professions, thanks to all the social and economic changes and, I like to think, to the example of those hardy Mitcham Beat ancestors.

The social character of Clarke County is reflected in its historic location—below the mansions and plantations of the Black Belt and above multicultural Old Mobile. The town settlers were hardly aristocrats. There was no planter aristocracy to speak of in Clarke County. What is referred to as the "middle class" existed without an established upper class. These town people consisted mostly of shrewd shopkeepers and their clerks, a few lawyers, doctors, and county officials, most of them better educated than us country folks but hardly refined. The worst of the lot had been suckled on courthouse-ring politics, and many had an eye only for the dollar. Of one of those skinflint merchants my grandfather said, with a knowing chuckle, "If he had all the money in the world but one nickel, he'd walk a rotten rail across Hell for that." That storekeeper's sort would have been as out of place in a Mobile mansion as anybody from Mitcham Beat.

There were fair-minded and good-hearted people in the towns, but they were overshadowed by what D. C. Mathews called "an overbearing commercial class." What did this class of merchant have to lose if the farmers prospered? Holding the generators of capital down made no economic sense—more prosperity by farmers meant more business for merchants—but money was not all the town set was interested in. The domineering, overbearing commercial class wanted to keep a foot on the neck of these plain folk. Without the country people remaining a lower class, these town merchants would have no claim to higher social status. And wouldn't that be a shame?

In both levels of Clarke County society, town and country, farmer and merchant, a snobbishness prevailed—and, as everybody knows, snobbism is one of the masks that fear wears. Now the old clique is largely dead and diluted, though, as in all close communities, those telling surnames survive. And so does the fear, on each side, the fear of the town class that they would lose control and the fear of the country class that they would regress into a trashy rabble and be cut off forever.

The official name for the voting district originally called Mitcham Beat became New Prospect before the end of the nineteenth century, and the term *beat*, a holdover from Alabama's days as a military territory, was changed to precinct. The old name for Beat 15, from a family of original settlers, has stuck because of the vigilante nightmare of the early 1890s that forms the first part of this book and informs the others. That bloody episode, largely lost in history, left the whole district terrified and stained. To some old people in Clarke County, Mitcham Beat is still a term of reproach, and those who lived there are low-rated as "Mitchamites," with negative, Old Testament connotations. The stigma, as I will point out, is the result of the Mitcham War and its rancorous foreground.

I knew that my grandfather, Lee Brown, was involved in that war, though how and on which side was not clear. He talked about it enough that the name of the famous gang stuck, and the alluring images of riders and guns, but I never picked up a story line. As it turned out, he and his family, like many in Mitcham, weren't on either side, but they caught fear from one and hell from another. Of much greater import to me is what role he played just after that county clique, backwoods community conflict. Forty years after Lee Brown's death, I began to learn what happened in late November 1894, when he was twenty-three years old.

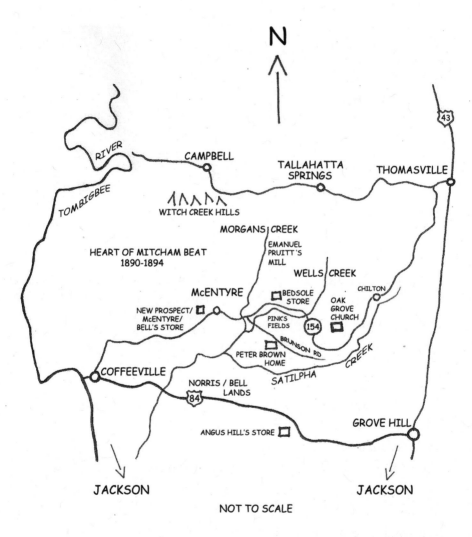

N

RIVER

TOMBIGBEE

CAMPBELL

TALLAHATTA
SPRINGS

THOMASVILLE

43

ΛΛΛΛΛ
WITCH CREEK HILLS

MORGANS CREEK

HEART OF MITCHAM BEAT
1890-1894

EMANUEL
PRUITT'S
MILL

WELLS CREEK

CHILTON

McENTYRE

BEDSOLE
STORE

OAK
GROVE
CHURCH

NEW PROSPECT/
McENTYRE/
BELL'S STORE

PINK'S
FIELDS

154

BRUNSON RD

CREEK

PETER BROWN
HOME

COFFEEVILLE

SATILPHA

NORRIS / BELL
LANDS

84

GROVE HILL

ANGUS HILL'S STORE

JACKSON

JACKSON

NOT TO SCALE

(MAP BY AUSTIN RHODES)

WHAT DOES THIS MEAN?
LORD, HAVE MERCY!

First, a summary, to help readers follow a story that's confusing even if, or especially if, you grew up trying to figure it out:

In the late 1880s, a local gang of hotheads, who called themselves Hell-at-the-Breech, was formally organized in Mitcham Beat. Its major mission became confronting the usurious lenders who preyed on the poor, pea-patchers and small cotton farmers. But first the gang quarreled with and terrorized, even killed, their own neighbors. These murders took place in 1890 and 1891. The pleas of those who saw what was coming to pass in their own settlement were ignored by Clarke County law enforcement.

Heady with their own local victories, Hell-at-the-Breech in late 1892 ventured outside Mitcham Beat, killed a merchant-lender, and threatened an entire incorporated town. Then a mass of outraged citizens rose up against them, in a vigilante, undeputized legion. Most people in Mitcham Beat were caught between these two forces, which I have called, respectively, the "gang" and the "mob." Because many members of the gang were blood or in-law kin, revealing Hell-at-the-Breech to negligent county authorities was out of the question.

Those who informed on the gang could be killed by their own neighbors. A reward from the governor amounting to $10,000 in today's currency went uncollected. To complicate matters further, many neighbors were Civil War comrades of members of the mob. And at one time they may have welcomed the vigilantes, hoping Hell-at-the-Breech could be disbanded. But presently the mob spun out of control and turned on the whole community.

The mob made no distinction between the local gang and the bystanders; these vigilantes pillaged, tortured, and killed. Thus, the people in Mitcham Beat for whom I write came to hate the mob more than the local toughs. From what I can piece together, my folks were against Hell-at-the-Breech, but either too weak or too savvy (or both) to take on anybody until they were directly threatened.

The man who fingered the merchant's assassins for the mob was a mysterious "detective" named John Robert Pinkerton but often referred to as Pink. He went even further and was also involved in the lynchings and torturing of those not involved in the assassination. The formal rule of law was ignored by the whole county. After the mob was routed in mid-1893, Pinkerton took up permanent residence, with his family, in the devastated community. What eventually came to be called the Mitcham War is prelude to his fate.

———•◦•———

Anyone seeking to understand the bloody episode should begin with the

1988 history written by three brave Clarke Countians, Hardy Jackson, Joyce White Burrage, and Jim Cox. Hardy is also a prominent professional historian and has written a scholarly article on the conflict. His great-grandfather was the county sheriff at the time of the war, but he writes with admirable impartiality. Both Joyce and Jim had ancestors who were drawn into the conflict. I will acknowledge their good work often, in italics, *MWCCA*, referring to *The Mitcham War in Clarke County, Alabama.* The history is fair, circumspect, and cogently reasoned. Readers should pay special attention to the appended interview with David Chapman Mathews, an educator, legislator, and old-fashioned Jacksonian Democrat who knew Mitcham Beat well and was among the few leaders who defended its people. Dave Mathews outlines clearly the melodrama that set the stage for the killing of Ernest McCorquodale, which started that so-called war. Following in the wake of Hardy, Joyce, and Jim, I examine the case involving my grandfather and how it illuminated the past and anticipated the future of Mitcham Beat.

To begin with the obvious, a bushel of factors figured in the outbreak of Mitcham War—class differences, national and local politics, commercial rivalries—but dry facts fight shy of the tangled, often terrifying story bred in the bones of Mitcham Beat children. Though facts have faded or become confused in retellings, that fearful feeling has been consistent: The voices have said, "Watch out. Never trust established power or be seduced into thinking those in power actually care about you, your kin, or your kind." And, contrariwise, *seek a champion.* That versions of this insecurity and longing are universal has occurred to me by slow degrees, over years of random reading.

However, speaking for those of us who grew up around those old tellers in Mitcham Beat, the fear we felt was entirely our burden and partly our fault. How people came to be so terrorized, why that terror lingered, and what effect it has on succeeding generations make whatever real history we can piece together important, or not worth attention at all, depending upon one's point of view. From mine, the surface story does not conceal a subtext relevant now, and perhaps forever, to people who never heard of Mitcham Beat, Alabama.

———••••———

In its violence and melodrama, the Mitcham War has the contours of an Old West range war or the bushwhacker violence and home-front anarchy before, during, and following the Civil War. In point of fact, it was about a backwater county's courthouse ring exercising control over a rebellious, even more backwater district. Just how many deaths directly related to it may be debated, but I fix it at ten, give or take. However horrendous those killings were, the terror the vigilantes spread and the way Mitcham Beat was regarded by the general public and characterized in the state press left the place stained.

One Mobile paper called it "Clarke County's Criminal Colony," which tarred all the residents with the broadest brush. That the beat resembled the stereotype of a Wild West community more than an 1890s Deep Southern settlement is no surprise because that corner of Alabama retained elements of the original Southwest long after that name had been displaced by the newer territories beyond the Mississippi. Clarke County existed in a time warp. What happened in Mitcham Beat was over and done with in most places, including the mountain South and even much of the Old West, a decade or so earlier.

Some trace the beginnings of the Mitcham War to the late 1880s when several young men, all of whom my grandfather knew but apparently did not run with, began gathering around Bedsole Store in the heart of the beat. The Bedsole family was a powerful force in

Mitcham—exceptionally energetic, intelligent, and ambitious. The general store was started by a man named Rafe Bedsole and operated after his death in 1874 by his son, Wes. The patriarch of the family was Edward Bedsole, Rafe's uncle, who had moved into Mitcham Beat from Walton County, Florida, in 1866. Somehow he had avoided serving in the Confederate army. Edward joined his sister Elizabeth and her three children—Rafe, Thomas, and Sarah—who had come from Lowndes County, Alabama, before the Civil War.

Bonded whiskey could be sold at Bedsole Store, legally, but the untaxed type, moonshine, was cheaper and in good supply. Right much of this liquor came up the Tombigbee, from Mobile or Washington counties, or across the river to the west from Choctaw County. From what's been passed down about their rituals, the fraternal group that gathered at the store seems a parody of the Masons (old Edward Bedsole was one) or a Sam Peckinpah version of *Tom Sawyer*. As the story was told, and I have no reason to doubt it, secret oaths, signed in blood, were required. Members swore not to testify against each other. They were bent on revenge against the overbearing white lenders who ran the county. They also hated the local people, even their relatives, who might have stopped them. Though racism was as evident in Mitcham as it was everywhere, I find no trace of Ku Klux Klan activity or hooded nightriders.

The gray eminence behind the gang was Edward Bedsole, a brilliant, driven frontiersman whose wife taught him to read and write. In 1892, he was seventy-three years old. If he did not directly encourage the mean bunch, neither did he discourage them after they began to do serious mischief amongst neighbors. His son, Quincy Farrington Bedsole, and his nephews, Babe and Mack Burke, were leaders of the Hell-at-the-Breech. Flush with ambition and meeting weak resistance in the beat, the

43

Mitcham gang also laid plans to take on the town-based power brokers who shut them out. Babe Burke was handsome, intelligent, bold, and five years older than Lee Brown, and he was married to the beautiful Sally Hare. Mitcham was his oyster.

A respected man in Mitcham, Joseph C. Anderson, then sixty-seven years old, knew Hell-at-the-Breech had burned the barn of a friend, John Hare, who also disapproved of their ways and was the father-in-law of another prominent gang member, Lev James. (*MWCCA*) A family confrontation resulted in the burning of that barn; it had nothing to do with the larger mission Hell-at-the-Breech would take on, but it demonstrated how violent and crazy these characters were. The fire killed a fine saddle horse and that particularly galled Anderson; he wrote a letter to *The Clarke County Democrat* decrying the lawlessness of Hell-at-the-Breech. It was a tacit call for help, which did not come. It also made him a marked man.

Anderson was a leader of the Mitcham chapter of the Farmers' Alliance, a national organization of the Populist era, similar to the Grange, that advocated fairer financing and better marketing for small farmers and encouraged improvement of their lands. Obviously, Anderson favored civility and order. The Populists were opposed to the merchants who denied them warehouse space and manipulated marketing—the same old pseudo-Bourbons that ran Grove Hill and wanted to keep the little man down. These were the power brokers who opposed taxes for public schools, better roads, and, later, rural free delivery of mail. Hell-at-the-Breech was not content to move through political channels, which were virtually nonexistent. Besides, in burning a neighbor's barn, they had ridden across a rural-code Rubicon. Not content to brook any opposition within the community, or to have a potential witness of sound reputation amongst them, or to face competition from a large political party with a base in the beat, in September of 1890 members of Hell-at-the-Breech ambushed Anderson, in the road, as he walked with two other men from an Alliance meeting. The killer, it was learned later, was Babe Burke, whose alluring, alliterative name has rung down the generations. Anderson's haunting, dying question was, "What does this mean?"

To Clarke County law enforcement, it meant nothing. Let Mitcham be Mitcham was their creed. Such backcountry people weren't worth the risk of trying to make a legal case. Besides, when rowdies were hauled in for moonshining or harboring sheep-killing dogs, their friends alibied for the accused, and no charge would stick. To hell with them, their inbred enclave, and their Populist politics. The independent voters in Mitcham Beat were not strictly loyal to the county ring's Democratic party machine, which further set them apart. The Farmers' Alliance endorsed its own slate of candidates. It was not forgotten by the ascendant Democrats who ran the courthouse that Rafe Bedsole had run for the legislature on, of all things, the Republican ticket nearly twenty years earlier, before Reconstruction ended. On the other hand, it was conveniently forgotten that, before occupying Federal forces left in 1877, the 1890s county judge, John Marshall Wilson, a Democrat during the Mitcham War, and his father, Jack Roper Wilson, who'd been the judge before him, had both previously politicked as scalawag Republicans. (J. M. Wilson's middle name was his mother's maiden name. It's an irony that he carried the name of the nation's first great jurist.)

Many local historians trace the roots of the Mitcham War to what happened when Rafe Bedsole, remembered as a Republican, dared to take on the now-Democratic county clique. (*MWCCA*) During the 1874 campaign, Rafe died—and not of natural causes, according to his family and friends. After a political rally at Coffeeville, at which Rafe ate a box lunch, he complained of a headache, and his opponent, Dr. R. H. Love, invited him by his office and administered a medicine. Rafe died on the road home. Another doctor, from Tallahatta Springs, just north of Mitcham Beat, was called in and pronounced the cause of death as poisoning. Dr. Love left the county. Conclusion: Love killed Rafe Bedsole because he was a threat to the establishment. The logic or illogic of this mix of politics and place, memory and amnesia, obscures the more fundamental differences between classes of citizens and control of money. Though the rancor and tenuous ties between Mitcham people and the county machine have been traced to Rafe's death, the festering humors lay deep in the whole body politic of that county.

Race was a sad but secondary factor, and the killing of three black men had to do with greed and party politics more than racial differences. Before the conflict known formally as the Mitcham War began, a black man named Emanuel Pruitt (variant spellings abound), who'd done no one any harm, was murdered for his money in 1891. As everybody knows, at that time a white who killed a black could, with a flimsy defense and after a judicial dumbshow, walk free. Pruitt ran a gristmill on Morgans Creek, not far from Bedsole Store, and raised cotton; he owned about 180 acres, forty of which he had bought from Jack Brown, Peter Brown's father. His killers hid in the rafters of his mill. When they shot Emanuel Pruitt, he fell headlong into a meal barrel. His remains rest somewhere in an unmarked grave. The killers dug holes around the mill, but they apparently never found Emanuel's cotton money. It was being held as a check at a cotton warehouse, waiting for him to pick up. My people in Mitcham believed that the killers were Sebren "Seeb" Hutto, my grandmother Brown's cousin, and his brother-in-law, a man named Pritchett. Both were probably members of the Hell-at-the-Breech, but there is no indication the killing was ordered by the gang.

Hutto and Pritchett, with some of their sons, fled to Louisiana, and cousin Howell Hutto, Seeb's son, told me and others many nostalgic stories of their journey—the camping out, the fiddle-playing by the firesides, the killing of game as they traveled—but he never mentioned why they left and stayed away about a year. In fact, Hutto and Pritchett were indicted in 1897, seven years after the killing. After a show to demonstrate that Clarke County justice fit the norm of the Southern day, the charges were dismissed. Though Howell Hutto was long-revered, a tall, handsome old man who wore bow-ties and looked vaguely Indian, Seeb Hutto's name was never spoken in our family, and he died not long after the indictment was quashed.

The shooting of two black men named Howze may also not have been the work of the Hell-at-the-Breech, though they were blamed for it. Both men died. According to the June 12, 1893, *Democrat*, William Howze was shot while working in his field, and "the weapon used was a .38-caliber Winchester Rifle"—a detail ironically parallel to another shooting which would occur seventeen months later.

The customary charge against black men—"outraging" a white woman—was brought up, but most knew it was false. Blacks were disliked by the Mitcham-Alliance set because they sided with the Democratic white power structure in the Jones-Kolb gubernatorial race of 1890. And members of the county machine would not admit that they'd bargained for the black vote, even though they'd thrown a big barbecue for their temporary allies. (*MWCCA*)

It was easy to lay blame for the killing of Lem and William Howze on Hell-at-the-Breech. Ever the apologist for white folks in the county seat and thus avoiding any mention of interracial conflict close at hand, Isaac Grant of *The Clarke County Democrat* said the shootings were due to some "color trouble."

The white-on-white troubles started coming to a head when the Hell-at-the-Breech turned its attention to the county merchants, dominated by flint-hearted men who preyed on the poor and ignorant without batting an eye. They had their ring, which they knew was stronger than anything Mitcham could muster. The county officials, the newspaper editors, the bankers, the merchants, and other "leading citizens" were all in league. These tanktown Babbitts didn't lose a wink of sleep after beating some rube out of his cotton and his land. In an age when crop liens were a necessity, manipulation by those who lent money and held power was easy. A man who could not pay off his debt in full, to the last penny, could lose the whole mortgaged property. Like the Mitcham gang, the merchants and bankers feared no legal authority. They were the law.

Hell-at-the-Breech thought differently and eventually concocted a scheme to take over the county—if we are to believe the old stories. Some even said they were into counterfeiting, a charge for which I find no scintilla of evidence. But they were not thought of as merely hotheaded hell-raisers. In the parlance of that century, they were regarded as anarchists; in our time, they would be considered terrorists or insurrectionists. To attract such massive opposition, they had to have posed a threat to vulnerable cotton crop-lien merchants who realized that these formally organized, politically driven backwoods boys were not your garden-variety outlaws. Sworn members of this countrified *cosa nostra* were packing guns and a head of steam—and more than a modicum of right.

One of the merchants who advanced money was Ernest McCorquodale, who lived in Coffeeville, a village on the Tombigbee, ten miles or so from Mitcham Beat. He was tied by marriage to the county political and social clique. The word in Mitcham was that McCorquodale took the mortgage payment of one of the Breech members, Kirk James, on a rainy fall night and told James he couldn't write him a receipt because his books were locked up and he had to get home to tend to his sick wife. He told James he'd give him the receipt later. The next thing James knew, as people in Mitcham would tell it, his property was foreclosed on, and, to no one's surprise, the county court upheld the judgment. When Judge John Marshall Wilson upheld the foreclosure, James allegedly told McCorquodale, as they were leaving the courtroom, "Well, Ernest. You have your judgment, but you won't live to enjoy it." It's a good line, and possibly true.

McCorquodale, like the other small merchants, had been in more of a bind than he'd let on. His money was lent out to the small farmers, and he had his own debts to pay—or not. Capital was short all over, and the small merchants let their wholesalers become *de facto* bankers, carrying their debts until the wholesalers had to sue. At least two Mobile wholesale houses won judgments against McCorquodale to collect the debts. The wholesalers were also in a bind, created by the cotton economy. The Mobile cotton factors who could fuel the economy were at the mercy of Wall Street manipulators. Cotton futures—or projected prices—would be churned upward during the borrowing season; then the actual paying price dropped as the harvest came in. Farmers and factors would be left in the lurch. Unfortunately, the cotton growers in Mitcham were certain that they had been swindled by the local merchants. And nothing in the calculating character of McCorquodale's set would encourage those ill-informed farmers to think otherwise.

So, Ernest McCorquodale had reasons to be sharp, even to engage in some double talking, but if he did so with the Jameses, he got himself engaged with the worst bunch in the county. Apparently, the experienced, fifty-year-old McCorquodale was not mealy mouthed when it came to collecting his money and protecting his interests. Despite his ties to the elite, he had been indicted a year earlier for "presenting a gun," though that charge, like those against the Mitcham men, was dropped. The county ring also had folks who would speak for them in court.

Given the reputations of the Jameses, the Mitcham people could have believed—maybe did—that Kirk was lying, but McCorquodale was a convenient lightning rod, though I find nothing to set him apart as exceptional. He had good reason to be worried about his business; he was also in financial straits. (That fact was learned almost immediately after his murder.) McCorquodale was an ideal target for a terrorist killing because he was so entwined with the Coffeeville–Grove Hill clique. His wife was a sister of the sheriff and first-cousin to the justice of the peace, Oscar York, who would turn out to be a central character in the conflict to come.

On Christmas night 1892, Lev James and Babe Burke staked out the merchant's house. McCorquodale was called to the door. His wife was standing by him, holding a lamp. Then a blast of buckshot struck him down. He fell into the yard. McCorquodale's holiday guests carried him into the house. His last words were, "Lord, have mercy!"

After his murder and a gathering of Masons had been summoned to his memorial service by Isaac Grant of the *Democrat*, Ernest McCorquodale's store stock was sold at auction to settle his debts. Lev James, it was reported, was there to bid on some of the items. It was later revealed that Lev James had been paid by his brother to do the killing, but Babe Burke was waiting at the back of the house in case McCorquodale tried to flee. The murder of McCorquodale sent the message to the merchant crowd that Hell-at-the-Breech must have intended: We are no ordinary outlaws, and we are coming after you.

And then a B-grade Western broke out across Clarke County and beyond.

A group of riders, called a mob or a posse but never formally sworn in as deputies, was formed to avenge McCorquodale's death and to stamp out this unprecedented challenge to the established powers. Virtually the whole county, aided by a few allies from adjoining counties, was pitted against that one beat, which says something about how the "finest and best citizens" regarded the threat posed by the "Mitchamites." In 1890, the county's total population was 22,916, of which 386 lived in Mitcham Beat proper. Residents in adjacent communities were also part of the conflict, swelling the actual number of those affected by the violence to, at most, 600. Nobody needed to ask why the killing of one river-hamlet merchant would trigger such prolonged, lawless, indiscriminate terrorism, directed at one backwoods settlement. Nobody needed to ask why the rule of law was ignored—it was Mitcham's fault. Was possible collusion amongst witnesses sufficient reason to abandon formal enforcement and to justify going into that community to "clean it out"? Was an understandable, forgivable outrage over a close relative's being gunned down on his own porch by two thugs just reason to purge an entire, largely law-abiding community, referred to scornfully by the county clique as "a nest of rats"?

The mob drew incitement from two weekly newspapers in the county and the dailies in Mobile. The story was eventually picked up by *The Montgomery Advertiser*, *The Birmingham Age-Herald*, and The *Choctaw County Alliance*, west, across the Tombigbee River, where an uprising against liquor laws, the Sims rebellion, had been put down, with the help of Clarke Countians, a few years earlier. (*MWCCA*) One barking-dog journalist was quoted as saying flatly that "Judge Lynch" would try this latest outrage. Suddenly Mitcham was a state story, ripe with melodrama, and the conflict was fanned into a fever by the papers. Some reports said 500 men—repeatedly referred to "best citizens"—were in the mob, though who knows how many best citizens were riding through the beat, and the adjoining beats, at any given time.

In the five months after Ernest McCorquodale's murder, the mob had made much racket, terrorizing the beat but making no headway in netting the assassins. The illegal posse met at Dead Level Church, on the edge of Mitcham, but before the vigilantes began their campaign the church was burned. *The Clarke County Democrat*, in its usual oblique way, dismissed the arson as related to the church's also being used as a school. For a while the mob was hamstrung by its own ineptitude and by the reticence of the Mitcham people who feared being killed by Hell-at-the-Breech if they testified against neighbor or family. But sympathy for the McCorquodale family also ran high. Ernest's brother Charles, who had come up from Salitpa, a community down the Tombigbee, to help his murdered brother's family, contracted pneumonia during that winter and died in April. That left two families without breadwinners.

Six months or so after the merchant was murdered, someone, probably in the McCorquodale-York family, brought in a detective bearing a well-known name, Pinkerton. He is often referred to as Pink, and that name appears on some of the land transactions. It must have been thought of as an acceptable, legal abbreviation of his formal name. Where he came from, who procured him, who paid him—none of these questions I can answer. Collateral descendants living in Choctaw County know little about him. He rides into the scene out of the mist, and into my imagination, as the essential mysterious stranger.

Because of his name, he was able to trade on the reputation of the most famous detective of that century. Allan Pinkerton had, in fact, come to Montgomery several years earlier to investigate a swindle, but a scholarly biography makes no mention of a relative named John, much less a county feud in South Alabama. True, the circumstances in Clarke County fit those in which Allan Pinkerton and his private agency thrived. Pinkertons were called in when police departments were understaffed, unschooled, incompetent, or corrupt. This description fits the state of law enforcement, across the spectrum in Clarke County of the late nineteenth century. In the summer of 1893, a sizable part of the famous agency was engaged in protecting the throngs attending the Columbian Exposition, which came to be called the Chicago World's Fair. The detective who came into Mitcham Beat had the advantage of a respected name, coincidental though it was, and he was paid not only to find McCorquodale's murderers but also to protect the fearful leaders in Clarke County: If this bunch would shoot one merchant off his own front porch on a Christmas night, who might be next? And somebody in that mob knew that this J. R. Pinkerton was as intrepid as he was unprincipled—a useful combination in a private detective of any era.

A shadowy figure assisting the vigilantes and Pinkerton was Charlie Coats, who had family ties to Mitcham. Allegedly, he was spurned at a dance by the saucy Rosie Burke, sister to the Hell-at-the-Breech brothers, and he became a recruiter for the mob. He was also familiar with the hired gun Charlie Smith. "Old Charlie knew how to place 'em," Coats is quoted as saying in *The Mitcham War of Clarke County, Alabama.* "He'd kill anyone for 50 cents if you put it in his hat." As we shall see, Charlie Smith's role as a hired gun did not end with the Mitcham War.

The first activity of Pink and Coats was to get a brother of Lev and Kirk James, George James, soused. In that drunken state, George James told them all they wanted to hear about the Christmas day murder. Whether what he blurted out was true was not tested. He said Lev James had killed McCorquodale at the behest of his brother, Kirk, who had been backed, he claimed or they said he claimed, by a Mitcham merchant-farmer named Sandy Norris. That was all the vigilantes needed.

Acting swiftly on the coerced testimony, the undeputized mob assigned a few of its members to take out Lev James. It happened on Monday, August 7, 1893. Lev James had been at a revival meeting at New Prospect Church, in the heart of Mitcham, across from the McIntyre post office and John R. Bell's store. The revival was being led by a legendary circuit-riding preacher, Wash Etheredge (or Etheridge), my mother's cousin. His sermon text was from Galatians: "Be not deceived; God is not mocked: for whatsoever a man soweth, that shall he also reap. For he that soweth to his flesh shall of the flesh reap corruption. . . ." Preacher Etheredge, who was described by Dave Mathews as a "Scotsman," exhorted loud enough for James to heed the stern message, though James, armed with a pistol, never entered the church.

Instead, Levingston James took issue with Preacher Etheredge's text, according to stories told years later. He walked around the churchyard cursing, sporting that pistol, as one would expect a stage villain to do. But God and frontier justice were not to be mocked, for Lev James was hearing his last sermon. On his way home, he was ambushed on the road, riddled with shot as he was riding, by a gang of assassins. Depending on the version, Lev either died there, after fighting off his killers, or rode his horse into his own yard and fell out of the saddle, dead when he hit the ground. Witnesses said the four killers were Will Harris, Sam Calhoun, Otway Dawson, and Carlos McCorquodale, the eighteen-year-old son of the Coffeeville merchant. Clarke County's own Hamlet had avenged his father's murder. An old McCorquodale told me Carlos often tried to retell his life story to relatives who did not want to hear about it. But the play didn't end there. A larger mission, the hunt for others in the initial plot, lay ahead.

Presently, the mob captured Lev James's brother, Kirk. My father said Kirk James fled from them and was found hiding under a cotton house. He was taken to a magistrate in Coffeeville, with Sandy Norris, and both were held overnight, at an encampment near present-day Center Point church. The magistrate was Oscar York, member of one of the few large-plantation families on the Tombigbee and a leader of the Coffeeville/Choctaw County portion of the mob. Of Kirk's role in the hiring of his brother to commit the murder there was little if any doubt, but Norris was a respected storekeeper and farmer, whose lands lay in the fertile Satilpha bottomlands. Sandy was known for his quick wit and his charitable ways. George James may have been trying to cover his own flanks by naming Norris as an accomplice simply because the country merchant had money enough to back the murder of a town counterpart. That was all—no motive, no evidence. Nevertheless, the mob captured Sandy also. A relative of his said Sandy prayed all night and Kirk cursed all night. Another source said Kirk slept like a "man in a field of fodder." The next morning, Thursday, August 11, they were trussed up and tied to the crossbar of a buggy seat for transport to the county jail. Before they had gone far, to the Cox Bridge, near Mitcham, the buggy was waved down, by none other than Oscar York. He was waiting for them with a mob estimated at more than a hundred armed men.

There was little doubt of the outcome. Flush with righteousness and crowd courage, these vigilantes flouted formal law, an abstract concept in Clarke County, Alabama, hardly comprehensible by such a mob, at such a heated moment.

Kirk James and Sandy Norris were dragged from the buggy and forced to stand on the bank of the road. James was defiant; Norris, terrified. Kirk James, in an act that says much about his character, took full credit for arranging the murder of McCorquodale and told them Sandy Norris had nothing to do with it. He himself had paid his brother, Lev. Weak-kneed, Norris was released.

In Sandy's story of Kirk James's last words, as remembered by Sandy's grandson, Basil Norris, Kirk bared his chest, looked across the road at the gunbarrels pointed at him, and said, "Not a one of you has guts enough to shoot me!" Mob leaders told Kirk that, yes, they were going to kill him, but they offered him the quaint courtesy of a final wish. He said, "THEN BURY ME IN A CHESTNUT COFFIN! I WANT TO HIT HELL SNAPPING AND POPPING!" True or not, that is a jim-dandy exit line. The rifles spoke, and the mob left James's body, described as a "mass of jelly," by the creek. Wherever his remains were interred, if they were, they were probably in a pine box, if in any coffin at all.

From there, the hundred-horse mob rode the four or five miles to Bedsole Store, galloping over the Morgans Creek bridge. At the store, they found Edward Bedsole's son, Quincy Farrington Bedsole, who had the memorable nickname Tooch. He was handsome, dapper, and smooth-talking. No one disputed that he had been a member of Hell-at-the-Breech, but no evidence existed to identify him as a killer. The mob really wanted his first cousins, Babe and Mack Burke, considered principal leaders of Hell-at-the-Breech, but, if my grandfather was right, they were huddled under the Morgans Creek bridge when the horsemen thundered over.

Tooch Bedsole may have been an accomplice when Joseph Anderson was killed by Babe Burke, but that point was never to be disputed in a court of law. The mob led Bedsole up the road from his father's porch, tied him between two trees, and riddled him with bullets. Cousin Howell

Hutto, who was a boy when the killing occurred, said Tooch had a plug of tobacco in his left shirt pocket. After killing Bedsole, the mob again rode away, leaving neighbors and friends to collect his remains in a bed sheet, put them on a cooling board, and bury him immediately. Howell Hutto said he counted six bullet holes in the tobacco plug.

Meanwhile, the Burkes, wiliest of the outlaws, had eluded the mob that had just killed their first cousin. They hid out in a near-impenetrable expanse of crawfishy, snaky, palmetto-flat land where the bamboo briers were as a thick as a man's thumb, the crooked-shank stink bays lay crosswise, webs of bullice vines hung from the larger trees, and twisted trunks of ironwood choked the stream banks. Even when I was a boy, you had to fight your way through that jungle, and you couldn't see two yards in front of your face. An old Mitcham man said, "It was too thick in there for you to pucker."

Surprising someone there would have been virtually impossible. Called Bear Thicket, it lay between Morgans and Wells creeks, two smaller tributaries of Satilpha. (The last organized bear hunt in the county had taken place there twenty-five years earlier, and a sizable bear was killed. A few bears were still around when the Burkes were hiding in that thicket. My father's sister, Vadie, gets credit for being the last person to see a bear there, more than ten years after the Mitcham War.) Bear Thicket is now mostly planted pines—as representative a place for these times as it was for the 1890s frontier.

The Burkes would have known Bear Thicket as well as or better than any other people living in Mitcham. Their lower fields, where some fertile ground was under cultivation, lay on the west bank of Wells Creek, a short stream that rose above their place, and flowed into the Satilpha down near where the Browns farmed. When it was known that the Burkes and their sidekick, Jim (Bud) Jordan, had escaped into Bear Thicket, it was surrounded by the mob. W. W. Waite, the twenty-eight-year-old sheriff and brother of Ernest McCorquodale's widow, arrived in Mitcham after the James brothers and Bedsole had been killed.

Waite did have bloodhounds brought in from Mobile. Sizing up the Burkes's hiding place and listening to stories that they'd even thought of erecting breastworks told not just the Burke bunch but everybody else in those parts how ignorant the mobsters were of Bear Thicket. Erecting conventional breastworks in that place would have been nearly impossible for a hundred axmen and shovelers. Somebody was probably recollecting Civil War duty. Waite even suggested that artillery be summoned (it wasn't). If the bloodhounds left any get in Mitcham, such mixed pups would have been the single blessing brought in by the mob.

Despite being surrounded by dozens of men, the Burkes eluded the trap set for them, and, with their father, Bill, and Bud Jordan, crossed the Tombigbee and made it to Louisiana. Other family members were either in the group or had left ahead of them. The Burkes and some of their Bedsole relatives never returned (at least not permanently, but some say they slipped back for visits) but Bud Jordan did, about six months later. Believing he had properly confessed to officials and had the protection of Clarke County law, he was killed in May of 1894. Most believed he was killed by Charlie Smith, and some contend that Smith was coached by Charlie Coats. My dad said that when Bud Jordan was killed he had a mouthful of raw peanuts.

While the Burkes were hiding out, the bloodlusting mob captured a man named Ivy Smith, no relation to the hired gun, who supposedly had taken food to the fugitives. He also never got the benefit of a doubt. Using another method of execution, the mob strung him up. Ivy Smith was, at most, a minor player; he was a man-of-all-work, who shows up on the ledger of a Mitcham Beat merchant, John Bell, as being paid for hauling merchandise from Coffeeville. The lynching of poor Smith provides the clearest evidence of how bloodthirsty and out of control the vigilante mob had become. They also took delight in putting nooses around the necks of those suspected of withholding information and trying to torture out information. (They had little success.)

It's worth noting that when the Mitcham War was done, the livelihood of three Mitcham Beat storekeepers—Bedsole, Bell, and Norris—had been threatened. The town merchants would not have grieved to see their country competition roughed up or, even better, driven out of business. The terrorized residents of Mitcham Beat stood by while the mob looted corncribs and haylofts, forced women to cook for them, and tortured men to give them information on the outlaws who'd escaped their rifles or noose. They were counting on Pinkerton to come through again.

On August 13, 1893, two days after Kirk James and Tooch Bedsole were shot to pieces, a group of Mitcham citizens, bedeviled by both mob and gang, caught between raging forces and mistaken for members of Hell-at-the-Breech, sent this letter to the governor of Alabama, Thomas Goode Jones:

Dear Sir:

We beg leave to call your attention to the fact that a mob of from 50 to 100 armed men are roguing [*a verb backformed from "rogue"*] in the central portion of this (Clarke County). Not only are they killing suspicious and accused carrectors [*sic*] but are killing some of our own quiet and best citizens by taking them prisoners, tying them, taking them off in the woods and shooting a hundred bullets in them and leaving them for the buzzards, presenting cocked pistols at women and children and scaring them almost or quite to death and many other things too numerous and rediculous [*sic*] to mention and we now appeal to your Honor for protection. Our sheriff has been unable or unwilling toward stopping it, as yet.

We will refer you to the following Gentlemen:

T. N. Griffin, Campbell P.O. Campbell beat

Henry White and Jas. Huggins, McIntyre P.O, New Prospect beat [*a phrase in the margin says* "where the mob is"]

E. P. Chapman [*and*]

S. P. Chapman, Grove Hill P.O., Grove Hill Beat

T. S. Bedsole, Tallahatta Springs, Ala. [*interestingly, a relative of Tooch and the Burkes, which says something about divisions within that family*]

J. D. Doyle, Coffeeville [*formerly of Mitcham Beat*]

Please send troops at once. Nearest point is Thomasville M&B [*Mobile and Birmingham*] Railroad.

We can also refer you to Jas. White agent at Thomasville.

We are yours respectfully &c,

J. T. McIntyre

George N. Huggins

Richard Ott

W. W. Truett

Address us at Tallahatta Spgs, Ala.

[*Scrawled at the foot of the letter, in other handwriting, is this postscript:* "Please let this be private & confidential as we will be killed if found out."]

You don't have to read between the lines: Everybody was threatened by the mob. In its way, this letter is eloquent, and it is evidence that some of the people in Mitcham could write as well as anybody in Clarke County of that era and could do so under fear of death. (A perfect word, *roguing*.) They were reaching out. Not all the townspeople were part of the anti-Mitcham machine. The beleaguered residents believed they had influential friends in the towns. Interestingly, though many Civil War survivors were alive and well, I find no evidence, in formal records and family stories, of Civil War veterans being directly harassed by the mob. The older men, leaders in the community, seem to have been advising behind the scenes. Clues exist in the names mentioned in the letter to the governor. S. P. Chapman was a lieutenant in Peter and Elijah Brown's Civil War company, which was raised in Grove Hill; a John Doyle enlisted in the company raised in Coffeeville, led by John W. Bell. (The likely role of Civil War veterans in the conflict I will treat later.) The letter also indicates that Mitcham people also had friends in adjoining beats. Mitcham had already become New Prospect beat; Tallahatta Springs was a village just north of Mitcham, in the Campbell beat; and some of the outlaws lived in another adjoining beat, Clarkesville.

In the "as yet" in reference to the sheriff's actions, the letter suggests that the people had some hope Waite himself might eventually come round, but he too was trapped between loyalty to his family and constituency and to his oath of office. And he was too smart to get into that Mitcham mess alone. In November 1893, the young sheriff himself wrote the governor, informing Jones that he "may have to call on you for troops." Waite stated twice in the letter that he wanted the correspondence kept confidential. His final sentence to the governor ironically echoes the Mitcham letter postscript: "*Please do not let this get in to print.*" If Waite's plea had gotten into print, it would have revealed the sorry state of Clarke County's law enforcement and might have placed him on a killing list.

Family complications typical in such communities are also evident in the letter the Mitcham citizens wrote Governor Jones. W. Wesley Truett's youngest sister, Docie, was now Tooch Bedsole's widow, and this Wesley (not to be confused with John Wesley) Truett was also the first cousin of Winnie Truett Brown, who was the mother of Lee Brown. The letter referred directly to Tooch Bedsole's body being left for the buzzards, but then so had Kirk James's.

The milquetoast governor already knew about the conflict because it had drawn such wide attention in the state press, and his office had begun to make mild inquiries before this plea from Mitcham arrived in Montgomery. When Governor Jones finally did send a representative to investigate and report to him, county officials made it appear that what had happened in Mitcham was lawful, that the mob was duly deputized, and that matters had quieted down. And that glossing over was accepted in the state capital.

Actually, Oscar York himself gets credit for stopping the mob's binge of violence. (*MWCCA*) The looting, torturings, and the hanging of a hapless fellow such as Ivy Smith should have satisfied the most sadistic, but the mob wasn't done. York allegedly stopped the riders in the road and said that enough was enough. He saw that with the killing of one innocent man, and the near-execution of Sandy Norris, matters had gotten out of hand. Vigilantism was playing to its customary conclusion. All that remained would be for the mob to disperse and slink into anonymity, ashamed of themselves and hoping history would forget them.

It hasn't.

THE GLORIOUS UNCERTAINTY OF THE LAW

On both sides, the 1890s Mitcham War adversaries acted out roles long defined in newspaper accounts and pulp fiction. That a pair of villains could be called the "James brothers" adds to the irony. The Witch Creek hills, the formidable northern boundary of Mitcham Beat, were used by a regional network of horse thieves, moving stock by night from the East to the West. Rumors were rife that Jesse James himself had come through. The natural Witch Creek lodgings were a perfect waystation for horse thieves—the cool limestone caves were especially pleasant during the summer heat, with ample water, swampy reed-cane flats nearby to provide forage, and plenty of fat pine and downed hardwood for fires.

Heroic outlaws would have appealed to members of the mob, who saw themselves as purging the country of a lawless gang of local ruffians.

Members of Hell-at-the-Breech, if they had had access to the literature, could have seen themselves as fighting tyrannical merchants. They had a role model in Alabama's most famous outlaw, Rube Burrow, who robbed the rich men's trains. A predecessor to Pretty Boy Floyd and Bonnie and Clyde, Rube Burrow was killed in 1890, and his death was reported in *The Democrat*. And the story of Billy the Kid, who was killed by Alabama native Pat Garrett in 1881, was widely circulated. But Hell-at-the-Breech was not interested in common romantic robbery or in personal tests of courage. They wanted political and social power. However doomed and preposterous they may appear in our time, the Bedsole-Burke gang was making a point.

If Mitcham Beat had been blessed with a writer of the Ned Buntline stripe, those bloodthirsty vigilantes would have made perfect countervillains, killing and terrorizing poor farmers at the behest of double-dealing, rapacious bigshots. The beat had all a Buntline or a script writer for *Deadwood* would have wanted—whiskey, murderers, a terrified populace, even a whorehouse located not far from Bedsole Store. Of less interest were a large number of respectable citizens not happy either with the internal strife fomented by the Hell-at-the-Breech or with the way they were being regarded by the outside world.

Among these were folks who formed a true middle class: indistinguishable from Hell-at-the-Breech, threatened but not killed by the mob, trapped for a while, tortured and terrorized but awake and watchful. Policing a gang that included relatives and neighbors with no help from central authority was more than those caught in the middle could handle. They were not respected by the vigilantes who considered the whole "colony" in cahoots with Hell-at-the-Breech. Yet, eventually, these seemingly passive people would be forced into action.

In the real-life melodrama of the Mitcham War, neither side won, and the story did not become the stuff of legend and song. Thus, to read the official record, you'd think the Mitcham War was over by August 19,1893, when *The South Alabamian* in Jackson, published by John Simpson Graham, ran a circuitous, three-column defense of mob law. Here are the headlines, a few excerpts, and my own italicized comments:

WAR IN CLARKE
THE MITCHAMITES ROUTED.
THE WILD AND WOOLY BOYS CURRIED.
THREE OF THE RINGLEADERS KILLED.

Never in the history of Clarke County has such excitement prevailed in our midst as during the whole of last week. On Monday morning of last week there was an up-rising of law-abiding citizens of our county for the purpose of exterminating the notorious outlaws of Mitcham's Beat. These lawless devils had reached a point where they could no longer be tolerated. It was impossible to reach them by law, owing to the fact that they always had witnesses who would swear to anything that might not be to their interest, therefore the people took the law in their own hands. At every term of the circuit court in this county some one of their clan was before it charged with some offense, but no case was ever sustained. [*Graham's hyperbole: Not every term, and who defined this singular "clan"?*] It was well known that they committed murders, burned houses, made and passed counterfeit money and planned to do many other atrocious crimes but those who knew these things were afraid to divulge it. . . .

They were repeatedly told that if they divulged anything that would bring trouble on this clan they would be killed. The

65

good people of that neighborhood lived in mortal dread. [*So far, so true. "Mortal dread" is exactly the right term. Those who passed along stories to me were trapped, and their fear of being trapped between two sides did not end with the Mitcham War. Then comes several hundred words of Graham's account of Hell-at-the-Breech, the killing of Joseph Anderson, the shooting of the Howze brothers, and the association of the Burkes, notably Babe, with Jim Jordan. Graham mentions the mistaken killing of a man named Keown, instead of someone named "Peters." No such killing was reported, and no "Peters" or "Keown" lived in Mitcham Beat, or for that matter, Clarke County. The one name that sounds like Peter Keown is Peter Brown, who was not killed. Graham also brushes across the relationship of Duncan Bedsole, an uncle of the Burkes, and their plans to kill a man named Foscue who lived in Coffeeville. All this rumor Graham had apparently gotten from an informer named Walter Deas, of an old family from that hamlet, who was said to be both a member of Hell-at-the-Breech and the mob.*]

And now comes Graham's ultimate defense of the mob's actions:

Under ordinary circumstances we [*Ah, the editorial "we"! That first-person plural reserved for royalty, editors, and best citizens!*] are bitterly opposed to mob law, but in this instance the law was powerless. Had these notorious fellows been allowed full sway for another 12-month the consequence would have been terrible. They were growing more bold every day. They made their boasts that the officers of the law dared not molest them. They said they cared not a d--n for the law or the officers. They threatened to clean out the town of Thomasville because one of their gang had been made to pay for a pair of shoes that he had stolen. [*And then the following statement, which counters the violent-hick stereotype of the people of Mitcham. It's worthy of bold-face in a larger type size.*] There is no necessity for these fellows to rob and steal, for most of them have good farms, plenty of stock, and promising crops. [*I give it Graham here: In this context "these fellows" refers to the community in general, not simply the outlaw "clan." These are the people whose land holdings and general character are borne out in court documents and in the collective memories I've been privy to. These subsistence farmers were mostly freeholders, not renters or sharecroppers. At the conclusion of this defense of lawlessness, Graham, who would be admitted to the bar the next year and then elected to the legislature, turned the Mitcham Beat episode into a reflection of state politics—the coming Kolb-Oates contest for the governorship, which pitted these yeoman-farmer Populists against the Black Belt–Bourbon oligarchy, of which Graham and other Jackson parvenus aspired to membership. His implication is as clear as his logic is skewed: These Farmers' Alliance people were not only Mitchamites, they were also Kolbites, and Reuben Kolb, the Populist candidate, was running against the Democrat William Oates, who was both a newspaper-man and a darling of the Old South aristocracy. After all, Colonel Oates had commanded the 15th Alabama Infantry regiment on the final day of the Battle of Gettysburg, considered by most historians as the turning point of the War and, need I say, of the United States. And, as Joshua Chamberlain, whose men turned back the 15th Alabama, had become governor of Maine after the War, so it seemed only fitting, more than thirty years after what was now a glorified defeat, that Oates become governor of the sovereign state of*]

*Alabama. Moreover, it must have seemed uplifting that a backwa-
ter fellow such as Graham would have wanted to stick like beggar
lice to the coat tails of a man of Oates's reputation. Ironically, many
Dale County relatives of Mitcham Beat residents had fought, and
many died, at Little Round Top.*]

To give John Simpson Graham the justice he never gave to the
poor people of Mitcham Beat, perhaps he grew ashamed of his role as
barking dog for the mob. He makes no mention of Mitcham Beat or
the Mitcham War in his 1923 history of Clarke County. He did not
want the mob episode or his role in it preserved. That smug, small-
town bravado, expressed in the headline about the "wild and wooly
boys" being "curried," is nowhere found in his history. He had stopped
his bragging thirty years later, and he apparently wanted to expunge the
episode from the printed record. He meant to promote the county, and
most of the "history" in his volume is lifted from the exemplary 1879
Timothy Ball volume.

At the conclusion, writing of himself in the third person under the
bold all-caps heading "WHAT THE AUTHOR STANDS FOR,"
Graham proclaims, "He stands especially for a strict observance of the
provisions of Article 6 of the United States Constitution, which reads
as follows: 'In all criminal prosecutions, the accused shall enjoy the right
to a speedy and public trial by an impartial jury. . . .'" The elderly pub-
lisher-lawyer-politician had conveniently overlooked his earlier disre-
gard for the rule of law.

His fellow publisher-editor, Isaac Grant, had begun reflecting on
the perils of vigilante justice within two months of the mob's departure.
In the October 5, 1893, issue, Grant, whose paper advertised itself as the
champion of "Democracy, Tolerance, Morality," published an editorial in

which the attempt to hide particular criticism behind the veil of general commentary is apparent. Taking to the pulpit, after he had himself stayed largely silent while the Mitcham Beat terror raged, he comes out strongly in favor of law and order (and competence):

MOBBING.

Where is all this mobbing and lynching to end? The country, north and south, east and west, seems to be running wild with it. The newspapers report cases of it almost every day, under all sorts of circumstances and conditions and in the most harrowing forms. It is teaching the young men of the country a fearful lesson in lightly taking human life and in disregarding the forms and remedies prescribed by law. Time can only reveal the magnitude and character of the bitter fruit of this unfortunately sowing. There are cases, now and then, where mobbing seems a necessity and where criminals can be reached and punished only in that way; but there are thousands of instances of lynchings where the law, if tried, would render full and speedy justice. Let us hope that some good may grow out of this alarming condition of things by impressing judges, and solicitors and juries and all officers entrusted with the enforcement of the law with the importance of prompt and speedy justice. Doubtless "the glorious uncertainty of the law" has had much to do in bringing about the present dangerous condition of affairs. Show the people the disposition to enforce the law without regard to childish motions and quibblings for delay, and soon they will manifest more respect for it and mob violence will become less frequent.

To well-educated subscribers, Grant's use of the "glorious uncertainty of the law" may have been familiar. It comes from the eighteenth-century Anglo-Irish playwright Richard Brinsley Sheridan, whose play, *The Rivals,* was widely read. I wonder if the Grove Hill journalist knew how fitly the full quote describes the division that sparked the Mitcham War: "The glorious uncertainty of the law was a thing well known and complained of, by all ignorant people, but all learned gentleman considered it as its greatest excellency."

There's little wonder to whom Grant was addressing his remarks in the fall of 1893, surely not to the "ignorant people." Though his own hands were not clean, he was taking a swipe at law enforcement. He does not appear to be on the best of terms with the courthouse ring. In February of that year, his obituary-eulogy for former probate judge Jack Roper Wilson, whose son was now running the courthouse, suggests sharp differences. It indicates more than the old rub between newspapers and public officials. Grant wanted to take a final shot at this fellow, else why would he have published this not-so-subtle description of the late lamented Jack Wilson: "He was a man of peculiar and striking temperament and disposition, and, having some faults and weaknesses, as we all have, possessed, also, many commendable and noble qualities, and while we should bury with his body the memory of his faults, let us seek to imitate his virtues and help others on to a better life." So much for the venerable Latin axiom, *de mortuis nil nisi bonum*: speak only good of the dead.

If accounts from the papers are an indication, in the fall of 1893, the county establishment considered the Mitcham episode over and done with. If so, they were wrong: The most baffling killing happened a year later.

SORE VEXED

True, by the fall of 1893, Mitcham Beat was considered by the general public to have been cleansed of its outlaws: The mob had done its bloody business; the Burkes and several Bedsoles had slipped across the Tombigbee, bound for Louisiana. Babe Burke remained under indictment for murder till 1910, a tactic that doubtless discouraged his return. Distant relatives said he did come back, under cover, and my grandfather said he saw him in Mobile and that he "was wearing a derby hat." The fact was emphasized every time Lee Brown told of this encounter; the derby hat may have meant Babe was still arrogant, but I'm puzzled by the repetition of this seemingly meaningless detail. My grandfather never said whether Babe recognized him or if they spoke. According to census records, William Edward Thomas Burke took his third given name and lived as "Thomas Burke" in the Ouachita Parish

area. Over the years, he was a bill collector and a Baptist preacher—
matched trades that could cover all bets.

Meanwhile, back in Clarke County, elected officials had successfully
misled a governor's investigator by claiming the mob had been duly deputized. The whitewashing, the cover-up, had to have been apparent, but
who cared? Only later would the ring's lying chickens come home to roost.
But Mitcham people had more on their minds than county politics.

The detective, Pink or Pinkerton, his work for the McCorquodales
done, had moved in, intending to stay. From all indications, he meant to
take over the role left open by the now-destroyed Hell-at-the-Breech
and to dominate the community. Even before he'd directed the mob
leaders to the Burkes and participated in the terrors, he'd gained possession of their land. The 1893 deed is on record. When Babe Burke, his
father, and brothers were hiding in Bear Thicket, Pink had had their
lives in his hands. I don't doubt for a minute that he could have ferret-
ed them out, or waited them out, but why should he? He had his blood
money, and, if Pinkerton family legend is true, a horde of gold. He knew
that the remnants of the Burke-Bedsole bunch had two choices: Stay
and face lynching or attempt an escape. But there was a third option: He
could surreptitiously buy their land, give a wink and nod to them as to
when and how to escape, distract those bloodhounds, divert the mob by
having an innocent man, Ivy Smith, lynched, and the chapter would be
closed. The Burkes, no fools, chose the sell-out/clear-out option. In fact,
the deeding of their land to Pink was recorded after they had crossed the
Tombigbee, toward Louisiana, never to openly return.

On the morning before Kirk James and Tooch Bedsole were killed
in August 1893, a *Mobile Daily Register* story on the war included this
paragraph: "Pink, the man who worked up the case on McCorquodale's
assassin, sent his son down to Babe Burke's to get his mule. On the way

the boy met a son of old man Burke who informed him that old man Burke and his two older sons, Jim Jordan and a man named Clarke were down in the woods."

Census records do not reveal a "son of Pink." The boy identified was probably Robert Wilson, whose unmarried mother was one of the women living in Pink's house. Much in this story rings false. The "son of old man Burke," probably Jasper Burke, was misleading the boy or the reporter, or the reporter got the story wrong, or both. By then, Pink had to have known that no Burke would ever again be plowing that mule, or any mule, in Mitcham Beat. Unless they were worked by womenfolk, the Burkes' fields had lain fallow for a least one crop year, while they were eluding the mob. Clarke's name never again enters the record. The name could have been Coats (a popular brand of thread was Coats & Clark), a likely fellow to cut a deal between Pink and the Burkes. Or Jasper Burke may have invented the name as a way of fooling the mob into believing that more folks than they supposed were hiding out in Bear Thicket. What Pink knew was that the mob was on its way, right then, to kill Kirk James and Tooch Bedsole.

We know precious little about this enigmatic man, the malevolent stranger. I can find no photograph of Pinkerton. The image of him that I will hold in my mind till further evidence arrives is of a mean, horny, pushy, scary character, with madness in one eye and shrewdness in the other. One collateral descendant recalls a reference to his having had red hair, unlike other members of his family. The relative remembered hearing stories that the man the family called "Robert" wore a moustache and was short in stature. (Once upon a time, Lee Brown said to me, out of the blue, "Keep your eye on a little man.") Pinkerton had lived amongst a tri-racial colony of people in Washington County, who stood apart from black and white societies and eventually were declared to be an offshoot of the Choctaws. They were called "Cajuns," but they in no wise were connected to the traditional Louisiana Arcadians. Pinkerton sired some children amongst them, if the family's surmises are accurate. The question of how he got associated with the mob remains unanswered. I figure some of those Jackson people fetched him in; they would have known that, with the famous name, he could be called a "detective" when, in fact, he was a sly, smart killer, a "spy," as a Mobile paper called him, though he seems to have operated openly. And why not, as an outsider.

Were it not for that name on the shattered gravestone in New Prospect Cemetery, some land records, and the old newspaper stories on microfilm few would know that a man who called himself John R. Pinkerton had ever existed. The National Archives records of the Civil War reveal the name of a John R. Pinkerton from Conecuh County who served a brief stint in an Alabama conscript unit and deserted. What he did thereafter, like his relationship to his own kin, nobody seems to know.

Behind the lines, military, bureaucratic, and paramilitary activities were often commingled and confused. My great-grandmother Mott, born Harriet Ann Hutto, said that during the War, when most of the able-bodied younger men were away, Hutto or Judah relatives in Dale County heard of their plight and sent hams, lard, and other foodstuffs, but these were all stolen by the "conscript officers," who may have actually been guerillas. She never forgot or forgave, though she did not know of a certainty who'd stolen the provisions. Such preying on the helpless would have provided perfect training for a man of John Pink's stripe. It could also have provided him with a fortune—that horde of gold John Robert Pinkerton is supposed to have accumulated. The loans he made to local folks and the land transactions that involved cash confirm that he had money, and it may have come from a combination of private stash and mob payoff. No matter, money or the rumor of money added to Pink's power and mystique.

Whatever his lineage, looks, physical stature, money, or past associations, this John Robert Pinkerton had to have been a threatening presence to be called a bully. Though he'd made enemies during the Mitcham War, he apparently didn't fear being killed by local people. He also did not mind their reactions to his setting up as a farmer amongst them and beginning to build a constituency that would fill the void left by the fall of the Bedsoles and Burkes.

I have now forgotten the context in which my father told me about Pink. He must have thought I'd picked up some information—eavesdropping was allowed, and exciting, but questions were ignored—and he spoke only in snippets, but he never discussed any connection with our family. He was fiercely protective of his father. (Of course, I now think I know why no anecdotes were circulated, and it has to do with shame, pride, and the statute of limitations.) My father spoke Pink's name with a sneer. Because he was born three years after Pink died, whatever my father told me was hearsay, though heard from how many people I'll never know. All I remember is that he said Pink was once in the hire of a Mitcham man, a miller who abused low-level whites and poor blacks. But my father could not or would not tell me all he knew. He was himself conflicted, wanting on the one hand to suppress the truth, and, on the other, to air it out. Killing, especially when a family member is suspected, has been known to trigger such a conflict.

Pink must have moved into the old Burke place at the end of 1893. Living with him and his wife were two unmarried women and the four illegitimate children of one of them. If the newspaper story is correct, Pink was "borrowing" a mule in August 1893, from the Burkes, who had already fled and would hardly be lending their nemesis a mule any-way. That time of year is too late to put in anything but a fall garden and too early for syrup making. By means direct and devious, Pink was pressuring some people and putting others in his debt. Among those to whom Pink had lent money was George Brunson, who owed him the equivalent of $3,600. Brunson's name would later be linked to Pink's as more than a debtor. Pink was also acquiring land, some of which he would convey to J. S. Pinkerton, who lived across the river. People must have thought the Pinkertons were going to team up on them. They knew John Robert Pinkerton had money, enough to buy land, and they had to have feared that he might have connections, families like theirs who would come in and take control.

Here is where the Browns enter the formal record.

In a deed dated February 4, 1894, and recorded three weeks later, Peter Brown and his wife Winnie Truett Johnson Brown bought 160 acres from J. R. Pink and his wife, Sallie, for $160. According to the Consumer Price Index, or CPI, an 1894 dollar equaled $25.70 in 2010. By the "unskilled wage" equivalent, $1 equaled $130. Thus, this piece of property would have been worth, at the lowest, $4,112. On February 12, 1894, the Brown couple sold 280 acres to the Pinks for $350[CPI=$8,995]. Almost immediately, Peter Brown bought another 280 acres, in another part of Mitcham, for $350. So, in these transactions, the Browns wound up with 440 acres and were out more than $4,000, but the acres they held were much less valuable as farmland and farther from home than the tract they had sold Pink. I smell a rat in these dealings.

I doubt that these land sales were made between friendly parties. The 160-acre tract Pink sold to the Browns was obviously land he did not want or need—it was worth only $1 an acre—and the 280 acres Pink bought from Brown was more valuable. Why would Brown, with his farming family, want to part with it? Pink wanted it because that larger tract, 280 acres, joined the Burke (now Pink) property on the back side, in the more fertile Wells Creek bottomland. Brown was not selling because he needed money, else he would not have turned around and bought more property after shelling out four grand for the 160. The complicated transactions suggest that Pink coerced Peter Brown into both the buying and the selling.

"Pressure" in Pink's case would be in the form of implicit or explicit extortion: He could, and would, kill any member of the Browns' family. It is highly unlikely the Browns would have willingly sold such good land to anybody, much less to a man so reviled. As family stories have it, Peter and his brother Elijah, both Civil War veterans, were normally fearless but not reckless. From time out of memory, these people had owned their own land and sought to acquire more if it suited their needs. But in Pink they were dealing with no ordinary man. This interloper was a devious killer, an agent of the mob. Long gone was any peace of mind these country folks had known before Hell-at-the-Breech had started its mischief.

By September of 1894, fear was rekindled amongst the neighbors who had suffered through the terrors of the past year. This new, more insidious danger had moved in, and people were talking about it and trying to figure out a way to cope with it. The community network was abuzz, and a consensus was building. We know now, from old court records, that one neighbor of the Browns was carrying a warning, channeled through at least two other neighbors, to another neighbor, who, they thought, was leaning toward Pink.

The brief formal record points to networking amongst only a few neighbors. To consider this group a small minority would be a mistake.

This community was tight-knit, and those few who would testify reflected a large, influential consensus whose passion was transcending mere concern, which in plainer English means they were scared, fed up with being overrun, and getting ready to act. Their community was a mirror of the town set—also intermarried and thick with each other—but what power did these country people have over their own lives? Short of moving away or capitulating, what means did they have to protect their own safety?

STORM CLOUDS RISING

An interloper of Pink's ilk would want to dominate a family like Peter Brown's. If it fell under his control, so would similar families, either by submitting or selling out. As one neighbor later testified, he was out to "bulldozer people." (The word *bulldozer* existed before it referred to tractors with blades. Arising in the 1870s, its original meaning was "a person who intimidates or coerces.") The land transaction with Peter and Winnie smells of extortion. Pink's behavior, inferred from land deeds and court documents, indicates that he believed that Mitcham was now his, not Babe Burke's, oyster.

By the standards of that time and place, Peter Brown was prosperous. Though not rich, by a long chalk, in 1894 he had money from cotton and cattle, perhaps some timber, and from his Confederate pension. The pension was small but enough to cover store staples, and he got a new wooden leg when he needed it, for free. The State of Alabama, in its largesse after Reconstruction ended, looked out for the CSA veterans, particularly those who'd lost a limb.

From whatever source, Brown had enough ready cash to participate in dealings involving Pink. He owned at least six-hundred acres, no more than a fourth of it arable, and his stock could range over many more. He was fifty-seven years old, and his wife, Winnie, was fifty-four. Moreover, they had a strong family around them. They had sons and daughters old enough for field and house work, in addition to the relatives of an extended clan. The Peter Brown family lived in a board-and-batten, dogtrot house on a knoll in a grove of live oaks less than two miles from the junction of Satilpha and Wells creeks, about three miles from Bedsole Store. It stood on the 79.8 acres patented to Peter Brown in 1860, in Section 35, Township 10-N, Range 1-E.

The Browns represented most of the positives and many of the negatives of the rustic, peasant way of life their people had followed for generations: They wanted to be independent, to get along with their neighbors, to farm and hunt and fish and sing and joke, to sit up with their sick and bury their dead, and to tolerate the dozens of quirks and spats in a clan so big it admitted a whole register of personalities, intelligences, talents, faults, eccentricities; they wanted good saddle horses, stout oxen and mules, productive cows, prolific hogs; they valued huge vegetable gardens. If they lived relatively happily in their backwoods hamlet, they knew what the trade-off was: Being left out, being shunned, being far too ignorant of the wider world. It was a tough bind.

Valuing hard work and practical skills over advanced book learning, they lived by a stubborn ethos, by varying degrees of resistance, defiance, and by a reluctance to surrender their own old ways of doing. But then right many did not want social mobility to begin with. And, considering what they saw in the towns, why should they want to be part of that set? On the other hand, Mitcham Beat was a social—what some might call ethnic—pocket, vulnerable and therefore defensive, with an attitude not unlike that of any group that flips the assimilation coin. The children of this old set would know a bone-deep fear unlike that felt by the old people—the fear of being stigmatized, cut off, without the education or advantages available to others. That anticipation of shame would have seemed strange to those older settlers who thought their way of life in that isolated hamlet was sufficient. If I read the old stories right, what the original Mitcham people wanted was simple and straightforward: safety, fairer treatment, and, of course, higher cotton prices. What else could have mattered?

In the 1890s the old homesteads were considered bulwarks, all anybody would need or should desire. They expressed what people stood for and against. The Browns' house resembled many in that community—nothing to brag about, nothing to be ashamed of. Its design is apparent in one old photograph. The roof was of cypress shingles, riven from the huge, gauzy-needled trees that grew in the oxbow ponds. The house and every other building on the place were built of logs or of heartwood boards from long-leaf pines, so laden with resins that they would resist rot and termites. The downside of fat pine is that it will inflame in a flash, which accounts for the absence of so many of these old places and the ruins of so many chimneys.

Across the front ran a porch, what my grandfather called a "gallery." Here would be hung a waterbucket and dipper, a shelf to hold a washbasin, and a drying rag on a nail. Here, of a morning, my father said, Peter Brown downed a dram of pure grain alcohol, ordered from Mobile on a steamboat that landed in Coffeeville. He then drank a dipper of water and went off with his boys to work the fields. Four or six rooms opened off the breezy open hall. To warm at least two of the high-ceilinged rooms of the single-gable house, there probably would have been two chimbleys—not *chimneys*, except in fancy writing. These were made of the soft, coastal plain limestone, quarried and sawed into blocks from an outcropping in the creekbottom near the Browns' place.

It would be customary for the main fireplace room also to be the parents' bedroom and nursery, a privilege of rank and age. The males and females, sons and daughters, cousins, passersby, would separate into rooms cold and drafty on winter nights. No matter if there were cracks in the floors you could throw a cat through and windows with shutters instead of glass-paned sashes, there would have been a weight of quilts to keep them warm. On any given night, there may have been three to a bed, another assist to warmth, if one sleeper didn't hog the covers. If there were young children about, sections of quilts would be held before the fire, and the warm blankets would be used to wrap them up in. Lee and Ferdie (and maybe Billy and Elijah) slept across the hall from their parents. Papa said that Ferdie was so smart he knew when their father was coming home after carousing with his friends. Papa said he and Ferdie would hear the extra-heavy thump of Peter Brown's wooden leg on the hall floor, and Ferdie would say, "Pa's drunk. He's putting down his stump."

It is likely that Ferdie played a strong background role in planning to dispose of Pink. He was brilliant, according to the old people, who generally speak glowingly of those who die young. His familial name, which my grandfather put on his tombstone, was Ferda, a shortening of Ferdinand, the name he was identified by in the 1870 census. The uncommon name suggests ties to Gen. Ferdinand Claiborne or to Prussian connections. He taught in a country school and wrote a beautiful hand, my grandfather said. He died of complications following a lower leg amputation performed by three doctors, one of them drunk, in the hall of that dogtrot house in 1898, when my father was a baby. Ferdie's father, Peter, who'd had a leg amputated in Tennessee, obviously had enough money to fetch a trio of surgeons. Ferdie was overdosed on chloroform, they claimed, and his kidneys failed.

When he finally awoke from the operation, Uncle Ferdie said ants were stinging his leg. He was told that the leg was off and had been buried. He kept writhing and pleading. Finally, to placate him, somebody went out and dug up the leg; it was covered in ants. He died a week or so later and is buried beside his mother in Oak Grove Cemetery. Ferdinand Brown left a bundle of his own writings that he entrusted to his brother Billy and requested he read them, destroy them, and never disclose their contents. Uncle Billy died sixty-five years later. My father tried him, time and again, but William W. Brown never broke that deathbed promise. Whatever Ferdie might have said that shed light on the Browns' role in the Mitcham War and the Pink episode was consigned to ashes by an honorable brother.

On the back of the house where Ferdinand Brown died there would likely have been another porch, perhaps with side rooms. Kitchens were in separate buildings behind the houses, to keep heat away in summer and to limit damage if a fire broke out. Often there was a roofed walk between house and kitchen. When I was a boy, it was not uncommon for those old people to say that someone was in the "house," meaning they were not in the kitchen. The cooking rooms were furnished with a table, chairs for the adults and a bench for the children, a range, and a woodbox, filled before bedtime with seasoned, finely split hardwood and fat pine splinters. A dishpan and a water bucket would have been on a shelf in front of a lone kitchen window, from which could be flung the dirty dishwater. I never saw such an old kitchen that also didn't have a slopbucket, where table scraps were thrown for hogs or chickens.

In the older houses, up in Mitcham, behind these one-room kitchens, sometimes with a lean-to pantry, there was usually a cluster of outbuildings—at least one corncrib and maybe a cotton house, a privy or toilet, a wagon shed, sometimes a blacksmith shop. There'd be a chicken yard and henhouse, and fenced lots for milk cows and their calves. One crib would have side-sheds to stall oxen, horses, and mules, and at least one outbuilding would be used for harnesses, plows, broad axes, froes, shovels, mauls, picks, prising bars, crosscut and hand saws, and whatever else might be thrown in by way of tools. A good distance from the house, in a vain effort to isolate the smell of pig manure and flood of houseflies, was the hog pen.

Often the vegetable garden, a critical component of this kind of homestead, would be beside the house, close enough so that at night dogs could run off marauding rabbits and other varmints. The cotton and corn fields were down in the fertile lands near the creeks. The contrasts on any given homestead were stark—walking ankle deep in cowshit, swatting horseflies, plowing and hoeing and gathering constantly, boiling clothes in smutty washpots foamy with lye soap, pressing clothes with "sad" irons heated on wood stoves, and then sitting in rooms with colorful quilted bed coverings, doilied chairbacks and, old prints and photographs, and then cooking and eating, after formal prayers, in kitchens with clean oil cloths and rich food smells.

In 1894, Peter Brown held lands that lay behind the house, toward the forks of Satilpha and Wells creeks, and in front, north of what is now called Brunson Road. From the tract northwestward, across this road, was the land he and Winnie had sold to Pink, above Bear Thicket. Behind the Browns' house was a tract that had been owned by

W. E. Burke, either Babe or his father, Bill, and I presume, after the Burkes left, by Pink. If Pink bought all of the Burke property—and I can't confirm that he did—then Peter Brown had Pink in front of him and behind him. That could not have been a peaceful prospect.

Peter Brown had plenty of land to farm; after all, he had homesteaded property as soon as he came of age, in 1858, and owned it outright two years later. Records show that several sales and purchases had taken place after the war. I can't figure out how much land Peter Brown had at any given time. In 1884, he and Winnie sold 360 acres to his brother Elijah, at the bargain price of $200. The next year he and Winnie sold the major portion of what appears to be about 120 acres to T. J. Gilmore, a veteran of the 32nd Alabama regiment and of the company raised in Coffeeville and led by Captain John Bell of Mitcham Beat. Gilmore's sergeant was John L. Brown, and his comrade was Samuel James W. Brown, the two brothers of Peter and Elijah Brown who died in the Civil War. Obviously Gilmore was an old acquaintance, and his name will appear in court testimony pertaining to the incident in question.

The 1885 deed to Gilmore contains an intriguing qualification: "except that portion lying north of Rocky Branch which we have sold to E. Brown; also our interest in land lying south of Rocky Branch, the Eligah [*sic*] Brown land being the amount received for the land lying north of said branch." These brothers were buying and selling land and swapping land with each other. The last tie to Dale County was broken in the 1880s, when Elijah Brown bought a 160-acre tract from Louis Brown, Jr., the first cousin who had come to Clarke and moved back to southeast Alabama. Some of the land the brothers held may have been inherited from Jack Brown or from the Truetts, since both Peter and Elijah were married to Truett women, who appear to be first cousins.

Their brother John L. had married Charity Truett, Winnie's sister. After he was killed in the Civil War, she remarried and moved away, and John L.'s place passed into the hands of her father, the Methodist preacher, William Hampton Truett, who went back to Dale or Henry county and died in 1870. In his 1923 book, John Simpson Graham simply identifies Truett as one of many ministers passing through Clarke County.

In 1888, Peter Brown sold 160 acres to W. L. Henderson, probably Wyley Henderson, who lived just north of Mitcham Beat, for $200. Whether Peter was strapped for money at the time is yet another unanswered question. A search of Clarke County records reveals only one mortgage taken out by Peter and Winnie Brown, which indicates their cash flow was rarely an issue. It was to N. B. Boyles, for today's equivalent of $3,750. Exploitation of this common practice of advancing money from merchant to farmer created the tensions that resulted in the Mitcham War. Significantly, this particular borrowing took place in January 1893, less than a month after Ernest McCorquodale was killed.

N. B. Boyles appears in census records to be Napoleon B. Boyles, who was born in 1855 in Monroe County, across the Alabama River east of Clarke. In 1880, he lived in Lower Peach Tree, a town near the northeast Clarke County line, and he settled in Choctaw Corner, just north of Mitcham Beat. He ran a store in Thomasville, the town Hell-at-the-Breech had supposedly threatened to capture. That episode is chronicled in *MWCCA*. It started with a quarrel over whether a Mitcham boy had stolen a pair of shoes from Boyles's store and ended with Thomasville's ordering fifty repeating rifles from Selma and asking for Army assistance to repel the invasion. It never happened. But the reaction indicates what a fright Hell-at-the-Breech had put into these town merchants.

For the purposes of this narrative, Boyles's lending money to Peter Brown a month after Hell-at-Breech killed Ernest McCorquodale indicates that he did not consider the Browns party to any rural insurgency. Of more importance, he believed that Peter Brown would repay the note and, if he didn't, the value of his property was well worth the risk.

The Boyles note outlines clearly how much a farmer stood to lose if a note was not paid in full or if some uneducated farmer was cheated by an unscrupulous lender. In this note Peter and Winnie borrowed against "our entire crop cotton corn &c raised by us or anyone we control in this year 1893, one sorrel mare, name Jennie, one Iron Gray Filly name Kate, one yoke oxen, name Brandy and Jerry, real estate [*fully described in surveyors' plattings*] 280 acres." Apparently, Peter and Winnie paid the note in full, as records show no sheriff's sale or foreclosure notices, and they got to keep their crop and stock, including the latter, well-named and surely off-ox. And so much for the notion that everybody in Mitcham rode mules with croker sacks for saddles, while the town people rode only blooded horses whose saddles were made of squeaky leather unfamiliar to these hicks. Other notes also show the number of saddle horses in that area of Mitcham Beat. (As a trade for a dog, my grandfather gave me a saddle with no stirrups or girth and a bridle with USA on it, probably brought home from the War. Both disappeared after my father's death.)

In 1894, in the household with Peter and Winnie Brown lived at least five of their children, in order of birth: Eula Ann (named for her grandmother, married John Hutto two years later), thirty; Ferdie, the club-footed brother, twenty-five; Lee, then twenty-three; Billy (William Wrighty), who was eighteen; Biddy Ann Idella, seventeen, named for an old Dale County cousin but called Della; and Elijah (not to be confused with his uncle with the same name), fifteen. Living either in the house or nearby was the half-brother, Fate Johnson, born in 1861, when Winnie was married to Joshua Johnson, who left for the Civil War and was presumed dead when she married Peter Brown in 1863. (That story later.)

In the vicinity lived dozens of blood kin—among them Peter's brother Elijah and his family, including a grown son, John Washington, and the whole Truett clan, relatives of Winnie, and the Wards, whose daughter Caroline had married Winnie's brother, John Truett. Nearby also lived the growing family of W. H. Mauldin, a celebrated hymn singer and teacher of singing schools. Mauldin proved how valuable a neighbor can be: He would play a key role in the major event to follow.

As I have pointed out, maybe far too often, many of these families had married into others, so a whole, close society existed, with relatives and neighbors intertwined, with some subclans at the center and others on the periphery. But to my knowledge there were no solitary souls, no hermits. The Mobile papers were right, in part: This was a colony all right, though hardly "criminal." And it not only was close; it became, for survival, collusive.

The Mitcham Beat network, like others in such communities, would not admit as allies certain outsiders who did not live by the same code or who were considered abnormal trash. Formal manners were the rule, and religion served as much for earthly bonding as it did for spiritual guidance. As noted, Winnie Brown was the daughter of William Hampton Truett, listed in the 1860 census as "clergyman, ME," which meant he was a country Methodist preacher. The church-going set were primarily Methodist or Baptist, with few doctrinal differences. Both hewed to the language of the King James Bible, and some churches were "union," meaning that both denominations worshiped together. There were some points of distinction: Methodists had that creed which spoke of "one holy and catholic church," which, to Baptists, hinted of papist sentiment. Methodists tended to be better educated, less emotional, and they were overseen by presiding elders and bishops. But they believed in "backsliding," which meant you can lapse and return to the fold, and Baptists held to the Calvinistic "once saved always saved" principle. Baptists were also more independent, with laxer standards for ordination, and were prone to fight amongst themselves and split off into new churches. No wonder that by the 1920s there was no longer a Methodist church in Mitcham Beat but at least four Baptist congregations.

Whatever devilment Peter Brown's family might have been into, there nevertheless was a standard of formal conduct: Off-color language in mixed company was taboo; men respected, and feared, good women; women had their own powers of enforcement; sexuality was regarded as private and dangerous. Bodily functions were not the stuff of ordinary conversation, and I never heard my mother or father use the word *pregnant*. A woman with child was "expecting." Who can believe that people who lived in such crude surroundings, where procreation was everywhere evident, could have also been, well, prudish?

As everybody knows, standards of propriety are necessary, lest a family or a community lapse into chaos, families be rent asunder, jealous murders to ensue. Which does not mean that this rural code, oddly reflecting the last decade of the reign of Queen Victoria, was unbroken. True to the nature of fallen creatures, these values were often honored in the breach. Far too many stories of secret genealogies and infidelities exist for us to believe that nobody fell through the thin ice of decorum. Unfaithful husbands and erring wives, lusty boys and hot-blooded girls, shotgun marriages, and bastard children were about as common in that settlement as anywhere else. And whispered accounts about such shames, involving families other than one's own, were as delightful then as they were in Stratford-upon-Avon—unless you were on the receiving end of the gossip.

In 1880, three households from the Browns, there lived a woman named Susan Wilson, who was fifty-nine years old, and two daughters, Annie, who was twenty-three, her sister Becky, nineteen, and the infant son of one of the daughters, Robert, who was eleven months old. No adult men were listed as part of that household then, or in later censuses. By 1894, Susan was dead, and her daughters and grandchildren had moved in with Pink; by this time, Becky had three more illegitimate children. These women would have known, Biblically or otherwise, the four Brown boys, Ferdie, Lee, Billy, and Elijah. Given the reputation of these women, it is impossible for me to believe that the young men of the neighborhood did not visit *in flagrante* with them, deny visiting them, and, by daylight, shun them. Among those young men, I suspect, was Lee Brown. As court records later revealed, the Wilson sisters had no reservations about testifying against Lee Brown. (There could be a countervailing argument, that these women of questionable reputation were scorned by righteous fellows, but, given human nature and the number of young men in that community, I doubt that few, if any, were either high-minded or, for that matter, choosy.)

There were other easy women in that neighborhood but most lived far in the backwoods or on the places of landowners who employed tenant farmers or hired hands and kept them in run-down shacks. I could name a few of these exploiting landowners, and the names of the poor folks who lived on their places, but I won't. I do remember such impoverished, tattered people showing up at dinners-on-the-ground and being fed and pitied by those who had brought baskets laden with ham, fried chicken, vegetables, and an array of cakes and pies. They were served without overt judgment, but people will talk.

I return to my grandfather and the family dynamic: Lee Brown was the third son. Ferdie was the second, and the first-born was John L. He was born a year after his namesake and uncle, Sgt. John L. Brown, was killed in the Civil War. The younger John L. died in 1885 when he was twenty-one. He was stricken in the field, turned blue, and was dead before they could get him home. He died the same year as his grandfather, Jack Brown, and is buried beside him in Oak Grove Cemetery. My grandfather, who was fourteen when his brother died, idolized John L.—he was a crack shot, he was more than his brothers could ever be, and so forth. Apparently, like his namesake, the younger John L. was a born leader. Knowing my own family's penchant for identifying such talent at an early age, I accept my grandfather's memory as more than mere grief. My grandfather never got over his brother's death, and he spoke of him often when I was a boy. Their birthdays were two days apart. I've tried to imagine what a promising young man this brother must have been, and I know that having such a role model die at a formative age for my grandfather moved him in some deep way. As an old man, after Grandma died, Papa bought a tombstone to mark John L.'s grave, to make certain his name was not forgotten.

It fell then to Lee to take over John L.'s role as oldest able-bodied son. He was a muscular, handsome fellow, and he must have been his father's surrogate. (Peter was able to help with the farming, but with his pegleg, he probably had trouble getting about.) From the records, Lee seems an audacious though not exceptional hell-raiser. There were hushed stories about his occasional drunken episodes in later life. In one remembrance, he tried to kill his wife with a butcher knife, before my father got there to calm him down. In another, he was an amiable drunk, who showed up and ran up and down the dog trot hall and said, "Old Jack's coming through!"

I never saw either the threatening or the humorous drunk. Papa could be a fiery old man when I knew him, but I never saw him violent or tipsy.

I don't know what to make of this Lee Brown's relations to his father, Peter. Family stories suggest Lee was the favorite, but then Peter Brown was hardly even-handed when it came to favoring sons over daughters. He left not a cent or an acre to any of the daughters, saying their husbands should provide for them, and he left Lee more than he did to his brothers. Yet even if his father favored Lee over the others, he kept their business dealings formal. A year before Peter Brown died, he lent Lee $124—about $3,000 today—as a crop advancement, and he paid the fee to have the mortgage recorded. If the son defaulted, the father would get three bales of lint cotton and cottonseed. By then Lee was settled, married, and the father of five children. I figure he either paid his father or Peter chose not to take him to law. Maybe he was attempting to show to his other children that, in fact, he was not favoring the son who had stood up for the family.

Peter Brown had to have known that this boy of his was a hellion. In September of 1894, Lee Brown and a neighbor, George Brunson, sixteen years older than Lee, had gotten into a spot of trouble. According to court records signed by Benjamin F. Elmore, the circuit solicitor, as district attorneys were then called, "Lee Brown did willfully injure or deface a building belonging to George James. The Grand Jury of said county charge that before the finding of this indictment Lee Brown did willfully injure or deface a building belonging to Charley Kearley." Who was this Charley Kearley? I can't find a trace of him in records. Perhaps he was a passer-through who lived briefly in Clarke County and was associated with George James, brother of Kirk and Lev. It was George James who, in apparent drunkenness, had confessed to the mob and nearly gotten a good friend and neighbor, Sandy

Norris, killed along with Kirk James a year before. One of the witnesses prepared to testify for Lee Brown was his half-brother, Fate Johnson. These indictments were thrown out, and I find no mention of them in the *Democrat*. I suspect that Brown and Brunson were both drunk, but I also believe this incident reflects a Mitcham Beat attitude toward folks who made threatening trouble, who were mixed up with Burkes bunch and Hell-at-the-Breech.

Hushed conversations must have been going around fields, fireplaces, and hunting grounds that fall of 1894. What do about this Pink? Obviously they wanted him out, but *killed*? And by *them*? And, if so, plans for such a killing would have to have been tightly guarded, else someone would tip off Pink. They were afraid, and mothers probably more so than the men who had been through the Civil War. Their sons were soon to be drawn into yet another, more immediate war. As the wiser heads knew, an act of such enormity could bring the wrath of the old mob back to Mitcham. But Peter Brown and others in that closed circle were not to be bullied and left cowering. Moreover, they must have suspected that this Pink or Pinkerton had run out his string with the county politicians and best-citizen mobsters. Whether they knew they had exceptional allies amongst the town set inspires speculation.

If there was fear, there was also a storm of anger and a powerful will at work. By that code, when you deliberately insulted a man, the offense was grave; the insulting of one's integrity or the impugning of one's honor demanded a response. Some call this mindset *attitude*, others *sensibility*. (The American historian Henry Adams, describing his Harvard roommate, who happened to be a son of Robert E. Lee, said, "Strictly, the Southerner had no mind; he had temperament. He was not a scholar; he had no intellectual training; he could not analyze an idea, and he could not even conceive of admitting two.") But even that offended temperament might not have been enough to bring a whole community to the final crisis, the pulling of triggers. Still, I take it that Pink did more than make lewd remarks or passes at women. Even if certain people thought him despicable for consorting with the Wilson women, that fact alone would not have prompted a confrontation. If his sexual exploits were offensive, such doings nonetheless were his business, as long as he kept his distance. On the other hand, if he had made unwelcomed advances on the wives or daughters of his neighbors, he would have been killed, or would have killed somebody, in an immediate show of passion. But however loathed J. R. Pink might have been personally, dealing with the threat he posed required reason, cooperation, and calculation.

As it turned out, many in Mitcham, not just the Browns, had specific reasons for wanting Pink out of that beat. One was John R. Bell, whose store at New Prospect was said to be the largest in the county, making him a competitor to town merchants. Bell was married to Sandy Norris's sister, Essie. Though Sandy is described as a cheerful man, who would stay up all night planning a practical joke, the Bells were old-time Scots warriors, known for seeking military conflict, according to one descendant. At least two from Clarke County had gone to the Mexican War—and returned. John R. Bell's father, Captain John W. Bell, had led the men of Mitcham Beat in Company H of the 32nd Alabama, recruited in Coffeeville. He had died near Chattanooga before John R. Bell was born. (The merchant who would figure in the Mitcham conflict was conceived when the Confederate captain was on a brief leave. The older children did not recognize their father when he returned and fled from him.)

Veterans of the Civil War—I can think of at least ten men, ablebodied, in their fifties, some of whose names would enter the court

testimony, who lived within a five-mile radius of Bedsole Store—
might have hated killing or seeing people killed, but they were hardly strangers to it. And those in the Alabama 24th, Company E, and
the Alabama 32nd, Company H, the two infantry units into which
most Mitcham men enlisted, had fought under that harshest of disci-
plinarians, General Braxton Bragg. He was notorious for ordering
executions, and Peter Brown had participated in at least one. (See the
Civil War chapter.) Like others who'd gone off to war, Peter Brown
had been educated in killing, and he returned to a South in which
anarchy and violence were commonplace. Everyone at that time,
especially the women, lived with the spectre of death and the memory of loved ones gone. Though family stories reveal Peter Brown's ten-
der side ("The Unclouded Day," that old standard hymn which speaks
of a land where no storm clouds rise, was his favorite), my grandfather said he had "steel blue eyes," like other old Browns, like Lee himself. In one photograph, Peter appears as a merry old man, sitting on
the porch with his second wife (Winnie died in 1900) and his two
sons, who are dressed in matching formal hunting garb, with canvas
leggings, and holding rifles. In a later photo, those eyes are looking
into eternity.

Unfortunately, we can find no pictures of Winnie, but she must
have been tall and slender, like her sons. Many of those later Truett
women were slim, with high cheekbones and sharp blue eyes, and I like
to think of her as the woman who taught her sons manners. I don't
know why my grandfather had ways that seem English—eating with
his knife and with his fork tines down—or why he was so particular and
formal. (When we were off in the woods, he always walked fully out of
sight to relieve himself.) I suspect that his sense of manners, the vanity
of his dress, the care he took to keep his sheds and home grounds so

orderly, came from his mother and her family. My father said he remembered seeing Winnie only twice: Once she was at a woodpile, gathering splinters, and the next she was lying in her coffin. He was only three, but he recalled his father lifting him up to gaze upon her form and saying, "We will never see Mother again." Why those Brown boys called Peter Brown "Pa" and Winnie Brown "Mother," rather than Ma, is a small hint as to differences between Browns and Truetts.

With eyes that could be both mirthful and piercing, and with hands that seem twice the normal size, Peter appears to be a man of sanguine temperament, welcoming but stern. He does not seem a man who would brook a blood insult, and, if he was like others I know, he did not forget an affront. He had seen much better men than John Pink killed. He and the other veterans were *de facto* leaders in that community, and they and their wives were a tougher bunch than Pink thought. Interestingly, during the Mitcham War, the vigilantes, some of whom were also Civil War veterans, had steered clear of these men and their families.

Apparently, this lesson was lost on Pink.

REGARDING THE AFTERNOON OF NOVEMBER 27, 1894

The setting: Through the palmetto and sweet-bay woods that lay between the field in which Pink was plowing and the Peter Brown house, across Wells Creek, there ran a wagon or then-public road, two miles at best. It would take no more than thirty minutes to walk it, ten to ride it, past the old Burke place, on what is now Alabama Highway 154, the main road between Thomasville and Coffeeville. Travelers would pass the fertile fields Pink had bought from Peter and Winnie Brown.

Why would anybody be plowing at that time of year? Even more so considering the turbulent fall weather? On Sunday, October 7, 1894, a two-day northeaster struck. *The Clarke County Democrat* called it a "big blow," with winds so strong that cotton left unpicked was blown out of the bolls and damaged. By Wednesday, the temperature had dropped to 48—cold for that time of year in Clarke County. On

November 29, the paper reported that a "heavy rain, accompanied by hail and gale" had moved through six days earlier. "Gales" were storms, sometimes in the backwash of hurricanes that might be reported but never predicted. Old stories tell of bridges being swept away and roads blocked by fallen timber and covered by the overflow of many creeks.

The rains, and floods (or *freshets*, as they were called) must have been general across the Alabama-Tombigbee basin. On the eastern shore of Mobile Bay, a jubilee took place in late November 1894 when the "single tax" city of Fairhope was dedicated in accordance with the writings of the social philosopher Henry George, who believed in commonly held property. The term "jubilee" refers to a rare phenomenon which occurs when a heavy influx of fresh water from inland—meaning the Alabama-Tombigbee-Mobile river watershed—meets abnormal winds and tides of the bay, causing an imbalance in oxygen content that sends suffocating fish—snapper, mullet, speckled trout, croaker—into a frenzy. They flop ashore, and folk living near the water reap a bounty, bringing out buckets and tubs and celebrating with neighbors.

Torrents are common in southwest Alabama any time of year, and usually jubilees come in summer. In 1894, the phenomenon happened in Mobile Bay much later than normal. What better omen could Fairhope settlers want? A hundred miles northwest, in this troublesome fall, the swollen streams in Mitcham brought no joyful jubilee.

In the best of times, after such autumn rains inland, the weather turns cool and mellow. Skies clear, and the air is clean and pure, purged of the dog-days miasmas. In that interregnum between seasons, farm people can rest a spell and reflect: cotton is ginned; notes and taxes paid; corn gathered; vegetables jarred; hog-killing done and smoke-houses filled; syrup made and canned; and woodpiles stacked high with split hardwood and fat lightard. Schools are in session. Women begin quilting, and men, their long labors done, can hunt day or night. Snakes are either dormant or sluggish, and the good dogs—hounds, curs, bulldogs, and feists—were not likely to get bit by cottonmouths or rattlers. And the families needed the game for food as well as for sport. But the fall of 1894 was not the best of times. Folks were trying to recover from what had happened only a few months before, and cotton prices were down to less than a nickel a pound because of the nationwide Panic of 1893. And, now, after all that strife and struggling, comes this alien.

Sandy soil dries quickly. The heavy rains had fallen four days earlier, but Pink must have thought the ground was not too wet to plow. Or maybe he was too inexperienced to know, or to care. Somebody knew Pink was in the field and had passed word along that he was in the open, exposed. It did not seem to matter that he might be accompanied by two of the women, Becky and Annie Wilson, and, Robert, the fourteen-year-old son of one of them, all of whom later testified in court.

Witnesses would say that on Tuesday, November 27, three men approached the field where John R. Pinkerton was plowing and either stood or stooped behind a rail fence. They were carrying guns, probably lever-action .38-caliber Winchesters, the favored rifle of the day because it also used .38-caliber pistol cartridges. They emerged from the woods and either knelt or stood—again, the testimony would vary—and Pink did not see them until the first shot was fired, and then he hollered. "Look out!" But by then it was too late. Eight or nine shots were fired. The shooters probably did not know if they hit Pink or not. But they were not firing randomly. No one else was hit; nor, for all I know, was the mule.

No one testifies to Pink's having fallen down. The black powder in the shells would have created a cloud of smoke, and unless the wind was blowing, some of the scene would have been hazy. Pink, a man of fifty-two, outran the fourteen-year-old boy, ducked behind a tree, and made it up a hill to the house. As the party was fleeing, the shooting continued. Those lever actions of the 1890s did not eject cartridges quickly; the action was awkward. The weapon had to be taken down and the spent cartridge ejected, and then the shooter had to re-aim. If visibility was perfect, and eight or nine shots from three guns were fired, the shooting would have taken less than a minute. If these rifles were fully loaded, sixteen cartridges—fifteen in the magazine and one in the chamber—it is possible that only one shooter fired. Possible, but, given the testimony, not probable. The most objective of the testimony indicates that the initial yardage was fifty-five yards, and, as the party fled, increased to more than a hundred yards. And how could the impeached witnesses be certain of the number of shots fired? Testimony varies on the number of guns and the actual shooters. Unfortunately, for one trying to imagine this setting—though, fortunately, for Brown and Brunson—these witnesses were apparently not exposed to grueling cross-examination. According to the Wilson women, the assailants were in full view, and after the firing they rose and walked, not skulked or fled, away. Hardly the action of ambushers fearful of recognition.

But they couldn't have been completely calm. Pink was not shot dead in his tracks. He didn't even fall. Unless they saw blood they couldn't have known he'd been hit, and they couldn't have known he was mortally wounded. He might have lived. And then what? Had Pink survived, more hell would have been to pay.

What the gunmen did not know right off was that Pink had been struck by only two bullets. These must have hit him in the guts (one newspaper report says "stomach") or nicked a blood vessel, or both, because he lingered until Thursday afternoon. J. S. Pinkerton, a brother, four years older, was called in from Choctaw County, across the river. (James S. Pinkerton is listed in the 1900 federal census as living in Choctaw County and his occupation was "mfg mineral extract." He was a prosperous landowner and storekeeper, and the extract he bottled must have been heavy on the alum. It was used to stop the blood from razor nicks.)

But no sheriff or doctor was summoned. Why? Did Pink know he was dying? Did he know he had been abandoned by the vanished mob? In the two days between the shooting and his death, the people of Mitcham Beat must have been more fearful than ever. There must have been a collective sigh of relief, not to mention a payoff, when the word circulated that the man memorialized in New Prospect Cemetery as John R. Pinkerton was indeed dead. I can't say my grandfather and his family were happy, but I also can't say that they were filled with remorse. I can believe they were relieved to have the necessary deed done.

I can find no obituaries for John R. Pinkerton, no records of who buried him, probably no more than two days after his death, in the graveyard in McEntyre, across from New Prospect Church, not two-hundred yards from the country school or John Bell's store. According to old timers, there had been, in pioneer times, another graveyard behind where the current sanctuary stands. If so, it is lost in the thickets, and it would take a necro-geographer to locate it. Of the nearly three-hundred or so graves in that cemetery we call New Prospect, almost all marked, only seven pre-date Pink's, and they are far away. He was a loner, buried alone. The name and dates on the fallen tombstone can be read, but the thick marble stone has been shattered, perhaps by rifle shots and the fragments placed at the head. The grave is less than a hundred yards from where Lev James a year earlier had raged around after hearing Preacher Wash Etheredge recite the Scripture, a passage from the epistle of a once-blinded convert renamed Paul to those licentious Galatians: "Be not deceived; God is not mocked: for whatsoever a man soweth, that shall he also reap. For he that soweth to his flesh shall of the flesh reap corruption."

On December 6, 1894, this item appeared on the front page of the *Clarke County Democrat*: "Mr. J. R. Pink, an old man, was shot from ambush and mortally wounded while at work in his field in Mitcham beat on the evening of the 27th, ult., expiring on the 29th. Before he died he swore out warrants against three suspects, but after examination they were released." (*Grant seems to be saying to the reader:"We all know this man and the backstory. No need to spell it out." Yet this matter was far from done with.*)

Like nearly every other word about Mitcham Beat that appeared in print in the 1890s, Grant's lone paragraph, formed in hand-set type, is laced with errors. Pink was only in his early fifties, hardly as decrepit as "old" implies. He must have been hale. According to witnesses, he took two bullets without falling and outran that fourteen-year-old boy, before dying two days later. That Isaac Grant of the *Democrat* published even the one paragraph is remarkable—and that he fell back to using the old name for the district even more telling. In September of 1893, more than a year before the Pink killing, after the mob had disbanded, Grant had written, "There is no precinct called Mitcham. For several years the beat has been called NEW PROSPECT. It seems that the organization known as 'HELL AT THE BREECH' was composed of members of 5 or 6 beats. NEW PROSPECT furnishing very few more than some of them." (Using all-caps for the church's name appears to be Grant's subtle way of implying that better days might be coming for the beat.) Grant had his own reason for wanting the illegal mob's ravagings forgotten: His former brother-in-law was Simeon T.

Woodward, a leader of the mob. So was the probate judge's future son-in-law Cobb Nichols, who would serve as a courthouse clerk, go off to medical school, thence to Panama, and become a farmer-doctor in the Tombigbee valley below Jackson. And Grant's dismissal of judicial proceedings as "questioned and released" was not the last word. A week later, Brown and Brunson would be within a hundred yards of Grant's newspaper office, in the Clarke County jail.

It's noteworthy that Grant used none of the available phrases to identify the victim. He could have been called "detective," or "the man responsible for routing the Mitcham gang" or, heaven forfend, a "best citizen." Pink, not John R. Pinkerton, was merely "an old man." Now he was a dead one.

Many who read the *Democrat* paragraph probably knew exactly how the killing of Pink was effected. From this distance in time, several interlinking, overlapping scenarios seem possible, some probable, to any who read the news story and understood the subtext:

Scenario I: Peter Brown, the old peg-legged veteran, with enough money in hand, simply called in a known hit-man. It was said Charlie Smith would kill anybody "if you dropped fifty cents in his hat." (*MWCCA*) This was the same Charlie Smith who allegedly killed Bud Jordan, a Hell-at-the-Breech outlaw who believed he could return from Louisiana and be left in peace. And this was the same Smith who had come in from Texas and, like Pink, had worked for a time as a goon for the cruel miller. He was associated with Charlie Coats, who arranged for him to kill Bud Jordan. (I cite this fact on the authority of a Mitcham woman I respect greatly. Her father or grandfather tracked Coats from Jordan's plowed field to Coats's own doorstep, and later in life, confronted Coats with the fact. She said Coats hung his head.)

Peter Brown, or an intermediary, contacted Charlie Smith and told him what was wanted. Smith was too smart not to know that Peter Brown spoke for more than himself. If he deceived Brown, he would not be paid—or, worse yet, killed. Peter Brown tells Lee to go with Charlie Smith, to make certain the job was done. And Lee, scared of both Pink and Smith, gets his sidekick and drinking buddy, George Brunson, to go with him. What Lee Brown might not have known is that Brunson owed Pink a chunk of money (the equivalent of about $3,600) and was being pressed to repay it in cash or perform other favors. Or Brunson may have told Brown, and Brown had thrown in with his buddy. Brunson already knew he was caught between sides, but, if Pink were dead, he was free of debt to the interloper and also free of doubt as to his allegiance to his neighbors.

Scenario II: Somebody else, maybe the most prominent storekeeper in the beat, John R. Bell, had contracted with Charlie Smith. Smith appears on Bell's ledger, in a strange accounting entry, for a lump sum of $10, in which one man buys for Smith and is repaid by Smith, who is responsible for the debt—with no items listed. (The exact date of this transaction is not revealed in the ledger, but the archival ledger, copied in garbled individual sheets, runs from the late 1880s to the early 1890s.) Bell had his own motive: His wife, Essie, was Sandy Norris's sister. Pink was the man who, with Charlie Coats, had almost gotten Sandy killed. If you think a Scotsman such as Bell, whose family was famous for fighting, would not want to get even, you don't know Scotsmen, Clarke County people, these particular Bells, or, for that matter, human nature. Bell could have paid Smith directly or joined in the conspiracy with Brown and others.

Scenario III: Somebody had to think of what would happen if *1)* Smith killed Brown and Brunson and fled, with the money; thus, Smith would have had to be paid in full afterwards; *2)* Smith merely informed Pink and the two of them fell into together; thus the presence of Brown and Brunson, armed, was a way of ensuring that Smith did the job; *3)* Somebody leaked word to Pink that he was a marked man, and he was waiting for the ambushers, and the hired killer and his accomplices failed—then what? Given these *ifs* a backup was required.

Scenario IV: This killing was set up with some bit of collusion from one of the Wilson women. Lord knows how many of these men had lain with them. And what would they do if Pink were killed? Being long-time outcasts, sad parodies of Mitcham people in the county's eyes, they knew the gamble: Pink might rough them up if he suspected them and wasn't killed; but if he was, they would get some freedom, and maybe money and maybe that place. If they had tipped somebody off, as this showdown was planned (whether they knew it was to be a slaying didn't matter) they were clear; if not, they were clear. Besides, they had been beaten around, abused, scorned for so long by so many hypocrites, what did they have to lose, either way? This theory presupposes, of course, that the Wilson women were intelligent and calculating.

Scenario V: Certain people who had sanctioned that mob, and who had much to lose, wanted Pink, with his knowledge of all that had happened, expunged from public notice, removed, forgotten, dead. The town set tacitly approved, possibly encouraged, what amounted to a planned execution. The go-between was Charlie Coats, who later became sheriff and a member of the state Legislature.

To my mind, the county establishment was deeply involved, no matter what the scenario. And the name of "old man Pink" was nearly erased, as virtually everybody wanted. But whatever circumstances one might presume, one fact may be documented: this Lee Brown was becoming a name in the news, a man with a known public presence.

The press coverage of the arrests was immediate, state-wide, sensational, libelous *per se*, and hugely erroneous. On Sunday, December 9, 1894, a front-page story appeared in the *Mobile Daily News*, from an "informant" who may have been on a river boat that had stopped in Coffeeville. Or, more likely, he was riding the Mobile and Birmingham down through Thomasville, Whatley, or Jackson, picked up a *Democrat*, and overheard talk around the depot or on the train. (This informant spoke in a hillbilly accent, unless the reporter was type casting. I never heard anybody from Mitcham pronounce the place "Meacham." This speaker probably said "feesh" for "fish" and "heel" for "hill." Also, I suspect that the intrepid reporter for this story was high on something.) The names of the "murderers" are among the few correct facts in this story.

Verbatim from the December 9, 1894, *Mobile Daily News*, with clarifying and critical commentary:

CLARKE COUNTYS CRIMINAL COLONY COMMONLY CALLED MEACHAMITES

———

Is again in an uproar—Three Men are Supposed to Have Been Lynched for the Murder of a Peaceable and Law-Abiding Citizen.

Ever since the Bob Sims affair in Choctaw County, there have, at times been manifestations of that cowardly spirit of assassination, which, at Bladon Springs, caused the death of an innocent man. [*A reference to the "Sims War," which involved a totally different set of circumstances in the county across the Tombigbee. It also involved lynchings of more than one "innocent" man, and some of the men who would later join the Mitcham mob went over to help administer justice. And, in turn, some of the Choctaw County vigilantes had come over the Tombigbee to assist their Clarke County allies. For a fuller description of this conflict and its link to the hysteria of the Mitcham mob, see* MWCCA.] The beat in Clarke county known as the Meachem beat has already been the scene of cowardly outrages, and last week a quite [*sic*], peaceable citizen, a farmer named Murphree Pink [*I'm guessing "Murphree" or "Murphy" was either a nickname or slang-of-the-day for detective or goon. The victim is referred to by these names in other stories.*] living in the eastern[*western*]portion of Clarke county, was regarded by members of the gang as a spy, and determined to rid themselves of him. Accordingly, he was fired at while at work in his field, three out of nine rifle balls [*See witnesses' testimony, to come.*]striking him in the stomach, from the affects of which he died several days [*two*] afterward.

Before he died Pink made an antemortem statement [*antemortem statements are generally, except in Mobile papers, made before one dies*] that three men, George Brunson, Charles Smith and Lee Brown had fired upon him from ambush. But at a preliminary trial they were acquitted [*no they weren't*]. Since then new developments have arisen which place the guilt upon the suspects. Indignation ran high, for ever since the memorable killing of the four [*two*] assassins of James [*Ernest*] McCorquodale in August, 1893 [*December 1892*] the respectable citizens of Clarke have pledged themselves to free the county of the lawless element, even if lynching has to be done. On Thursday night, Mr. Tom Webb [*probably Sam or Will Webb—no Toms in the censuses of 1880 or 1900*] and S. D. Roberts [*again, no such Roberts with these initials appears in records*] of Coffeeville arrested Charles Smith. Constable Tom [*perhaps Oscar*] York and his posse brought in on Friday, Lee Brown and George Brunson. The citizens commenced to gather immediately and couriers were sent out to notify others. There was no time lost for it was feared that the Meachamites would ride into town and demand the surrender of the three murderers. A general feeling prevailed that the county would be far better without such men and it was self-evident that Judge Lynch would soon hold court.

Several hundred men, many of them armed with winchesters, shotguns, revolvers etc., with a look of determination on their faces, stood around the stores and talked over the situation. There is no telegraphic communication from Coffeeville, and the informant of the NEWS, who came down from that locality, could not positively say that the three men had been hung, although he believed that the aroused citizens would not stop until Pinks' [*sic*] assassination had been avenged.

Further information will be anxiously looked for.

Another *Mobile Daily News* story ran, again on page one, two days later. Though the trailing paragraph guts the article, the paper could not hold back from stirring the pot.

Because this story bears a Birmingham dateline, it likely came in by telegraph:

PUNISHED PINKS
—

MURDERERS-THEY ARE REPORTED TO HAVE BEEN LYNCHED.
—

There is a Rumour From Coffeeville That the Three Men Have Been Sent to the Other World by the Rope Route-The Rumour Denied.

Birmingham, Ala., Dec. 11—Three of the notorious Meachamite gang in Clarke County have been sent to eternity by the rope and limb route. The Meachamite gang has for years run illicit distilleries; made counterfeit money [*how, pray tell, in so backward a place?*] and committed robbery [*stolen shoes?*]and murder [*true, in the case of Emanuel Pruitt, Joseph Anderson, and Ernest McCorquodale.*] For a person to give them away meant death. In August, 1893, James McCorquodale [*error repeated, probably taken from the* Mobile Daily News]and citizens drove the gang from the county. No less than ten men met their deaths.

A short while ago, the Meachamite's [*sic*] returned to their old haunts and began to wreak vengeance. Murphree Pink, a farmer was shot down. Pink made a dying-statement charging George Brunson, Charles Smith and Leo [*sic*] Brown with the shooting. They were arrested and upon preliminary trial [*this was probably a coroner's jury, though a preliminary hearing was held later*]accquited [*sic*, also *reproba, falsus*]. After being turned loose other evidence was found that they were members of the Meachamite gang. [*evidence? guilt by residence?*] The scene is some distance from the telegraph station, but a man just arrived at Whatley, the telegraph office, says the men were lynched.

The *Mobile Daily News* must have regretted having to publish the following paragraph at the foot of such a juicy story:

A FABRICATION
Special to the Daily News.

Whatly [*sic*], Ala., Dec 11—No truth in report of lynching at Coffeeville. The murderers of Murphree Pink are still in jail. There is no mob and no trouble is anticipated.

Who wired in the lead story and then the correction? Regarding the first, I suspect someone who knew what made news. Isaac Grant, with connections to the Mobile journalists? Of the second, someone who knew what the informant was up to. No report of a lynching appeared in *The Democrat*. Regardless, neither my grandfather nor Mitcham Beat was the real issue here. The focus was shifting to those who had helped the mob, hired Pink, and lied to state officials by saying the undeputized mob was a legal posse—not to mention letting its killings go uninvestigated and unprosecuted. No wonder the courthouse ring was beginning to consider just what readers across the state considered the actual "criminal colony."

What it came to was this: George Brunson and Lee Brown were apparently questioned, then released, then subjected to a coroner's jury. Then came the arrest warrant, eleven days after Pink died.

The State of Alabama
Clarke County to the jailer of Clarke County

—

On examination of Lee Brown charged with the offense of murder it appears that such offense has been committed and there is sufficient cause to believe that Lee Brown has been guilty thereof. You are therefore commanded to receive him into your custody and detain him until he is legally discharged. Dated this the 10th day of December, 1894.

J. O. York, J.P

Brown and Brunson were held in what must have been one of the county's most impressive buildings. Though the courthouse was in a frame building, the "new jail," built in 1870 after prisoners had tried to burn a hole in the old log structure, was made of brick. Graham, in his 1923 history of the county, said that around the structure was a wooden wall eighteen feet high. This wall consisted of seven-by-ten-inch fat-pine beams, set in a ditch twenty-four feet from the jail. Two-by-twelve boards were nailed to the beams, creating a double wall, and the whole wall was topped by two-foot planks to prevent rot. However proud the citizens were of this secure structure, they paid little attention to the comfort of the inmates, who were held in steel cells, which the *Democrat* called "cages." Brown and Brunson must have shivered through their three nights. The jail was so cold prisoners complained, and the next spring a grand jury recommended sashes for the windows.

While Brown and Brunson were literally cooling their heels behind bars, a Grove Hill lawyer, J. T. Lackland, had been retained, and he filed for a writ of *habeas corpus*:

Expartee—George Brunson and Lee Brown

—

Petition for Writ of Habeas Corpus
The State of Alabama
Clarke County
In Probate Court [*then a trial court*]

To Hon. John M. Wilson, judge of said court your petitioner J. T. Lackland who makes this application on behalf of George Brunson and Lee Brown respectfully represents that the said George Brunson and Lee Brown are imprisoned in the county court jail of said county by W. W. Waite, sheriff of Clarke County by virtue of two several *mittimus* [*a now-archaic legal term referring to the transmission of a document from one court to another, in this case from the coroner's inquest to the county court; it seems that an "or" was omitted between "two" and "several" or that one of the words should have been struck*] charging the offenses of murder issued by one J. O. York, a justice of the peace of said county. Copies of which *mittimus* are hereto attached marked "Exhibit A and B" and constituting a part of this petition and petition alleges that the said George Brunson and Lee Brown are charged with and held for the alleged murder of J. R. Pink and are not as petitioners is informed and believes guilty [*a translation: who, represented by Lackland, have been charged by misinformed petitioners, who believe them to be guilty, but who are wrong, and upon such false information they have been arraigned on the false charges for which they were arrested, and jailed, and who believe themselves not guilty*] of said offense, and are held without probable cause of guilt thereof and that said detention is illegal, wherefore petitioners pray for a writ of habeas corpus directed to the said W. W. Waite commanding him to bring the bodies of the said George Brunson and Lee Brown before your Honor at a day and place to be by you appointed together with the cause of their said detention and may it please your Honor upon the hearing of said writ. Discharge the said George Brunson and Lee Brown from the custody of said W. W. Waite, sheriff of said county and that other further and general relief may be awarded in the premises as are neat and proper and the petitioners will ever pray to.

J. T. Lackland
Sworn to and subscribed before me this 13th day
of December, 1894. Jno M. Wilson, Judge

The two were apparently released that day, though I find no indication that bond was set or bail paid. Records in the Clarke County archives show jail fees charged for a three-day period, December 10–13, 1894, and other court costs, but these were not exacted by the county until April—judgment, $10; clerk's fees, $5.10, sheriff's fees, $8.30; witness fees, $7.50; solicitor fees, $7.50; jail fees, $3.30. These fees amounted to about $950, in today's currency, using

Consumer Price Index 1895–2009 equivalents. The fees were not settled until October 10, 1895, after the cotton had been ginned. If Mitcham farmers got the standard price, cotton sold for nearly eight cents a pound, up from less than a nickel a pound the year before. The fees for Brown and Brunson, if the figures found represent a total, equaled almost exactly the income from two bales of cotton, a hefty sum. The invoice was marked "satisfied in full," and it was signed by W. W. Waite, sheriff. But it does not say who paid the fees or that actual money had changed hands. I have my doubts.

A LARGE CROWD CAME IN

So, three weeks after the shooting of Pink, the accused men, Lee Brown and George Brunson, stood before Judge John Marshall Wilson, and with them their lawyer, J. T. Lackland, who either provided his services gratis (hardly likely) or was paid by the Brown family, which had money for fees. Not until 1932, in *Powell vs. Alabama*, related to the famous Scottsboro Boys case, did the Supreme Court require the state to provide counsel for indigent defendants charged with murder. The district attorney, Benjamin F. Elmore, was responsible for representing the state. The objections indicate the presence of a prosecutor, and the solicitor's fees are part of the record. Behind the accused pair was a large contingent of Mitcham people, not merely the witnesses but others who had wanted John R. Pinkerton dead.

As if to set an exact span on the Mitcham War, the preliminary hearing, which was, in effect, a trial, took place two years, less one week, after Ernest McCorquodale had been murdered. On December 27, 1894, *The Clarke County Democrat* published this skeletal paragraph:

Messrs. George Brunson and Lee Brown, who were committed to jail recently under a charge of complicity in the shooting of Murphy Pink, had a preliminary hearing on Wednesday [a week before the publication date of the *Democrat*] before Judge John M. Wilson of the county court. A large crowd came in and a number of witnesses were. examined. It was shown they were elsewhere on the day and at the time of the shooting of Mr. Pink. They were both discharged.

"Came in" is the telling phrase. It was customary in those days for large crowds to gather on what was called "court day" to hear lawyers orate and spar, to recall the turns of wit, to hear sordid details of criminal cases, usually involving murders, to hear prisoners ordered either to the coal mines or the gallows (the last hanging was in 1911), and outside of court, in a phrase of the day, to "swap snuff."

Grove Hill, located on a plateau, the highest point in the county, consisted of one main street, with the courthouse at its end. There were fewer than twenty businesses and about that many lawyers. The first bank was seven years away from being established, and in photographs the town looks like an Old West set—board sidewalks, a couple of two-storey buildings, and perhaps four stately homes. But the town was well laid out: a grid of broad, level streets, with only one block lined with stores, and the wood-framed courthouse and the brick jail, facing east like a graveyard, at the end. In 1901, a three-storey brick-and-stone courthouse, with a Richardson Romanesque rabbit-hole arch for an entrance, a four-storey clockless turret, and a mix of rectangular and arched windows, tall and narrow, would replace the old wooden building in which Brown and Brunson were tried. Fewer than 150 homes existed, and the town had a raw, striving look, unlike Mobile, Demopolis, or Selma.

In 1894, the *Democrat* office was located in what once had been a saloon—though by this time the temperance movement was popular, and the prevailing Protestants were openly against legal liquor. Most of the homes had kitchen gardens, henhouses, stables, and cow lots, with much the same arrangement of wells and privies as the cruder Mitcham homes. On the road to the east, which intersected the Old Federal Road, were broad fields, which fell off into more scrublands, till the road reached the valley of the Alabama River, dividing Clarke from Monroe County. To the west ran the twenty-mile route to Mitcham Beat, an unpaved road that alternated between hilly yellow-clay barrens, lined with piney woods and stands of blackjack oaks and small creekbottoms often deep with black mud.

A one-day trip between Mitcham Beat and the county seat would, in the best of times with the best of teams, take the better part of the day. In mid-December, with the daylight shortening, those who attended the trial probably came the day before and left the day after. The travel may have been arduous, but it was familiar to Peter Brown. In 1868, he had served as the election official responsible for carrying the locked ballot box from Mitcham to the county seat, which meant he probably traveled part of that route after dark.

Some matters required visiting the county seat, and court days provided more than the spectacle of the trials. Itinerant dentists advertised in *The Democrat* that they would be on hand to pull teeth. And there was government business to attend to: the paying of taxes, the reassigning of deceased Civil War veterans' benefits to widows, and, of course, requests for new wooden legs. Merchants might expect an increase in trade, but, given the division within the county, most of the people in Mitcham dealt with community merchants or bought directly from Mobile. Distance between the beat and Grove Hill, and over those hateful roads, was a factor, but another was the certainty that they were not much respected amongst the quality in the county seat. Better to trade with John Bell, or Wes Bedsole, or Sandy Norris. These backwater farmers were the people who, in the eyes of Isaac Grant and others of the Grove Hill establishment, "came in." The phrase makes clear the distinction between those folks who lived in the towns and those who were from the outback. And the size of this country crowd must have been extraordinary for editor Grant to have taken notice.

Those attending the trial heard their neighbors spell out the relationship between the long-time residents and J. R. Pink. The testimony, recorded by clerk W. W. Daffin, makes references to the "trial at McEntyre" (sometimes McIntyre), the post office at New Prospect, though the place was still known as Mitcham Beat. It is not clear how much of this testimony was transferred from the mittimus and how much was from the stand. There appears to be a mix of recorded and live testimony, else why would a "large crowd" come in?

The State of Alabama

Clarke County Probate Court held 19 Dec. 1894

No. 1

J. S. Pink being first duly sworn deposies [*sic*] and says, I knew Jas [*Jno*] R. Pink, he is dead. He died last Thursday evening two weeks ago to the best of my recollection. Was with him before and at the time of his death. Died in Clarke County,

Alabama. Died from two wounds in his body, supposed gunshot wounds. He said Mr. Smith shot him and Mr. George Brunson and Lee Brown were with him, Smith at the time of shooting. Took plow in field working 1/4 [*a quarter mile*] from his house. Think he said was 8 or 9 gunshots. Told me that night he was shot on Tuesday morning. [*Other witnesses say he was shot in the afternoon.*] He lived from Tuesday morning to Thursday evening at the time before he told me when and by whom he was shot by [*sic*], said nothing about dying or whether he thought he would die. This is all I know.

– Signed J. S. Pink [*As this is only testimony "signed,"
it may have come through the mittimus.*]

No. 2

Annie Wilson who being first duly sworn deposies and says, I was in field 20 steps from Pink when he was shot, saw 2 men standing at fence about 40 steps from Pink 9 shots were fired. When they shot him he hollered once or twice "look out." I recognized the persons do[*ing*] the shooting they were Mr. Brunson and Mr. Brown, the defendant. Shooting took place Tuesday November 27 about 2 o'clock. Him and my sister and a little boy were in the field with him. They were on the opposite side of the fence, rested their guns in crack in the fence. When I saw them they were in stooping position behind fence. After firing the 9 shots they walked off. Nothing between me and the fence.

– Annie Wilson

No. 3

Becky Wilson who being duly sworn deposies and says as follows, I was right by Mr. Pink when he was shot about 2 weeks ago. Don't remember day and week. Three men at side of fence, recognized the men they were George Brunson, Lee Brown, and Charlie Smith. 9 shots fired. George Brunson fired the shots, were resting guns through crack in fence. They were in stooping position. Have known defendants 7 or 8 years. After shooting parties walked off. Pink was 30 or 40 steps from fence. This was 2 o'clock in the evening. Think it was on Tuesday. This is all I know about the matter.

– Becky Wilson

Becky Wilson being recalled testifies as follows, I am not married woman have 4 children. I did not tell Mr. Gilmore, when Mr. Pink was a corpse, that when shooting occurred Pink ran off and I followed him.

– Becky Wilson

No. 4

Robert Wilson being duly sworn deposies and says, my name is Robert Wilson, 14 years old. I was in field when shooting took place, was about 5 steps from Pink when shooting occurred. 55 steps from fence Mr. Woodham stepped it. I looked in that direction, I saw 3 men they were Charlie Smith, George Brunson, and Lee Brown. They were side of fence one was standing and one was sitting by tree, one was stooping down on knee shooting. Don't know who was shooting. 9 shots were fired. I did not count them. Pink ran towards house stood till shots fired and ran to a tree and started behind it. I reckon tree was 75 or 100 yards towards house from Pink, I ran up on hill in same direction as Pink and watched them when men quit firing. They wheeled around and went off, had back to me when about 10 steps from fence. All 3 men looked back at once, I was about 100 yards from them when they looked back. I recognized them. It was only one gun. I have stated all that I know about this matter.

– Robert Wilson

No. 5 [*Census records reveal no Robert Small. The witness was probably Peter Small, the only grown man of that surname in Mitcham Beat at this time.*]

Robert Small being duly sworn deposies and says, I knew nothing of the killing of Pink. I conveyed a message delivered to me from Mr. Brunson to Mr. Mosely to the effect that Mr. Mauldin said from what he knew Pink's reputation was not good as he was trying to bulldozer people, he would be likely to go the way the Burkes did and if Moseley was taking sides with Pink he would go the same way. This was September 1894. This is all I testified before jury [*the coroner's jury*] at Pink's death. This is all I know. Defense counsel moved to exclude the testimony upon following grounds. 1st- because it is irrelevant and immaterial, 2nd- because this is hearsay as far as Mosely is concerned, 3rd- because it in no way connects the defendants with the death of the deceased.

– Robert [*Peter*] Small

No. 6

W. H. Mauldin being duly sworn deposies and says, I testified in this case at the trial in McIntyre [*which must refer to the coroner's jury hearing*], I know nothing about the killing. I live about one mile from Pink, did not hear shooting. I am aquainted [*sic*] with Annie and Becky Wilson, have known them 20 years, am aquainted [*with*] their characters in the community, their characters are bad, would not believe them on oath. The shooting occurred Tuesday 27 November. I saw Brown and Brunson that day about 150 yards from Brunsons house. I live about 3 miles from road, saw them at 20 minutes till 3 o'clock. It's 4 or 5 miles from where shooting took place by nearest route. [*not true*] Lee Brown, Ferdie Brown, and George Brunson were there, had 2 ox wagons, Mr. Brunson lives about 3 miles from my house. I was getting out some rock. [*probably hewing out the soft limestone for chimneys*]

– W. H. Mauldin

No. 7

Bob [*"Babe" or E .B.*] Mosely being duly sworn deposies and says, I knew nothing of killing of Pink. Mr. Small came to me with a threat, said Pink had a bad reputation in the county [*notably, "county," which suggests he was regarded as a pariah beyond the boundary of that community*], said they understood I was talking to him, that Pink would very likely be run out of the county and I would be run out too if I took sides with him, said Brunson said so. Same objection as to testimony No. 5.

– E. B. Mosely

Thus ends the extant record. Isaac Grant was right: "Brown and Brunson were discharged," but the charges were not dropped. They were actually bound over to the grand jury. In January, the case must have been presented, for scrawled diagonally across the front of an indictment document, which is in the archives of the Clarke County courthouse, are the words "No Evidence." Because this was a murder charge, there was (and is) no statute of limitations. Should new evidence arise, Benjamin F. Elmore, or another prosecutor, could reinstate the charges. This legal possibility, however unlikely of ever occurring, put the lid on all commentary about this case. Collective memory was far too much a part of that community for those who attended that trial to forget, but to speak openly? Never. Too dangerous.

. The testimony confirms how this community worked in concert, even if they did not do so intentionally. The preliminary hearing "depositions" also point to what questions might have been asked if this case had come to trial.

J. S. Pink attended J. R. Pink during the last moments of his life and swore that the victim said the shooting took place on a Tuesday morning and that Pink died on the following Thursday. J. S. does not specify any specific kinship, and his distinct physical differences prompt speculation that the two were not full brothers by blood. The witness testified that Pink had been shot twice. Pink was able to run from the scene and to talk until near his death. Perhaps he didn't conclude right away that he was mortally wounded. He waited until his brother arrived to identify his killers, and he had to have known that Charlie Smith was a contract hit man. But if more than one gun had been fired, and him running for cover, he could not have known of a certainty that it was Smith's bullets that hit him. No doctor or sheriff was called to his bedside, which suggests J. S. Pink himself provided information for the warrants.

The testimony of the Wilson sisters and fourteen-year-old Robert Wilson differs markedly from that of J. S. Pink. The Wilson women both say J. R. Pink was shot at 2 p.m. Annie Wilson does not mention Charlie Smith. If eight or nine shots were fired in a short span—the witnesses must have settled on a specific count after the shooting—the smoke from the black powder might have obscured Pink's location. Of the eight or nine shots, only two struck Pink, if we are to believe his relative's testimony. Annie Wilson says the men were standing; her sister Becky says they were shooting through a crack in the rail fence and stooping. If the shots were fired through a fence no more than four feet high, usual in that time of free-range cattle, whoever was doing the shooting had to have been lying down, kneeling, or standing, probably not stooping—as Becky and Robert Wilson testified. Becky Wilson said Charlie Smith was there but that George Brunson did all of the shooting; Annie says one of the gunmen was Lee Brown.

In short, if eight or nine shots were fired from a distance described by various witnesses as from thirty to fifty-five steps and six or seven missed, perhaps it was because the shooters misaimed intentionally or were too shaky to hold the bead; regardless, it would be difficult to hit a man running for cover, much less ducking around trees. If there was no wind, or if it was blowing from behind the shooters, enough haze could have been created by the black powder smoke to obscure both the target and the assailants. No mention is made of how long the shooting went on, but Robert Wilson's testimony suggests it continued after he'd run up a hill toward the house. Over that length of time, one shooter could have done all the firing, but not likely. Charlie Smith may have been the actual killer, but, given the time span and the action of those .38 Winchesters, Brown and Brunson may also have fired.

It's noteworthy that the Wilson testimony stresses how casual the killers seem. They walked away, hardly, as I have noted, the actions of men who had lain in ambush and feared recognition or punishment. And they looked back. What they wanted to see was whether they'd hit Pink. Lawyer Lackland did a fine job of impeaching, on moral grounds, the testimony of the Wilson woman who had four children and no husband. Where the other three children were is anybody's guess. These were women of whom W. H. Mauldin had said, "Their characters are bad."

Taken together, the testimony of Robert Small and W. H. Mauldin provides a clear indication of how the people who'd been terrorized felt about Pink. (At the hearing, no mention is made of his wife, Sallie, whose name appears on land deeds.) He was a man who was out to "bulldozer" people, and he was recruiting allies within the community. Babe Mosely had been courted by Pink. There was no doubt that Pink was building himself a power base; he already had George Brunson deeply in his debt. With the Bedsole-Burke set out of power, he would be the boss of Mitcham Beat.

But Peter Small was spreading the word: Don't consort with Pink or face exile, or worse. Small threatened Mosely at the behest of one of the Brunsons, possibly George, who was speaking for Mauldin. "Going

125

the way of the Burkes" suggests that the community may have played a part in the Burkes' and Bedsoles' escaping Bear Thicket; if so, it was with the clear understanding that these troublemakers would never set foot in Mitcham Beat again.

William H. Mauldin, who provided the springing alibi for Brunson and Brown, was also at one time a close neighbor of Peter Brown. He was famous as a gospel singer and a teacher at "singing schools," popular sessions of instruction usually held at churches. A native of Chambers County who fought with the Alabama 14th through Gettysburg to the surrender, he probably came to Mitcham to join a relative, named Mauldin, who was in the company of S. T. Woodward, leader of the Jackson faction of the mob. W. H. Mauldin's family, which eventually grew to eleven children, traveled far and wide to singings. His first four children were sons, a male quartet—Willy, Henry, Marshall, and Harris. In 1894, their ages ranged from twenty-three to sixteen. My father said W. H. Mauldin was so caught up in singing that he let his crops go one year, and he came to his one-legged neighbor and asked to borrow some corn. Peter Brown said to him, "Mr. Mauldin, you have a bunch of strapping, strong boys. You could raise a plenty of corn for your family." Mr. Mauldin replied, "You are right, Mr. Brown. I do have a bunch of strong boys—strong enough to lift your corncrib off its blocks and carry it home." He got his corn, and that story was always told with a chuckle, never with any scorn of W. H. Mauldin. My grandfather was fond of all the Mauldins, and no wonder: Singing-master Mauldin's testimony at the trial must have sounded to Lee Brown like the songs of celestial choirs.

The inclusion of the neighbors' testimony, over Lackland's nominal objections, suggests that the objections were overruled by Judge

Wilson. Lackland had nothing to lose in the comments from neighbors of "good" character. He was merely appearing to represent his clients against some unanticipated testimony from immoral women.

The Mitcham citizens referred to incidentally in the testimony, T. J. Gilmore and W. P. Woodham, were community leaders. It appears both had served on the coroner's jury. Gilmore had served under John Bell in the Alabama 32nd regiment, with two of Peter Brown's brothers, one their sergeant, the first John L. Brown. Both he and his brother, James, had died in the war. And, like many other Mitcham veterans, they had fought under Bragg, later Hood, all the way from Murfreesboro to Spanish Fort, where, in the last days of the war, Gilmore was captured. He himself had also bought land from Peter Brown in 1885. And Becky Wilson's testimony included a telling post-script: *I did not tell Mr. Gilmore, when Mr. Pink was a corpse. . . .* So, some Mitcham people had been at the wake and probably helped in the burying of John R. Pinkerton, not two hundred yards from John Bell's store. To any from Mitcham who might have doubted, Gilmore could confirm that the evil man was, indeed, dead and in his coffin.

W. P. Woodham—the initials stood for Wright Pleasant—was another immigrant from Dale County, from an old family connected to the vast Dowling-Boutwell clan. He was related by marriage to the Norris family. Wright Woodham's sister Hester was married to Henry Hawthorne Smith, who'd been a cavalryman under the command of Fightin' Joe Wheeler, and they were near neighbors of the Norrises. In 1880, Henry Hawthorne and Hester, their names eerily echoing the names of the author and the protagonist of *The Scarlet Letter*, had lived less than a mile from the Peter Brown family. (I know generally where they lived because they were my mother's maternal grandparents.)

As the testimony indicates, Gilmore and Woodham had been to the scene of the shooting, stepped off the distances, and talked with the witnesses before the first "trial" was convened. The tone in the Wilsons' testimony suggests these two men were acting as members of a coroner's jury, directed to investigate the slaying of "Mr. Pink." (How these neighbors refer to each other points out that even in a clannish, backwater community certain formalities are observed.)

When proceedings of the trial were presented to a Clarke County grand jury in February and the bill of indictment was returned with the words "No Evidence" scrawled across the front, it was signed by the prosecutor, Benjamin F. Elmore. There was, of course, ample evidence already and more could have been gathered. Why did the Clarke County machine not want to see these country fellows in the dock? I doubt that it was out of compassion: Such would not be consistent with the prevailing mindset. I doubt that Peter Brown and Mitcham Beat had enough money, certainly not enough votes, to sway anybody in the courthouse. Lee Brown was released, but not acquitted or otherwise exonerated. He could have been rearrested, tried, convicted, and hanged.

Why then was he let go—and where to?

I can respond quickly to the latter half of that inquiry. My father said Papa somehow acquired a fast horse and lit out for Texas. Though my father did not relate this departure to the Pink case, he said that Papa was in Texas for a year before returning to Clarke County. He and Mattie Mott were married in September 1896, and my father was born in August of the next year. While he was in Texas, my father said, Lee Brown lived amongst Indians, who came to him one evening and told him white men were coming that night to kill him. (Heaven knows if this is true and, if so, why anybody would be after him.)

Again, a fast horse was made available, as the story goes, and he lit out, equally fast, for home. By the time he returned, Judge Wilson was in his final term of office and would depart in a few years for Mobile where he became, fittingly enough, a cotton broker. In the life of this family of Wilsons—so opposite that of the poor Wilson women of Mitcham—we can see a final light shining on the Mitcham War, the execution of John R. Pinkerton, and the motives that, I believe, lay behind the decision not to proceed with the indictment and conduct a full-blown murder trial.

THE WILSON ANGLE

The Wilsons of Mitcham Beat were resigned to their low reputation. They had little to lose. The Wilsons of Grove Hill, however, had much on the line. They had money, political power, influential friends, and statewide ambitions. Brother Timothy Ball in his 1879 history said that Joshua R. Wilson, grandfather of the 1890s judge and a descendant of Connecticut Yankees, sold $50,000 worth of cedar in 1837. (The CPI equivalent for today is $1.2 million.) His son, Jack Roper Wilson, served as probate judge from 1868 to 1888, and his grandson, John Marshall Wilson, from 1888 to 1904. Together, the Wilsons, with their relatives and minions, bestrode Clarke County business and politics for nearly a century.

Judge John M. Wilson had attended West Point for a year before returning home and taking his law degree at the University of

Alabama. In appearing to vigorously prosecute Brown and Brunson, all the while planning how to let them go, John M. Wilson had more than his own reputation to protect. His younger half brother, Massey Wilson, was a rising star in state politics. A brilliant and handsome young man, Massey started as clerk in the office of brother's probate court. Then he studied law at the University of Virginia and at the University of Alabama. In 1890–91, he was working in the House of Representatives as "engrossing clerk," which meant he wrote the final drafts of the acts of that body. From 1892 to 1898, he was clerk of the house, and in 1900 he was elected to represent Clarke County. By 1894, he had had enough contacts with the state press to have floated stories about how indignant Clarke Countians were when their good name and character and law-abiding nature were impugned. Who else but a man of his political position would have had access to the state's lazy reporters, who never asked if the accusations were justified?

During much of his career in the legislature, Massey Wilson was also nominally a practicing attorney in Grove Hill. The bulk of the practice was apparently conducted by his partner, notably J. T. Lackland, defense attorney for Lee Brown and George Brunson; their shingle was advertised on the front pages of *The Clarke County Democrat*. The county seat paper kept close tabs on Wilson's doings, in the short paragraphs that amounted to local news. For sure, young Massey was headed for bigger things, and any stain on his family's reputation would reflect on him, particularly if it related to murder and the rule of law.

On the same December 1894 day that *The Daily News* reported the lynching of the defendants, the following mysteriously tentative stories ran on page three of a rival paper, the Mobile *Daily Register*:

THE CLARKE COUNTY AFFAIR.

THE ACCUSED DOUBTLESS SAFELY HELD IN GROVE HILL JAIL.

Judge Wilson, of Clarke county, was in the city Sunday. He came direct from Grove Hill. Asked as to the reported uprising of the Meachamites in that county he stated that the reports which had been sent out were calculated to place the county in a bad light before the public, and, while he could not positively say that the men had not been lynched, yet he was positive that the intention of the citizens was to accord each of them a fair trial. [*Some kind of convoluted sentence! The main thing on Wilson's mind was the county's reputation, which each story buttressed as less than wholesome. These murderous "Meachamites" may have been lynched—no loss there—but the "intention of the citizens" was to give them a fair trial. While I cannot positively say that Judge John M. Wilson was throwing up a straw conspiracy that was out to besmirch the sterling image of Clarke County, it is my intention to overlook the manifold irony in this nineteenth-century version of political spin. But I digress. . . .*] The three men arrested on the charge of murder were George Brunson, Charles Smith and Lee Brown, and they were sent to jail at Grove Hill on Saturday in charge of an escort of officers and were safely lodged in jail. [*Smith? Could the county not have known what the next story, appearing on the same page, revealed?*]

So much for the *Daily News* as a mouthpiece for the Wilson ring, which is presented as either too pure or too oblivious to know whether lynchings had occurred. Actually, of course, the Wilsons were neither clean nor blind: They knew precisely what had happened and how the story was taking a treacherous twist. Certainly a lynching was out of character for the county's "best citizens," the same who had lynched at least four people, to date, not to mention refusal to lawfully investigate and prosecute at least six other killings. Immediately below the above story, the Mobile paper published this paragraph from the *Montgomery Advertiser*:

SMITH ESCAPED.

—

Montgomery, Ala., December 10.—A special to the Advertiser, from Grove Hill, Clarke county, speaking of the Meachim trouble in that county, says Smith and Brunson, accused of killing Pink in that county, waived examination. Brunson is in jail and Smith escaped while on his way to jail. Everything is quiet and there has been no lynching, as was reported. [*No mention of Lee Brown? More importantly, how could a fellow like Charlie Smith have escaped two captors? Could the likelihood that he had received hit-man money have been a factor? And if so, how did he come by that money? Of course, he could have simply been turned loose, given more money, and told to skedaddle. Or he could have been shot. Searching records, I find no trace of Smith, not even a fugitive or alias warrant.*]

The pressure must have been on, from somebody, to defend the reputation of the Clarke County justice system. Twelve days after Judge Wilson suggested that persons unknown were out to cast the county in a "bad light" *The Birmingham Age-Herald* published the following front-page story:

CLARKE COUNTYITES INDIGNANT.

—

Mobile, Dec. 21—George Brunson and Lee Brown, men presumed to be outlaws of Meachams beat, Clarke county, were reportedly lynched, but safely lodged in jail at Grove Hill, were tried December 18, proved an alibi and were discharged. [*Again, not exactly true.*] Clarke county people are indignant that wild reports of their character for absence of law have been circulated. [*wild reports of their character for absence of law—but not false reports. And who could these law-abiding "indignant" Clarke County people be?*]

To a journalist trained in the 1960s, these yellow-journalism-era stories tell a familiar story about our scurvy trade: These papers had no reporters on the scene, no knowledge of the people, no interest in any contrary views, no fact-checking, and no favorable "Meacham" readers. Moreover, they were listening to one source. I believe it was the said Massey Wilson, who would have fed them other leads pertaining to state political intrigues. Yes, the Wilsons knew that the vigilante action was turning sour. And they absorbed another possibility, that they, meaning Massey, had political enemies outside the county who might capitalize on the role of the Wilson family in the Mitcham mess. Unbenownst to the Mitcham Beat executioners of Pinkerton, the tables were turning in their favor.

If—another big *if*—the slaying of Pink had resulted in a jury trial, with vigorous prosecution directed from the state capital and a spirited defense of the accused, all or some of the following could have happened:

1. The relationship between Pink and the mob could have been explored.

Witnesses would have been subpoenaed, and the names of terrorizers, among them Simeon Woodward and Cobb Nichols, put on record. Were members of this mob ever legally deputized, and by whose authority did they kill at least four men, torture people, and invade households? Could any individuals ever have been tried for any of these offenses?

2. J. S. Pink could have been called to testify about the relationship of his brother to the mob, to his neighbors, and to the Wilson women. And whatever checkered past John R. Pink had would be exposed, especially his relationship to Charlie Smith, whose "escape" was shady from the outset.

3. Sheriff Waite could have been subjected to lengthy examination about his role and the subsequent cover-up. If so, the links between Waite, the McCorquodales, Oscar York, and John M. Wilson would have been presented. How could such well-educated people have thought they could get away with their own breach of law? Did nobody think the frightened people of Mitcham capable of writing such a letter to the governor, which could have been entered as evidence, against the mob that murdered and tortured and frightened women and children "almost or nearly to death"? Was it assumed that the people of the backwoods had no one in the towns to speak for them in court? What about Napoleon Boyles, the Thomasville merchant, who had lent Peter Brown money? He would testify to the family's character.

4. A skillful defense team could present Mitcham people as salt-of-the-earth sorts, nature's noblefolk, heroic and wounded Confederate veterans, bereft widows whose larders and harvests had plundered by the vigilante mob—the picture is easy to see. What sympathy would a jury

have for Ferdinand Brown, a hard-working cripple who probably knew more inside dope than anybody else and how to articulate it?

5. The papers could have had a field day, and the Wilson family would not have come across entirely as heroes. John M. Wilson's protesting about the lawful nature of Clarke County would have seemed ludicrous, even laughable. If there had been a jury trial, an outside judge who knew that his rulings were being monitored by state government and perhaps by a fickle press would be cautious about favoring the Clarke County establishment. The whitewashing lies told by the county ring to the governor's emissary would have been revealed. And how many more political fires would the Wilsons be called upon to smother?

I suspect the Wilsons were aware of all of these possibilities, and perhaps more, and realized they had much more to lose than did two plain country fellows. As this drama unfolded, they had taken on a community that was not as backward as they thought, and with enough spit and vinegar to fight back. Political backfires have been sparked by much less.

That state politics might turn on what happened in Mitcham Beat is amusing—and instructive. The Wilsons had little to fear within the county, as far as I know. The editors, Isaac Grant and John S. Graham, saw no reason to investigate, much less report on, the suspension of murder charges. Benjamin F. Elmore, the prosecutor, had bigger fish to fry, and he may have chosen not to press the case for reasons not apparent to me. Some people must have believed that he was instrumental in refusing to prosecute Lee Brown. (My father named his first-born, a son, Elmore, and he told me it was for Benjamin F. Elmore. But he never told me the back story.)

Not to put too blunt a point on it, the killing of Pink was as much a favor to the Wilsons as it was to the Mitcham neighbors. They could hardly have left killers unaccused–that would merely confirm the public's notion of lawlessness in the county. But they had to manage the proceedings carefully. Giving this matter the appearance of proper handling and then getting it out of sight and hushed up required artful political joinery.

Lawyer Lackland, later to be circuit judge, was part of the Wilson ring. So was Prosecutor Elmore. And John Wilson himself was the judge of the court of record. (A separate criminal court for the county was not established until 1907.) As further insurance, John R. Bell, the Mitcham Beat merchant—the same whose brother-in-law, Sandy Norris, was nearly lynched by the mob—was on the grand jury. Bell was anything but a friend of Pink's, and he was set to buy the land of Pink's brother, removing the whole family, bag and baggage, from Mitcham Beat. And the deep ties between Bells and Browns, from the Civil War onward, were evident. It would hardly serve Bell's business interests to alienate himself from his community of customers. This home-cooking must have been as aromatic then as it is now, but whether Lee Brown sensed what was aboil or to what extent is now sealed.

Eventually, the successful suppressing of the whole Mitcham Beat episode redounded to the younger Wilson's benefit. Massey Wilson was elected to the Legislature in 1900, and in 1901 he ran for a state office— notably, for attorney general—and won. The chief law enforcement officer of the state was never to be associated with a set of killings and an adroitly managed cover-up. There was to be no blot on Massey Wilson's record, no mention of any Mitcham War. Wilson took office in 1903 and served one four-year term. He appointed as his assistant in the attorney general's office a young man, fresh from passing the bar exam,

Thomas W. Martin, whose father, William Logan Martin, had been appointed to fill an unexpired term as attorney general in 1889 while Wilson was building a career in the legislature. William Logan Martin was often mentioned as a gubernatorial candidate; he was already a powerful force in state politics.

As the elder Martin mentored Wilson, so did Wilson mentor Martin's son Tom. In the formative stages of hydroelectric power in the state, Wilson proved himself adept at crafting riparian laws that would allow for dams to block rivers and for thousands of acres of land to be flooded to provide water to power the turbines. The history of Alabama Power reveals much about the general state of Alabama's turn-of-the-century politics and economy and points out that Wilson was involved with the group that owned the Muscle Shoals site on the Tennessee River and the Cherokee Bluffs site on the Tallapoosa River. The laws that Wilson so carefully crafted passed through the Alabama Legislature in 1907 when William Logan Martin was speaker of the House of Representatives.

Shortly after the laws were enacted, Martin died. After Wilson left the attorney general's office, he continued to mentor the young Thomas Martin, and Tom joined Massey Wilson's law firm about 1910. A decade later, Martin became president of Alabama Power Company, a company that later became one of the state's "big mules." The investor-owned Alabama Power Company was founded in 1906, and Martin became involved in the corporation in 1912 only because Wilson had left the state. Though much good came from this company, it paid little heed to appeals of landowners protesting the inundation of their lands. The fledgling, capital-strapped company of the early century also hotly contested opposition from those who favored state-owned utilities; the political and legal savvy that Wilson brought to the drafting of riparian laws made them defensible in the courts. The legislation would prove a key to the success of Alabama Power Company.

Whatever his big mule notions, if any, Massey Wilson proved himself a principled man—at least to his own class. In 1911 or 1912, he left Alabama to head the International Life Insurance Company headquartered in Saint Louis, and, when it was failing during the Depression, he poured his fortune into it and lost that fortune, entirely. He kept his reputation and his standing, as his brother had forty years earlier. The daughter who'd been born in 1894, the year of the Pink episode, was dead by 1901, when Wilson ran for attorney general. Broke and childless, he spent his last thirty-plus years in rustication, at his wife's family home in Wilcox County, across the Alabama River from the county his family had dominated. Over the years, he received some small fees, commissions, and charitable favors from Thomas Martin, who had risen to fame and riches with Alabama Power, but, unlike his former protégé, Massey Wilson received no honorary degrees or wide acclaim, so far as I know, nor is there any evidence that he sought either. He lived to be ninety-eight and is buried in his wife's family's cemetery.

His counterpart, a Mitcham Beat farmer, returned from his year of exile in Texas, married a woman of good standing, raised a big family, and, to my knowledge, never again had his name appear in a docket book. That man, my grandfather, presented himself as a public man, laughed often, and lies buried in Oak Grove Cemetery, between ancestors and descendants.

PART II

EXPLORING THE MITCHAM MINDSET

In this section, I present five essays, dealing with the migrations and interminglings, the folkways, the impact of Civil War, civil accord, and the last pioneer family in Mitcham Beat. To spare the general reader, I've kept the begats to a minimum. Some matter is repeated from the previous section, for continuity's sake. My intention has been to investigate how the political attitudes and social structure developed and were sustained within and by the community.

When I was a boy, it was common for us children to sit on the porch after supper and listen to the old people go through family connections, reaching back two hundred years or more. The old people corrected each other and clarified the lineages and dropped anecdotes. Many of those strange and often euphonic names still float through my head, and I have dug through records to place them. The old people had no such problem, and no need for documentation, and the accuracy of their memory has astounded me. What they said was significant then. What they did not say is equally significant now.

The Civil War–era settlers did not consider themselves inferior to anybody, but that attitude was changing as the Mitcham War approached. It became important that people cast as lower on the social scale know about those who considered themselves superior and held the power. Country people eventually knew more about the pedigrees and secret doings of townspeople than did most of the forward-looking, laughable uppercrust. Many of these town people had no interest in examining pasts that were not much different from Mitcham Beat's; they'd simply moved out and up faster, become better educated and connected, and got a chokehold on the economy. And few knew anything at all about the relationships within the terra incognita called Mitcham Beat.

The pattern is a familiar one. If you rank low on a social scale, it's wise to study those who consider themselves above you. Knowledge may become power. If there was a thread of resentment or envy running through this talk of outsiders, there was also amusement, throaty chuckling, and, occasionally, deep respect for individuals.

MOVING AND MELDING

The existence of an area of free land,
its continuous recession, and the advance of American settlement,
explain American development.

—

FREDERICK JACKSON TURNER
The Significance of the Frontier in American History and Its Surroundings (1893)

By the time the Dale County wave started arriving in the 1850s, Mitcham Beat was only partially settled, but the attitudes that led eventually, or inevitably, to the Mitcham War and the killing of Pinkerton were already formed.

Pioneers had been drifting in, even before Andrew Jackson had opened the Alabama River valley after the Battle of Horseshoe Bend, in 1814. About 1805, three Mott brothers, sons of a Revolutionary War soldier, whose family was probably named LaMotte, had arrived with their families, and in 1810, Benjamin DeLoach had come, rolling his worldly goods in a hogshead, or wooden barrel. At some time in this early phase, Josiah Wells had established a grist mill on the creek that would bear his name, near land claimed and bought in 1860 by Peter Brewer where later the Seaborn Goodman family lived. Bears, panthers, deer, and huge rattlesnakes were abundant. At night, to fend wolves off livestock that were penned in makeshift corrals, the settlers built fires. They also dug holes, baited and overlaid with brush, to trap wolves. I never heard stories of success, but the remains of one old wolf pit were still visible in the 1960s.

Mitcham was a pristine, raw, border country, hard to reach by mainland roads. It was close to the Tombigbee River, though, with numerous landings where hand-drawn craft and later steamboats (the first came up in 1821) dropped off goods from Mobile and took passengers down to the port city, which was ceded by Spain to the United States three years after Benjamin DeLoach arrived. Thus began a long relationship between old-time Mitcham Beat residents and the merchants of Mobile, and thus were planted seeds of resentment of those middle-men storekeepers in Coffeeville, Thomasville, Jackson, and Grove Hill.

Benjamin DeLoach stated to W. D. Council, a newspaperman, that he was born in 1770 in Virginia. County historian T. H. Ball said that when DeLoach died in 1876 he was probably the oldest living person in Clarke County. An encomium written by Council before DeLoach died and published in Ball's book details how plucky and hardy he was:

> "Uncle Ben" was a great scout and fighter; was in the fight with the Indians at the "Bully Hill," on the road now leading from Tallahatta Springs to Wood's Bluff, and was also in the "Edwards Field" fight on the road now leading from Linden to

Coffeeville. At the "Edwards Field" fight turkey tails were suddenly elevated above the heads of the savages, as a signal for firing and for the purpose of halting the whites. Uncle Ben, being wide awake, cried out "Indians!" when a volley of rifles was fired at the noble little band of white men, consisting of Silas Scarborough and three sons, David White, David Phillips, Joab White, [*no first name listed*] Bradbury, and a few others. Col. McGrew and a man named Griffin were killed on the ground. Bradbury was mortally wounded and died on the road to the fort [*Fort Easeley*].

At Fort McGrew, farther down the Tombigbee and south of the stockade where Bradbury died, DeLoach was with Darling Peevy, Joseph Mott, Jonah Mott, William Mott, the McGrews, Callers, Scarboroughs, Whites, Pughs, Rutledges, Trawicks, the Hicks and Webb families, Mathew Brewer, Richard Odom, and others, Council said, "whose descendants are living in the county."

After the threat passed, DeLoach returned to northwest Clarke County, and on January 1, 1818, married Isabella Leach. Beginning with a 40-acre parcel registered in Isabella's name in 1839, the DeLoaches held twelve tracts, totaling 720 acres, by the outbreak of the Civil War. Benjamin DeLoach, Council said, "has been a practical farmer ever since and a citizen of this county." In 1872, DeLoach stated to Council that he "was one hundred and one years old, the 15th of last December." His stamina amazed Council, who wrote, "Twelve months ago he was his own mill boy, and two years ago he visited Mobile on business. He is now in good health, and has not approached imbecility." One of Jonah Mott's sons, Marion DeKalb Mott, married Ben and Isabella's daughter Sarah, and to that union was born in 1840 Andrew Jackson Mott, who named one of his sons Benjamin. Mott, my father's grandfather and mentor, died in 1917, when my father was twenty years old. Generations living in one place over such a span of time figured strongly in the fixing of traditions and manners.

The Motts showed an enterprising spirit common on the American frontier. Joseph Mott, Jonah's brother, had a store and several lots in Clarkesville, the first county seat, and later, when a lack of good water made settlers abandon that place, he moved to Choctaw Corner, the old dividing post between the Choctaws and the Creeks, and there he established another store and sought official recognition. Mott's Post Office was located near what would later become the town of Thomasville, easterly from Choctaw Corner when rail lines were laid. My grandmother always insisted, though I was skeptical, that Motts deserved credit for being the first settlers of Thomasville. As it turns out, Mattie Mott Brown was only a few miles from being right.

When Texas opened, many of the Motts left and prospered there, one becoming a judge. They were part of a massive migration to the Texas republic that included William Barrett Travis, who practiced law in Claiborne and Clarkesville before heading to his mortality and immortality at the Alamo. The GTT—Gone To Texas—Motts left behind brother Jonah, his son Marion, and others, who were too broke to travel, too grounded, or too hopeful that prosperity might come to that section of Clarke County. After Sarah DeLoach Mott died, about 1850, leaving two children, Marion Mott married again and raised a large family near Wood's Bluff, on the Tombigbee, north of Mitcham Beat. After Marion Mott began his new family, he left his son, Jack Mott, and a daughter, also named Sarah, who disappears in history (though rumors about her abound) to be raised by Benjamin and Isabella DeLoach.

The Dale County migration began nearly fifty years after the Motts, DeLoaches, and others had come to the unsettled country. So many came from that southeast corner of Alabama, carved from Henry County and named for the famous pioneer Sam Dale, that Mitcham Beat in the decade before the Civil War, and just after it, could have been called Dale County West. Whereas almost all the Mitcham settlers to that point were of British Isles stock, primarily English, Scottish, and Welsh, those from Dale brought Teutonic blood. Many of the Dale settlers were primarily of German-Swiss or German stock, the former from the area around Basel called the Palatinate, in the upper Rhine Valley, and the latter from a nearby province, Baden-Wurttemberg. Most of these settlers migrated to South Carolina from Europe over a thirty-year period, beginning in 1735.

The first came at the behest of the crown, which offered free or "bounty" land, fifty acres, plus tools, to farmers and tradesmen. Most expanded these allotments considerably. Fertile land west and north of Charlestown was plentiful, and the settlements could both provide produce and services for the city and serve as a buffer against French and Indians.

As Val McGee points out in his well-researched history of Dale County, *Claybank Memories,* many of the settlers in the Choctawhatchie valley were described by their new neighbors as "generally Dutch," which meant they came from Deutschland, not Holland. In 1880 Jack Brown stated that his father's birthplace was Prussia, which suggests that the original Brown (or Braun or whatever our original name was) came in a later, separate migration. A professional genealogist in South Carolina searched that state's tangle of records but could offer only suggestions, given the commonness of the name—Brun, Bruner, von Braun? Or perhaps some other name, possibly Jewish, that had been changed? One John Brown served on a petit jury in 1780 in the Camden district "eastward of the Wateree."

Most of these immigrants were interested in farming and moved from the "low country," to the "backcountry"—a significant distinction. Away from the swamps, the climate was healthier, the countryside more open, and large plantation owners less dominant. An insular culture developed for two obvious reasons: The immigrants were farmers, generally, not merchants, and living in their own community was a set way of life, protecting but isolating. They didn't fit in amongst the city people.

The first colonists had lived nearer to major cities in Switzerland or Germany, but not in communities as remote and tight as those formed in South Carolina. The settlements would come to resemble Scottish clans, which is no surprise. That was the most satisfying, perhaps natural, system of community organization. Besides, Scots were liberally sprinkled among them; their Calvinism was similar to the Swiss Reformed beliefs; and Scots were dominant all over the South. Intermarrying and living in close communities contributed to this model of clansmanship. Scots were a powerful constituency wherever they settled—fecund and full of fight. They had come from a tradition of raiders, borderland "reivers" or cattle thieves, and militantly religious. The paradox was expressed in the old saw, "The Scots prayed upon their knees, and they preyed upon their neighbors." Behaving like a Scot was a key to survival, and the Germans must have taken to Scots' ways quickly.

Distinctions between Scots and other British Isles settlers are lost in the welter of names and intermarriages. Truetts, Hugginses,

Hutchinsons, and Wigginses probably came from the Scottish borderlands in North England, Urquharts from around Loch Ness, Bells from anywhere in Scotland, Woodhams, Motts, Hawthornes and Etheredges from English stock, Hares and Bedsoles from Ireland. Many immigrants from Ireland were Ulster Scots, Calvinists who had sought asylum, and French-sounding names sprinkled amongst the settlers (DeLoach, for instance) could have roots in Normandy, from the descendants of Frenchmen who followed William the Conqueror to England, or in Scotland, where the French Huguenots sought refuge amongst fellow Protestants after the Edict of Nantes, which had ushered in a period of religious toleration, was revoked in 1685.

Early settlers from sundry lands of origin passed through ports all over the Eastern seaboard, though most apparently through Charlestown. Some Germans came down from Pennsylvania, Virginia, or North Carolina, to join the South Carolina settlements. British Isles stock was soon intermarrying with them, and perhaps Jews as well. Charlestown had the largest Jewish settlement in the colonies. Who can say what happens when the spirit meets the flesh? Many of the Old Testament given names would fit Christian or Jew, and Jews were encouraged not to distinguish themselves from the *goyim* colonists. DNA evidence from one descendant of Jack Brown suggests the possibility of intermingling, though no genealogical connections have been documented.

In our records, the primary progenitor, John A. Brown, is listed with his wife, Miss Brooks, as the parents of the five brothers who came to Dale. A son of one, Jacob, was named Bors, probably Boris, a name more popular in northeastern Germany, nearer to Slavic/Baltic lands; that fact, slender though it is, makes me believe that Jack Brown was right about his father's natal place. (Ironically, like Mitcham Beat, Prussia no longer exists except in references to history.) Lee Brown said our ancestors were Germans, and, though he was three generations away from the original German settler and was seven-eighths of British Isles blood, that settled the matter. In fact, his own children had more German blood than he did, because of the Hutto-Judah connections of Mattie Mott. German-Swiss surnames traceable to backcountry Alabama, many of the names Anglicized, were, and some still are, sprinkled across Mitcham and the rest of Alabama—Hutto, Ott, Geiger, Gartman, Snell, Till, Bamberg, Gissendanner, Friddle (Freidel), Miller, Shamburger, Judah (originally Tshudy), Funchess (Pfunzius), Turnipseed (Ruebsamen, meaning "rape or oil seed"), and many others.

Our set of Browns came in the 1830s to Dale County, to the valley of the Choctawhatchie River, in southeast Alabama, from backcountry South Carolina, Kershaw County, near Camden. A nineteenth century historian, William Preston-Mathews, compiled a list of heads of households in that small valley, the state of their birth, and their sons' names.

In the list are the five original Alabama/Dale County Browns:

- Brown, Henry- SC Sons Nelson & Henry.
- Brown, Jack- SC Sons James, John L., Peter I. & Eliga.
- Brown, Jacob- SC Sons John P. & Bors.
- Brown, Lewis (also Louis)- SC Sons William, David Euriah, Lewis & Jonathan.
- Brown, Peter- SC Sons Peter, Richard, David & Sidney.

These names—John, Peter, and Elijah, for instance—have floated around in the family, generation to generation, over the past two hundred years, ensuring challenges aplenty for future genealogists. Amongst the first Alabama-born daughters were Melissa and Missie, whose mother's name is recorded only as Miss Brooks. And Miss had a granddaughter named Melissa.

The pioneers no doubt followed the same route as most immigrants to Dale; much of the way, they traveled over the Old Federal Road through Georgia and the Creek Nation, passed present-day Columbus, Georgia, crossed the Chattahoochee River there, and took the fork that ended in Pensacola, Florida. Stopping in Dale County, they homesteaded land they hoped would be good for cotton. Jack and his wife, Eula Ann Ansley, already had one son, named Samuel James Wesley (called J. W. in the Civil War records). The land Jack homesteaded was well away from adjoining tracts settled by his brothers, but in the late 1840s, he moved closer, to land near the Truett clan.

Jack and Eula's second son, John L., married Charity Truett, the daughter of William Hampton Truett, who is listed in the 1860 census of Mitcham Beat as "clergyman, ME," meaning Methodist Episcopal. John L. went with, or led—for he was, as his military record indicates, a leader—the Dale Countians to the Satilpha bottomlands in the mid-1850s. In that entourage was W. H. Truett's family, and also that of his brother, Elisha. Their old father, Elijah, and maybe their mother, Susannah Wiggins Truett, came with them. Handmade, primitive tombstones, without dates, stand in Oak Grove Cemetery for Elige and Sue Truett, though, given the repetition of names, these may be Elisha Truett's son and his wife.

If the customary pattern prevailed, the Dale settlers came because they'd discovered, possibly through a scout or maybe the toutings of speculators, that land more fertile than the sandy soils in Dale was to be had in the upper drainages of the Tombigbee River in northwestern Clarke County. John L.'s parents and two younger brothers apparently joined the united and extended family in Mitcham Beat, maybe a year later, about 1858. A first cousin, Louis, is also listed as a landowner, but he went back to Dale County. J. W. Brown married and stayed in Dale County until the Civil War broke out. Then he too came to Clarke County and enlisted in the company being formed at Coffeeville, of which his brother John L. was sergeant.

Some of these settlers in the Choctawhatchie valley owned slaves, inherited or purchased. That they bought some land in Mitcham, rather than homesteading it all, indicates they had acquired some money—perhaps from selling their slaves. A relative said the black dead were buried outside the Brown's Methodist Church cemetery, on land that later went into cultivation. "The old folks said that when they were plowing and the leg of a horse or mule sunk deep into the ground," a distant cousin said, "they knew they'd broken into the grave of one of those slaves."

Another family that migrated to Mitcham in the 1850s was that of John Andrew Jackson Hutto and his wife Lucy (or Louisa) Ann Judah, both of the old Orangeburgh Swiss–German stock. Hutto is listed in the 1860 census as "teacher, community school." They had a large family, mostly girls, and left the eldest back in Dale County where she was listed as a "student," probably in a female academy in Newton. Among them, one was named Martha and another Matilda. Harriett Ann Hutto of Dale married Jack Mott, grandson of Benjamin and Isabella DeLoach, and she named one of their daughters for her mother and two of her sisters. Martha Ann Matilda Mott Brown—a grandmother, we used to say, who had five names—was called Mattie, which is the name on her tombstone in Oak Grove Cemetery.

To see these ancestors identified as teacher, student, or clergyman is to be reminded that we should not submit to the negatives in the caricature of cracker. Since we often stereotyped ourselves, evidence that we did not fit the world's notion of us as hookwormy hicks was unknown or ignored. Those old people did not think poorly of themselves, perhaps because they grew up in a time when the contrast between social classes was less stark. Images of Mitcham people are complex—and confusing. My grandfather ate with a fork and a knife, British style, and he pronounced bottle as *bot'l* and cattle as *cat'l*. Where did that sort of elision come from? He called a front porch a *gallery*, and he dressed as close to a gentleman as he could. Just when you thought you had an old person like him pigeonholed, you'd get a surprise.

It was the same with most of those people. My dad would refer to a bed-spread as a *counterpin* meaning counterpane. Once I was reading a book on the front porch and came across the word *syllabub* and asked him what that was. "Oh, it's a whole lot like eggnog, makes a white froth," he said. "People used to whip a big bowl of it for the holidays." (He did not say that it contained spirituous liquors.) Just when I thought I had him pegged, he blindsided me again. He often affected antique speech. For instance, he would pronounce garden *g'yar-den* and use *a* before those *ing* words that grammarians call present participles: "Alliene," he would say to my mother, with a lilt in his voice, "I'm a-goin' to the g'yar-den." He liked lapsing into old dialects—saying *c'yarn* for carrion, and *agger* for ague, and *mastah* for master. When my mother used a phony formal voice when talking to strangers on the telephone, he would laugh and accuse her of "talking proper."

Recalling the rich lexicon at our disposal, I hear mountain, low country, African-American, and King James English, reflecting roots and wanderings and defined against the conventional pronunciation and grammar we learned in school.

All down the line, the trickle of book-learning and the flood of folkways flowed together. Harriett Hutto Mott lived to be eighty-five and served the Mitcham community as a nurse, traveling far and wide to tend the sick. My father, who was approaching age thirty-five when Grandma Mott died in 1932, said that when he was a boy he went around with her in the woods and swamps to gather medicinal herbs and that when she was away for long periods sitting up with the ailing and dying, he stayed with his grandfather, Jack Mott, the Civil War veteran, helping him in the field and in the kitchen and picking up countless stories. Grandma Mott had been taught treatments for fevers and croup and how to find purgatives that would cleanse the body—folk remedies that would have been learned by the first European or African immigrants. Others in Mitcham knew these old cures. William Wrighty Brown, Lee's brother, treated a sick grandson with two teas, made from elderberry and mullein. (The tonic must have had special powers, for the grandson became the probate judge of Clarke County and still enjoys robust health.) The colonists had a long association with the Indians of the Carolinas—after all, they caught the brunt of the Cherokee War of the 1760s, just as the British hoped they would—and, like as not, the whites learned some of the Indians' herbal medicines.

Coming up from the lowcountry of South Carolina, the back-country immigrants also learned rice cultivation and carried that knowledge from South Carolina, through Dale, to Mitcham Beat. My grandfather pointed out a crawfishy flat near the old road to Oak

Grove Church, where, he said, rice was grown when he was a boy, in the late 1870s.

Soon the settlers gave up rice, which required more work than corn and took energy away from cotton raising, which was on the economic throne long before the Dale settlers arrived in Mitcham. In 1851 the editor of *The Clarke County Herald*, James T. Figures, scolded farming friends for planting so much cotton and advised them to "go to planting more corn, potatoes, peas, beans, pumpkins, wheat, rye, oats, rice, and sugar cane." Unless they lost their lust for cotton, he said, they would "wear out and render worthless the best land the sun ever shone upon." The lesson that Figures could not teach about diversification was driven home by the boll weevil more than half a century later.

Because of the Mitcham settlers' remoteness and standoffishness, the old habits of farming, housekeeping, and thinking, of working toward what might be called "common sense" prevailed, even as they adapted to changes. If they were behaving more like people of three centuries past, they probably did not know it, or, if they did, didn't care. Obviously, they believed their way of looking at the world concretely, with every person having a place in the society and every phenomenon worth pondering and talking about, was right.

Every person was judged on the basis of his or her character, and being able to judge people and especially to view them against the backdrop of their families—which ones did they take after, if any?—was a key to stability. The status quo was not valued in itself; the residents of Mitcham Beat were not immune to change or overtly resistant to it, as a deliberately closed society might be. Change came slowly for several reasons: little capital, little formal education, little association with town society. Also, many of the old ways they clung to had been tested and proved true by time. Besides some doings—killing hogs, making syrup, quilting—that might by others be considered utilitarian were near–religious rites, ceremonial and celebratory.

Memories were long amongst the intermingling and extended generations. When my father heard his grandfather, Jack Mott, tell stories, he was absorbing a sensibility and a history that had been handed down from grandfather to grandson (and many relatives in between) through parts of three centuries. The birth-to-death span from Benjamin DeLoach, through Jack Mott, to John Coley Brown ran from 1770 to 1970. DeLoach had been Mott's mentor, and Mott had been Brown's. In his last years, my father was speaking from a perspective conveyed by only a handful of people, but these were men and women, who, in their overlapping lifespans, had witnessed or directly experienced every war from the American Revolution to Viet Nam. Henry James, an American writer not closely related to Kirk and Lev James of Mitcham Beat, said that art grows where the soil is deep. So does folk history. In old, settled, backwater cultures, where attention spans might cover a couple of centuries, the oral tradition was a source of education and entertainment. I could add "identity" if I wanted to stretch this point.

Dates of death and birth were recalled as concrete events, not abstract figures. For instance, my father said they buried Grandma Mott on April 13, 1932, in cold ground, and every year since, around the thirteenth of April, there had been a chilly spell. When he told of that burial, my mother would add, "I was in the bed with your sister Christine, who was five days old." This way of chronicling public and private histories was common in Mitcham, as it has been in other old cultures in which the five senses of intelligent people have not been displaced by written records and electronic devices.

Descendants of our set of Dale settlers are exceptionally fortunate in having a printed genealogy, and a story to go with it, because how the pedigree came to be, and from whom, is as remarkable and revealing as the document itself. We have that archival treasure, rare amongst country people, because of a quarrel between two hard-headed brothers over religion, a unifying and divisive force everywhere. The reasons rural Americans (and everybody else, for that matter) divided often appear comic and petty in retrospect: Should the hymns of Isaac Watts be allowed? Was Moses actually found in the bulrushes? Is it a sin to cook on Sunday? Once-saved-always-saved, or is back-sliding allowed? If people wanted to find a forum to elevate animosities to some higher plane, they found it (and still find it) in religion.

Our family quarrel was a departure from the usual spatting over how to interpret and follow Biblical teachings. Ours pitted brother against brother, Methodist against Mormon. The quarrel reveals much. The Methodist brother was not pleased that the Mormon brother had set himself up as superior—the One True Flock!—and the Mormon brother was showing that he was not afraid to buck the constricting opinions of the community. That is how the long quarrel between Peter and Elijah Brown appears to me now.

Why Elijah Brown "went over" (my grandfather's term) to the Mormons is not known for a certainty, but one of his daughters, Allie Sophronia, who was my grandfather's age, married a Geiger. Somewhere down the way, maybe during the Civil War, some of the Mitcham Beat Geigers had converted to Mormonism. It was not a general Southern phenomenon, and the church historians I consulted called it an anomaly.

As my grandfather and father told it, Peter and Elijah engaged in a long, bitter quarrel and did not make up until late in their lives. They had fought the Clarke County wilderness, and against the Yankees, and when they'd recovered from the Civil War, they fought each other. Peter, it was said, believed that Mormons wanted to take the families out to Utah where the church elders would send the men off in the hills to tend sheep so they could ravish the womenfolks. The general public was well aware of the Mountain Meadows Massacre of 1857, in which 120 or so Arkansas pioneers en route west were slaughtered by Mormons near Salt Lake City. In the 1890s *The Clarke County Democrat* was still taking swipes at Mormons.

Peter Brown also saw the paradox in his brother's separating himself from his family and yet yielding to the absolute authority of a church, any church. To men of Peter Brown's temperament, that was surrender, whether it be to the Pope of Rome or the Quorum of the Twelve Apostles. People who cut themselves off from their families and their community—forget the irony of secession and the isolation of the Mitcham yeomanry in Clarke County—galled Peter Brown, and later his son Lee. It violated some code in his thinking. My grandfather felt the same way Peter did about those denominations, notably the Campbellites, who also believed only their flock could pass through the Pearly Gates. And yet he respected those rigid, righteous Christians. "If you want to know the Bible," he said, "go talk to a Campbellite."

The two brothers obviously thrived on the argument. Peter wanted his younger brother to see through that Mormon foolishness, and Elijah wanted Peter to join with him in another war between Us and Them. The most-often-told story about the differences between the two involves a spoken pun. Peter Brown was at his woodpile one day and saw two men coming toward him. He knew, so the story goes, that they were Mormon missionaries and went to the gate to meet them.

They were polite. "Mr. E. Brown sent us to you with some tracts on Mormonism." Peter Brown said, "Damn you and damn E. Brown! The only tracks I want to see are yours, in the road, heading the other way!" (That Elijah Brown sent his brother tracts puts to rest any notion they could not read.)

When I was about twelve, Lee Brown, then about eighty-five, gave me a green, oblong binder containing pedigree sheets compiled in the 1920s by James Joseph Zachariah Geiger, widower of Allie Sophronia, daughter of Elijah Brown, who had died in 1892, at age twenty, and left one son. Papa's first cousin, Allie was a year younger and appears in a photograph as sadly prim. Zack Geiger was the son of Harriett Hutto Mott's sister, Sarah, which made him Mattie Mott Brown's first cousin. Zack traveled amongst Motts, Huttos, Truetts, and Browns compiling the names for his church records. And he compiled them by family.

In the list of children of Peter and Winnie Brown, only two exact birthdays are recorded—John L. Brown's on September 14, 1864, and Lee Brown's, on September 12, 1871. John L. was the oldest brother, the one who was stricken and died in the field in 1885. Because only those two birthdates are listed specifically by day as well as month, we may infer that it was Lee Brown who gave Zack Geiger such precise genealogical information: Lee would have remembered because his birthdate and John L.'s were two days apart. Lee was the one with the archival memory of the settlers. And before he died, he bought tomb-stones for his grandfather, Jack Brown, for his brother John L., for Ferda, the club-footed brother who taught himself to read and write and became a schoolteacher, and for the infant children of Lee and Mattie.

Before Peter Brown died in 1907, the brothers had reconciled. I don't know when or what caused Peter and Elijah to set aside their differences. No story was handed down. Maybe they simply tired of the fight, or one needed the other in a time of crisis. That Peter named his youngest son Elijah, even though the name was common, suggests they had been on good terms in 1879. I find no indication that Elijah the elder remained a practicing Mormon. My grandfather and father both looked up to him; he outlived Peter by thirteen years and became the patriarch. I'm guessing he disavowed Mormonism; in any event, religious differences ceased to separate uncle from nephew. I am not guessing that my middle name comes from that Elijah Brown.

When my father and his brother Connie, one year younger, were big enough to work in the fields, Lee Brown would send them over to help Uncle Lige. My dad said the old Civil War veteran would have them up, dressed, and fed long before dawn and send them out in the yard to see if they saw light breaking in the east. He meant to get every minute of work he could out of his nephew's boys, and if he had tried to convert them to Mormonism, my father would surely have remembered. None of Elijah Brown's other children were Mormons, and, except for a generalized residue of prejudice, Mormonism did not exist in the beat.

The only sign of that bitter quarrel is not obvious to those who stroll through Oak Grove Cemetery. Peter Brown and his descendants are buried against the west fence and Elijah Brown and his against the east. Tombstone dates tell the tale: While they were quarreling, members of their families died, and they wanted their respective plots as far apart as possible, but neither was taking his dead to another cemetery. Then, though Peter and Elijah had made up when the time came to bury them, it was meet and right that they be put with their own closest kin. Thus their families lie, separated till

Judgment Day. Elijah Brown and his family will get to see the Resurrection first, and I hope that does not renew the spat.

The division between Peter and Elijah was more dramatic at first, but it became less obvious over the years, as the empty space between their plots was filled with gravestones. People in Mitcham had to have known about these brothers' quarrel, but I doubt if they made much of it. In the extended families of that place, somebody was always on the outs with a relative—though no family that I know of left such a monumental sign.

The old printed genealogy has served us well over the years. One can track the pattern of migration by looking at where the children were born, for mothers always remember. The arabesque pattern of blood and community is evident in the many marriages of Browns to Truetts and Truetts to Wigginses and Huttos to Motts. I don't know if Zack Geiger depended on interviews and family Bibles or had Mormon data at his disposal back then—probably more of the first—but the dates in his record are generally accurate. Geiger had religious zeal and family manners, a rare combination. For my grandparents' assistance, he gave them a copy of the genealogy, a reconciling act in itself, and my grandfather, knowing I was a bookish boy, passed it down to me.

When Papa gave me the pedigree, he pointed to the right columns in the ledger, detailing how Zack Geiger had claimed our dead ancestors—by the Latter-day Saints they'd been "baptized," "endowed," and "sealed"—and he said, "Pay no mind to that Mormon business. They were trying to pray our kinfolks out of hell."

THE WITCHES OF MITCHAM BEAT

*I have ever had pleasure in obtaining
any little anecdotes of my ancestors.*

—

BENJAMIN FRANKLIN
Memoirs (1790)

Now I heard this story when I was a boy: Old lady Daisy Brunson was telling my father that she was a little girl in the room the day Jack Brown died. The year was 1885, and he had passed or was approaching his eighty-third birthday. I don't know the exact date he died, but it had to have been in warm weather because a window was open by the bed, and it was night. She said that as the breath was leaving Jack Brown's body, a black spirit flew into the room, through that very window, and crouched behind a trunk, and that when Jack Brown's breathing stopped the spirit flew back out of the window and chains could be heard rattling in the "ellyments." My father listened to that story and glanced away. It was accepted as fact that Jack Brown was the meanest of men, for the devil had come for Jack Brown's soul. My maternal grandmother, Alice Camilla Smith Etheredge, who was born in Mitcham Beat and was four years old when the old progenitor died, told a version of the same story. The link between Jack Brown and the witchcraft conventions was firmly fixed, community wide.

No bill of particulars against this ancestor has been passed down the line, a significant absence that points to how people were judged in those days. The tree anticipated the fruit: Character dictated the pattern of deeds. If you knew one's character you were prepared for his or her actions and to deal with them, without being blindsided. When a distant relative appeared, and seemed in good health, a common greeting was, "You look just like yourself." An ailing person would say, " I just don't feel *at* myself." If this way of judging meant people were often not given the benefit of the doubt, it also meant fewer surprises or disappointments. In this peculiar skewing of pure Calvinism, character was not necessarily predetermined by the Almighty working through bloodlines, for great character often appeared in the worst of families and vice versa. People called "mean" in Mitcham usually had a hard heart, the most dangerous of all conditions. People who merely committed despicable deeds were generally called "sorry," or, if they were lazy and shiftless, "no 'count." A permanent change in behavior might occur, but the change was suspect—"beauty is skin deep but ugly goes to the bone"—and change was accepted as a final mark of character, after the funeral.

In the one ghostly image we have of Jack Brown, a tintype too faded for reprinting, he looks formidable, a big square-headed man with a beard, looking straight into the lens. He's wearing a flouncy bow tie like Walt Whitman's. He does not look like a man you'd want to cross. He may have come from the womb that way, or he may have been bitter because of the great losses he had experienced since leaving South Carolina fifty years earlier—Dale County dirt turning out too poor for cotton, two of his and Eula Ann Ansley's sons lost in the Civil War, and then, the next year, her dying as they were traveling to or from Dale County and him having to wrap her body in a quilt and bury her in the corner of a farmer's field over near the Alabama River. Maybe he had a blunt German temperament. No descendant was described as he was.

If he had powers as a witch or a warlock, they were not enough to protect him from life's vicissitudes or to provide him great fortune. And he was no hermit. Four years after Eula died, he married a Civil War widow, and in the 1880 census they had in their household a white woman, age twenty-nine, named Mary Philemon, listed as "servant," and her young daughter.

Whether he deserved that reputation as a man of dark spirits, and whether he got it as an old man or a young, may never be known. Lee Brown took me to Jack Brown's grave every time we were at Oak Grove Cemetery. It used to be marked with a piece of railroad steel at the head, with a big sweet shrub growing round it. Before he died, Papa had a store-boughten headstone put on his grandpa's grave. Two descendants later replaced the small marker with a larger, bearing the old man's full name as recorded in the Zack Geiger family pedigree: John Andrew Jackson Brown.

What is known is that, until well after the Mitcham War, country people lived in a world of light and dark, and, between, in flickering shadows. Lives were ordered by the rhythms of the sun, moon, and seasons. To approach empathy with those ancestors, I have to imagine a world with no electric light, no television, no Internet, where darkness was penetrated only by open flame—fires, candles, torches, or kerosene lamps. It was world in which nature prevailed, in the seasons, in floods and freshets, or dry spells in which they lived (or nearly starved), in the deep, dark forests of the Satilpha swamp. Anyone who has been alone in those woods during the newing of the moon is likely to have felt the presence of spirits and to have longed for comforting company.

The Devil and other dangers lurked in those haunted woods, just as they had lain in ambush for Puritans in the foreboding forests of New England. In those borderlands between nature and supernature, witches and their ilk wielded great power. The northern boundary of Mitcham Beat was the Witch Creek hills, through which ran the creek by the same name. It was a wild and wicked region, laced with limestone caves, a perfect place not only for horsethieves but for folks up to more heinous mischief.

Peter Brown, his son, and his grandson—and a whole lot of those old people—believed in witches and spells. Lee Brown's mother, after all, was a Truett, a family in Dale County well known for its practice of witchcraft as well as its profession of Methodism—not mutually exclusive. One of the old Truetts was said to be a warlock, with the power to break spells. If, say, you discovered a horsehair tied to a bush in your yard, you knew that some enemy was putting a hex on you, and a trip to the warlock was necessary. One story provides an example of how the beliefs figured in that society.

Peter's brother Elijah, Uncle Lige, as my father called him, with reverence, "was not afraid of the Devil." And, it follows, witches. Apparently he had had a falling out with Betty Bedsole, the sister of Edward Bedsole. She had first married Uriah Brown but refused to let her three children, among them Rafe, bear the Brown name. The Uriah Brown who was her first husband may have been kin to our set, but I can't establish a tie; Jack Brown had a nephew named David Euriah who died in the Civil War, but it's doubtful he was the father of Betty Bedsole's children. Nonetheless, because of what happened between her and Uriah, she'd come to hate the Brown name and I reckon all called by it.

Before she and Elijah Brown came to their confrontation, she had been married to a man named Montgomery and carried his name, but he too had disappeared. In the story my grandfather told, Uncle Lige's cows came up one evening, but instead of milk they gave blood. He knew right off that the woman, referred to as "old Montgomery," had cast a spell on them because of some quarrel. In the story told around our hearthstone on winter nights, she is a hag and a harridan, with long white hair, the epitome of witches, much like the old Scottish witches and spirits, like the Bean Nighe, of whom and whose kind the Urquharts and other displaced Scots crofters would likely have known. Elijah Brown went to the old woman's house with his knife open in his pocket. He called her to the gate, grabbed her by the hair of the head, bent her over his knee, and put his knife to her throat. "If my cows are not giving milk tomorrow," he said, "I am coming back here and cutting your goddam head off." The next day the cows did give milk, and, as our version has it, "Old Montgomery" had disappeared.

Actually, Elizabeth Bedsole Brown Montgomery went to Louisiana with the Burkes, her nephews, at the end of the Mitcham War, and she lived to 101 or so years of age. A descendant of the Bedsoles said Betty had once cast a spell on her own brother, Edward, who was the brains behind Hell-at-the-Breech. I don't know if the spell worked, but Edward lived a long life and was a plucky survivor. So was Elijah Brown. He served in the Confederate army throughout the whole war, receiving only a slight wound, and died in 1920, near his eighty-first birthday. Mormon or not, he obviously believed he knew a witch when he saw one.

Though almost all of these people were practicing Methodists, the dark spirits were ever near, and, in the prevailing sensibility, no conflict existed between these worlds of the supernatural. Had not Saul, when he was unable to summon the dead prophet Samuel, whom he needed for counsel before a big battle, gone to the Witch of Endor for help? And was this not the same Saul who had driven out the necromancers? He did not get the message he sought, for when the ghost did come to him it correctly predicted not only his death in that battle but also the death of his sons. Had the witches paid King Saul back in kind? Should not one interpretation of this passage be that it is not smart to try to banish witches? Unless they cast a spell on you, your kin, or kine, is it not best to tread lightly past these creatures of the dark world and move swiftly along? You may need a witch, or some other threatening minority, yourself one of these days.

Ample evidence exists that these so-called semi-literate people, like their counterparts all over America, knew the Bible thoroughly, and, like theologians everywhere, disputed interpretations, sought guidance, and looked for omens. One spring in the mid 1950s we had a late frost; new leaves froze, turned brown, and dropped. Old man Leonard Horton told my dad that "we were living in the last days. It says in the Good Book that in the end time, you won't be able to tell the seasons of the year by the falling of the leaves." As we drove back home from Mr. Leonard's place, my dad sought comfort in dispute. "The Bible also says not even the angels in Heaven shall know when the Son of Man cometh," he said, by way of instructing me and steadying himself.

Knowledge of obscure Old Testament passages, the ones that don't make standard lectionaries, is also especially evident in the naming of children. People who read the King James Version (I know, the proper title is *Authorized Version*, but I prefer KJV), or had it read to them, looked to the Bible not merely for polysyllabic, euphonious names that would baffle generations of genealogists to come, but to find those associated with values that amplify the standard Christian virtues. Lee

Brown had a niece named Barzilla Hutto, for that Old Testament person who had gained a place in the Good Book for showing hospitality to the fleeing King David, and hospitality was a virtue highly valued in Mitcham Beat.

As the passage from the First Book of Samuel also indicates, witches, and ghosts, and visions were all of a league. Like the Hebrews of old, the backcountry people of Clarke County believed that the dead move amongst us, to instruct and to advise, not merely to frighten. The dead know what the living doeth, went the saying, and by that is meant a warning: We are all being watched as well as being watched over. Rarely, and to few sane and mortal people, do the visions of that other world come.

All of us grandchildren of Lee Brown have this chilling story etched in our memory: Once when he was leading his plowhorse, going home for dinner, the horse began to pull back and wall its eyes. Something in the tree limbs hanging over the lane was spooking him. Papa said he looked up into the branches and saw a small coffin swinging slowly through the leafy limbs. When he got within earshot of the house, he heard Grandma Mattie screaming, "The baby is dead!" Little Grady Duroc, thirteen months old, had died unexpectedly. He is buried beside them in Oak Grove Cemetery.

Papa said that when Bill Edwards—he pronounced the last name *Edderds*—died, he was walking to Bill's funeral at Oak Grove. The two were almost the same age and had grown up in Mitcham together. Bill died in 1934 when he was sixty-one years old. Papa said he was passing a fence with a gate in it, and there sat Bill Edderds. He was smoking his pipe. Papa said they nodded and spoke, and he walked on to the burial. He felt some awe at the sight, apparently, but he was not upset by the thought that the dead live on, in their own realm yet free to present themselves to us as they wish.

Descendants of the Browns now living in Dale County tell many stories of witchcraft, spells, and charms. "Those old Browns were superstitious people," cousin Jesse Snell of Dale County told me, "and you could not talk them out of it." In the graveyard behind Brown's Methodist Church, near Ozark, Jesse said, a man was buried, and the next day, in the fresh ground raked around the grave after people had left the funeral, were found circles of footprints, where, it was believed, the demons had come to dance, another soul claimed.

Witchhunting was an obsession of colonial Puritans, a fact familiar to all who've studied the Salem trials, Nathaniel Hawthorne's works or Arthur Miller's *The Crucible*. The Elect of Massachusetts were merely following a tradition established in the British isles. But witchcraft was also persecuted in Germany and other countries on the continent. Fear and appreciation of witches' power existed in the collective memory of settlers from all across Europe, especially the peasants who settled South Carolina. Witchcraft stood for rebellion against the social code, against people who set themselves apart, with the power of dark arts and the freedom to indulge in carnal acts and go unpunished, on this earth. Thus the witches and warlocks were feared, envied, and respected.

Some of these settlers in the Dale County community owned slaves, who added their ancient African folkways to the lore—amulets with power, cures, and ways of dealing directly with the spirits. For instance, bottle trees were in yards to trap invading spirits, and newspapers were pasted on indoor walls not as insulation but to distract the haints, who had to be literate (and probably white) because they suspended their temptation to do mischief while they read the news, and those about to be hainted could get away from them. (A lesson for journalists there.)

In South Carolina, the white pioneers lived near enough to the black people, among them the Gullahs and Geechees, to have picked up ancient African secrets as easily as they learned to grow okra and water-melons. A black woman, Aunt Ida Brown, worked for my parents when my older siblings were little, when my dad had money from his logging work to pay her a pittance. She also worked for other families and served as a midwife. When one of my brothers developed a rash, Aunt Ida advised the application of a poultice that included amongst other ingredients "sheep shank." The boy, who must have been about five, asked her what "sheep shank" was. "Honey," she said frankly, "Dat is sheep shit."

As the story about Jack Brown's death shows, the association of witchcraft with Satanism had not disappeared completely; it is safe, and important, to believe in the presence of an All-Powerful Evil, whose first wile, a French writer said, is to convince us that he does not exist. But even by Jack Brown's day, most of the practices called witchcraft did not concern the capturing of a soul. They were used primarily to cure, to ward off evil, and to encourage good fortune. The pagan rituals held on tenaciously, despite the spread of evangelical Christianity, because they served the people. God had been moving in a mysterious way from the beginning of time, long before the line was penned by the mad English poet William Cowper, the same fellow who wrote the ghoulish and graphic old hymn, not surprisingly a favorite in Mitcham Beat, "There is a fountain filled with blood, drawn from Emmanuel's veins."

Some of the incantations have roots traceable to Anglo-Saxon gnomes and charms, now considered paleopoetry, the stuff of dull scholarship. Lee Brown knew how to "talk out fire." If someone, say, got burned on the fingers by a hot poker and Papa could get to the victim before the wound blistered, he could whisper a charm that would ease the pain and heal the wound. The chant was repeated three times and the burned skin was rubbed with the chanter's spit. (Our Lord used spit, as some old-fashioned Bible readers would know.) Papa taught me that charm about a year before he died, and he told me I could pass it on to a grandson. That means he must have learned it from Jack Brown, but I am not done with it yet. It works, if the timing is right and the burned person believes. That makes it fall into the category with the conjuring off of warts, which also works. But our family is not in sole possession of the charm to talk out fire. A version of that same incantation was found in a daybook kept by Edward Bedsole, written in his own bold hand in the early 1890s.

There were other incantations, which I do not know. One is the verse used to stanch blood. A charm could be uttered after a person had been cut, and the bleeding would cease. Some who used this charm also included a poultice made of smut from a chimney and spider webs, reinforcing the old spiritual way with a rational practice—the carbon from the chimney had been sterilized by the heat and the spider webs made a coagulating bandage.

In following these old ways, the people did not think of themselves as heathens; they simply had a sense of awe and knew that this world is not our final home. Like the American Indians with whom they had associated in South Carolina, they found this belief in a spiritual world confirmed in dreams, which came from that other world, which was also rooted deep in the tradition of Jews and Christians. And interpreters of dreams played an important role in the community. Some dreams had formulaic meanings: If you dreamt of a death, say, it meant someone was going to get married. People who wouldn't have known a Jungian archetype if they met one in the big road were strong for dream study.

My mother, born to an Etheredge (spelled five ways over the years) of Black Belt stock on her father's side and to a mother whose parents came from Dale County, believed firmly in the messages that come to us in dreams, and with good reason. Married at thirteen—her parents were witnesses to the wedding, which was performed by Adlai Bell, grandson of the Civil War captain—to a man who was twenty, she had given birth to three sons before she was eighteen. When the youngest of the three, my brother Roy, was a baby, he developed sore eyes, or what is now called conjunctivitis. Doctors were of little help, and the young couple was desperate. My mother dreamed that if she mixed rich cream with powdered flowers of sulfur and made a yellow paste to put on the baby's eyes, they would get well. She did and they did.

Some of the old cures are obscure in origin. When the oldest son, Elmore, was a baby, he took sick, and Coley and Alliene thought he would die. Her old maternal grandfather, Henry Hawthorne Smith, who'd been a Confederate cavalryman, told my father to take his straight razor and nick a fold of skin between the child's shoulder blades, or, as he said, to "scarify" the skin. He said the child's blood would be as thick as molasses. Then my father was to mix that blood in a teaspoon of my mother's breast milk and give that to the infant. My father said Grandpa Henry was right: the blood looked black and syrupy, but after my parents followed the old man's directions to the letter Elmore quickly improved.

Premonitions and intuitions were not ignored. Many of the stories included "*something* told me. . . ." My dad was working in the woods one hot summer day when something told him to look behind him, and there lay coiled a gigantic diamondback rattler. Almost all these stories of miracles, and the marveling over miracles, follow the theme of survival-in-the-wilderness. Once a drought (or "drouth," as it was called) was so prolonged that creeks ran low and wells and springs went dry. When ours did, my father found a spot near our house where free-range hogs wallowed because the ground stayed moist. He sank a shovel in that spot and heard "a rumbling deep in the earth." Soon water was bubbling around his feet. The new spring was boxed in and covered over, and its flow served our family until we left Mitcham in 1946. God had again delivered his people from the brink of disaster, just as He had the Israelites in another dry place.

One might conclude, after pondering the spiritual life in Mitcham, that such unschooled country folk would be susceptible to Pentecostal religions, but they were not. People may have argued about which denomination offered the road to salvation, yet they were suspicious of religious fervor, or what used to be called "enthusiasm." Emotions are fickle, dangerous forces. Holy-rollerism never caught on. A relative told me he knew of one tent revival that was held in Mitcham. The Pentecostals came in to evangelize and asked to use the old Methodist church but were refused, so they pitched their tent beside it. As the service reached its fevered pitch, the preacher called on the congregants to come forward and unburden themselves of their load of sins. One woman, who had married an old widower and had given birth to a child, rose and confessed that the natural father of the child was the old man's young son. Those gathered were shocked into silence. The revival abruptly closed, and the Pentecostals left, never to return. The Holy Rollers were more fearsome, more upsetting of the social order, in their way, than were the witches.

People in Mitcham enjoyed their kind of religion—awe before the presence of the Almighty, frightful musings on mortality and immortality, eloquent and entertaining preaching, long and lusty singings of the old hymns, and gathering for dinners-on-ground—but religion that went too far, that was disrupting rather than unifying, was frowned upon. As old-time Methodists, mainly, their attitude toward religion resembled that of low-church Episcopalians. It was a way to practice Christianity in a ritual way, satisfying and uplifting; it introduced authority and order into a world of chaos and uncertainty. But the practice of religion also required the use of what they would have called "common sense," which the more learned call commonweal, knowing that *weal* means "good."

The miracle stories existed in counterpoint to stories of failures—How We Almost Made It But Didn't. Indeed, the dark side of the survival story is revealed in accounts of missed opportunities, the shifts of Southern family fortunes. I've heard dozens of stories about some ancestor who sold for a song lands that would later become fabulously valuable. If only that old grandpappy hadn't a-done that, we would not now have to keep plowing that damn mule and we'd have so much money we wouldn't care if syrup went up to a dollar a sop. By far the stronger and more positive theme was: Disaster Averted by Mysterious Intervening Forces. The first theme prevented presumptuousness and reminded everybody that none of us can see through the thickness of time; the second offered inspiration and hope. Who knows whence deliverance cometh? The woods were full of those tales of being rescued by dreams and by visions and voices speaking in the wilderness and of ancient cures that worked when modern medicine didn't.

Make of these stories what you will. Some will wonder about sanity or about how strong the proof was in the distillate some of those tellers and practitioners of ancient lore imbibed. Such searches for explanations or such pat dismissals are to be expected from those whose way of thinking has been confined and channeled by the Enlightenment or the Age of Reason, which, I rejoice to report, failed to reach full flower in the shaded glades of Mitcham Beat, Alabama. Call the people of that remote settlement uncouth, if you must, but don't dismiss the possibility that they drew sustenance and strength, like sweet well water, from deeper springs.

HARD TIMES, HARD LESSONS

*Jealousies and prejudices which one part of the Union had imbibed
against another part. . . . What, but the mixing of people from
different parts of the United States during the War,
rubbed off these impressions?*

—

GEORGE WASHINGTON
Farewell Address (1790)

If the Mitcham War was a factor in bringing that community into the
politics of Clarke County, the Civil War was a factor in bringing many
backcountry Southern people into a surer sense of the Union. Many were
named for Andrew Jackson and shared his belief in united states. By the
time I was born, members of my family considered themselves first as
Americans. In fact, I did not think of myself as a Southerner until I was
twelve or so. There were few Northerners around to call attention to the
way we behaved and talked and to trigger defensiveness.

When I was growing up, after World War II, we sang "Battle
Hymn of the Republic," with no notion that it was the Yankee anthem.

The fathers of many of my classmates and two of my older brothers and many cousins were considered Yanks in other countries. After the United Daughters of the Confederacy was founded, in the fateful year of 1894, and other groups sprang up, it became fashionable in upper classes to think of oneself as a Southerner, though, in point of fact, I never fully felt the reality of being different until I went off to other parts of the country and people heard me speak. Then I truly became a Southerner, an outsider, quaint, accented, and immediately typecast by region and by people, my fellow Americans, who were surprised that folks from my benighted region could utter a word that was intelligible, intelligent, and informed by reading.

My first recollection of a Southern identity came when I meddled in a big Bible on a washstand in my grandparents' fireplace room. It was crammed with old newspapers and clippings. My grandmother must have kept every obituary of every Mott who'd died in the last fifty years. My grandfather kept those special sections that Alabama newspapers used to publish to commemorate Confederate Memorial Day, the last Monday in April. In his young manhood, Lee Brown's father and uncle Elijah had attended those reunions. Papa went through those newspaper pullouts and tried to explain to me what that war meant. All I remember is his saying, "Pa never spoke ill of Yankees." Those editions carried early 1900s photographs of the county-wide reunions of the Clarke County veterans, most with long beards, many with a leg or an arm missing. I can pick out a few peg-legged men who might be Peter Brown. None seemed to be glorifying their cause so much as celebrating their survival and camaraderie. My father said that his grandfather was angry because one young orator, rising to the occasion, celebrated them as "the great men of yesteryear." Peter Brown said, "Great men of yesteryear! We are great men today!" To have a glib young whippersnapper patronizing him and his comrades struck Peter Brown as the height of uppityness.

As survivors of the War, Mitcham Beat ancestors talked little about it, except in these concrete shards of war memory, but their sons and grandsons glorified the Lost Cause. My father absorbed those little pieces and his readings of the apologists for the Confederacy. His accounts remain vivid, but I can't quote from specific sources—Peter Brown? Elijah Brown? Jack Mott? Henry Hawthorne Smith? Other old veterans with whom he associated as a youngster? As records became available, many blanks could be filled.

I like to think Peter Brown fully became an American of the post–Civil War period earlier than most, on January 1, 1863, during the Battle of Stone's River, fought near Murfreesboro, Tennessee. As I will note, it was a fateful day for him personally and for the nation. Peter, with his brothers, cousins, and neighbors, was then in the process of being educated, led out of the provincial backwoods into a larger understanding of human nature, a wider knowledge of peoples from all over the country, and a fuller understanding of the faults and virtues of leadership. Prisoners such as Peter Brown not only mingled with fellow Southerners, they also got to know, and some even to like, Yankees, and Peter himself traveled in every Confederate state east of the Mississippi. Returning home, Peter and other veterans brought an education gained involuntarily but nevertheless useful. They would look at the world from a more national perspective, and they would regard the term "war" as more, exponentially more, than a small-town merchant–backcountry farmer feud.

———•·•———

Even before the battle in which the four Brown brothers and other farm boys would learn in the hardest of ways the importance of intelligent, inspiring leadership, winter had already successfully invaded middle

Tennessee. After a balmy opening, December 1862 had turned bitter cold, and by Christmas, waves of rain, sleet, and snow were falling on Confederate troops huddled in makeshift huts, with firepits in the center. Mitcham Beat men were being primed for their first major engagement with the enemy. They did not know, as we do, that the fighting to come over that frozen ground would prove prologue to the many casualties, the loss of life and limb, the protracted retreat, the increasingly inept leadership, and, finally, to the shame of defeat. They did not know that if they survived the long campaign from Murfreesboro, through Chattanooga, Atlanta, Franklin, and Nashville, the experience would amplify an attitude toward formal authority long established in the mindset of Mitcham Beat.

The deepening chill had come in from the northwest, where the Yankees were. Union and Confederate armies had been preparing to lock horns for more than a month. Where the battle would take place, but not exactly when, had already been decided. The Army of Tennessee, commanded by General Braxton Bragg, took up its position at Murfreesboro, thirty miles southeast of Nashville. Most of Bragg's force had marched from eastern Kentucky, where in early October Bragg muffed a chance for a major victory at Perryville. As Bragg's army, numbering about 40,000 actives, had moved out of Knoxville toward Murfreesboro, it passed through Tullahoma and picked up the Alabama 24th Infantry, a regiment that had come over from Corinth, Mississippi. Among the Mitcham men in that unit, in Company E, called the Dickinson Guards, were Peter and Elijah Brown, the elder twenty-five, the younger twenty-three years old. Peter said he and his comrades thought the war would be a "breakfast task," a small morning chore; why, they'd whip the invading Yankees and be back by planting time.

The 24th regiment was placed in the brigade of Colonel (later General) Arthur Middleton Manigault (pronounced *man-e-go*), a rice planter of Huguenot stock from near Charleston, collateral descendant of a signer of the Declaration of Independence, and a veteran of the Mexican War. Manigault may have been the first bona fide aristocrat any of the Mitcham men had seen. And to call him rich would be an understatement. One ancestor's estate was the largest probated before the Revolution, amongst the holdings 32,700 pounds sterling and nearly 300 slaves. His grandfather's estate included 490 slaves and 47,532 acres of land. Yet General Manigault, unlike Bragg, must have worn his rank as well as his social station lightly; in the leveling brought on by war, leadership was based on character and courage.

Manigault's men respected him, and the soldiers must have appreciated his care for them. They even serenaded him one night. His memoirs were written two years after the war, for his family, and lay unpublished for ninety years. Manigault's account lacks Lost Cause bloviation—regrets, blamings, and defense of the secession mistake. Instead, *A Carolinian Goes to War* offers sharp insights into the life of the common soldiers—their games of "Base Ball," their snowball fights, and the preaching and stealing that went on behind the lines. His brigade consisted of three regiments from Alabama and two from South Carolina. Some of the Alabamians were only a generation removed from South Carolina and had cousins in the South Carolina regiments, which include surnames familiar in Mitcham—for instance, Hutto, the most easily traceable to South Carolina. Manigault stayed with his men in the thick of battle and received a head wound at the second Battle of Franklin. He died of the lingering effects, two decades after the surrender.

Other leaders, among them Nathan Bedford Forrest and Joseph E. Johnston, were also admired for their bravery and ability to inspire men to fight. Colonel Newton Davis, who survived, and Captain John Bell, who didn't, were likewise strong leaders. As Sam Watkins's account of the war indicates, the private soldiers were close observers of their leaders as well as their messmates, and they saw character tried in the hottest cauldron. What the men from Mitcham Beat learned about admirable leadership would stand them in good stead when they returned and found its opposite in the clique that ran Clarke County.

Peter and Elijah's two older brothers, John L. and Samuel J. W., were in Company H of the Alabama 32nd, recruited in Coffeeville by Alexander McKinstry, a Mobile lawyer. Though that regiment was raised in Coffeeville, many of the men were from Mitcham. The beat had voted 12–0 for secession; the low turnout, far fewer than the males of voting age in that settlement, points less to apathy than to a unanimity of opinion. All the Mitcham men whose companies would become part of the Alabama 24th or the Alabama 32nd enlisted early. It's doubtful that the primary motive behind their volunteering was a desire to see slavery protected. The only person in the district owning more than twenty-seven slaves was William Levi Beckham, whose slave quarters were located where a brisk stream, now silted in, flowed into Satilpha Creek. (I was born in a log house called the Sigler Place, owned by the overbearing sawmill baron White Smith, a few hundred yards from Beckham Branch.) My father showed me the foundations of the old cabins and pointed out what he called the "Indian" peach trees that were still growing there in the 1950s. Beckham owned other plantations and far more than the minimal number of slaves cited in the census. He probably lived elsewhere, and an overseer lived near the quarters, in a handsome, log, dogtrot house farther up the stream. After intermarriages, deaths, and migrations, the Beckham name had disappeared before the turn of the century; now only that dry branch bed remains as a ghostly reminder.

The presence today of a black community at Dead Level, around present-day Greater Ebenezer Church, and census data for 1860 in an adjoining beat, Clarkesville, indicate that several families in Mitcham, among them the Bells, owned slaves. By contrast, the Coffeeville beat, where there were large plantations, was firmly anti-secessionist and voted against it 84–32. The unionist sentiment may have been influenced by some slaveowners who, perhaps not ironically, had migrated from Maine, or perhaps from other, Southern-bred slaveowners who feared insurrections by enraged slaves and wished to appear in sympathy with the Unionists. Tension between Negroes and whites is understandable: The population of Clarke County in 1860 was about 15,000 and racially equal in numbers, and it has remained so to this day. Most blacks (only a few were listed as free) were concentrated on larger plantations on the Alabama and Tombigbee rivers.

Taken together, these facts, and some knowledge of the Mitcham sensibility, suggest that men from the beat, preparing for battle at Murfreesboro, were there because they valued independence, considered themselves part of the state and the Confederacy, and welcomed a challenge from invaders. John W. Bell, who farmed just across Satilpha Creek from the Browns, was named captain of Company H of the 32nd regiment. John L. Brown was his sergeant, and his oldest brother, Samuel J. W. Brown, a private, had come over from Dale County to join up with John L. Also in their company were Rayford H. Bedsole and his brother Thomas. Other soldiers bore familiar Mitcham Beat names—Brazzeal, Brinks, Coate, Gilmore, Howze, Hutto, McIntire, Pugh, even Mitcham.

By the fall of 1862, Mitcham Beat men in the first regiments to be raised in Clarke County had had time to make the transition from farm boy to soldier. The 32nd saw action at Bridgeport and Stevenson in north Alabama, and in early December 1862, the regiment fought under General Nathan Bedford Forrest at LaVergne, between Nashville and Murfreesboro, before falling back to join the larger force at Stone's River, just west of Murfreesboro. The 32nd regiment, in a brigade commanded by General Dan Adams, joined members of Bragg's army who had been in fighting at Corinth, through Shiloh, a deadly draw, and on to Perryville, where Bragg had stalled, giving the Yankees time to slip away to Louisville and avoid a major defeat. But that was Braxton Bragg for you. His soldiers said that if the gates of heaven opened for them Bragg would order a fallback.

After Shiloh, Bragg began to acquire a reputation as a martinet, a stickler for protocol, who, unlike General Nathan Bedford Forrest, loved in-fighting and disciplining his troops better than keeping after the Yankees. By the end of his eighteen months of command of the Army of Tennessee, most of his top officers had turned against him; from their comments and subsequent history Bragg emerges with a string of negative descriptions attached to his name, among them sadistic, vindictive, stubborn, and duplicitous. The officers' opinion echoed that of the soldiers, and several of his generals pleaded with President Jefferson Davis for Bragg's removal. But Davis had faith in his old Mexican War comrade, who, like Davis, was a West Point man. The president did not transfer Bragg to a desk in Richmond until February 1864, after the disaster at Chattanooga. Captain Bell of Company H was happy to see Bragg gone; and Colonel Newton Davis, who took command of the 24th Infantry after the original commander, Colonel William Buck of Mobile, got a thumb shot off at Stone's River, felt much the same. Even General Manigault, though he labored to be fair in his postwar assessment, saw Bragg as a failure. He was the antithesis of Robert E. Lee, who was beloved even after he had blundered.

The most-often quoted assessment of Bragg came from a Tennessee soldier, Private Sam Watkins, who was in the brigade that fought alongside Manigault's at Murfreesboro. After the war, he wrote that soldiers followed Bragg only because they feared him. He became infamous as an executioner. "Every day," Watkins said, "someone was being led to the stake." Firing squads killed not only men charged with desertion but others who were considered insubordinate. Bragg, like most bullies, wanted sycophants around him, and he spurned the generals who tried to convince him to alter course.

The Union forces, recently named the Army of the Cumberland, were massed in Nashville, and their commander, a quirky Roman Catholic zealot named William Rosecrans, was dragging his feet and irking Lincoln. The Union had already suffered a major defeat at Fredericksburg, and Lincoln wanted a victory to stave off any notions the English might have of joining the Confederate cause. General Henry Halleck, the commander-in-chief in Washington, sent Rosecrans a telegram that said, essentially, go out and fight Bragg, or you'll be forced to step aside.

Bragg got to pick the battle site, and he chose the open fields and cedar thickets near Stone's River, a few miles west of Murfreesboro, near the Nashville and Chattanooga Railroad and major pikes to Nashville, Lebanon, and Nolensville. Here was yet another mistake, which cannot be laid to anybody but Bragg; the roads gave the Yankees a way to approach Bragg's army from three sides, and the railroad led back to Nashville, where Rosecrans had ample supplies and 30,000 troops in reserve. Why did Bragg choose such a place, with the enemy near its supply base, and particularly in such open terrain, when he could have positioned his troops, outnumbered by 7,000 when the battle started, in the wooded hills to the south and west? Outflanking the enemy was out of the question, because, if it succeeded, Bragg might be trapped between the main force in Nashville and the outlying Federals. In hindsight, this analysis is facile. Perhaps Bragg chose Murfreesboro because he and his generals wanted to be feted in grand style.

Christmas had been a time of celebration in the old Tennessee town. A grand ball was held for the officers, and the Confederate cavalry general John Hunt Morgan married a local belle. The officiating clergyman was General Leonidas Polk, one of Bragg's corps commanders, another West Pointer, and a bishop in the Episcopal church. Many of the officers had been on a drinking spree—and no doubt many of the foot soldiers also. They deserved a drink, for, as Manigault wrote, they were "much in need of rest and refreshment." Many had made the long march to Murfreesboro in rags, barefoot, and near starving. They had run out of bread and had been living off meat and parched corn. One Mitcham Beat veteran, Jack Mott, said the private soldiers got that corn by waiting for the officers' horses to be fed and grabbling the kernels that dribbled from the horses' lips. If corn had been scarce on the march, a clear liquid distilled from it became abundant, for barrels of whiskey had been liberated from a Yankee depot at Stevenson, Alabama. Sam Watkins claimed the officers were still soused or hungover as the Union army approached. A division commander, General Frank Cheatham of Tennessee, under whom Adams's brigade, including John Bell's company of Clarke County men, had been placed temporarily, was so drunk he fell off his horse while addressing his troops.

On the eve of the battle, December 30, as the armies were facing each other, an event occurred that is too patently Hollywood to be believed were it not so well documented. In the memorable cadences of historian Shelby Foote, "the military bands began to play their favorite tunes. Carrying sweet and clear on the windless wintry air, the music of one band was about as audible on one side of the line as on the other, and the concert thus became something of a contest, a musical bombardment." A Confederate band answered "Yankee Doodle Dandy" with "Dixie" and "Hail, Columbia" with "The Bonnie Blue Flag." Eventually, one band struck up "Home, Sweet Home" and soon bands on both sides picked up the melody. Rebel and Yankee soldiers sang the sad old song together. Far from pleasures and palaces, they were preparing to kill each other the next day.

Yankee and Confederate battle plans were mirror images: Bragg would hit Rosecrans's right, and Rosecrans would hit Bragg's right—two big armies attacking on opposite sides of the field. Each thought he could get the jump on the other, and the Confederates succeeded, dramatically. Bragg's left corps surprised the Yankees at daybreak. The shocked bluecoats, still at their breakfasts, flung skillets and coffeepots and fled, running over men to their rear and deaf to officers trying to halt the rout. Panic ensued, and the screaming Confederates were too thrilled to leave off their pursuit and regroup with the main body. Meanwhile, the sleet and rain continued.

As the Federals were launching their less-successful attack on the Confederates' right, anchored by the corps of General John Breckinridge, Manigault's South Carolinians and Alabamians were clustered with other brigades in the division commanded by General Jones Withers, a West Point graduate and Mobile lawyer, in Polk's corps, near the center. The major thrust was to their left. The order for Manigault's brigade to attack did not come till 10 a.m., and by then the Yankees were braced and ready. As unfortunate as the Mitcham Beat boys were in being under Bragg, they were equally unlucky in being sent to attack the Michigan, Indiana, and Ohio troops in their front under Philip Sheridan, a fierce little Irishman who was one of the ablest leaders on either side. His command took losses more terrible than the Confederates, and his line wavered, even ran out of ammunition once, but it always regrouped.

The 32nd Regiment, Company H, under John Bell, was in fierce fighting throughout the three-day battle. In a letter sent to his wife a week after the battle, the captain spares her the goriest details but provides a day-by-day account of his company's actions in what some Southerners of the time would call the Battle of Murphreesborough. On December 31, his unit was moved a mile from where the battle would start and placed in a small grove of cedars. Soon they were ordered into the thickest of the fighting. They forded the river, crossed an open field, and marched toward unseen enemies. A single shell from the masked batteries found Bell's company, killing three and wounding six.

When his men got within two or three hundred yards of the Yankees, they also came under small arms fire. Two more soldiers fell on either side of the captain. Bell wrote that his only fear was that, when the retreat was ordered, he would be shot in the back. Of the twenty-seven men in his company, thirteen were killed or wounded. Throughout the battle it had rained "incessibly," Bell wrote. On New Year's Eve night, he could not sleep and then, after the second day, he "lay down upon rails to keep out of the water and slept until I was perfectly saturated."

On New Year's Day, Bell's men were joined by now-Colonel Alexander McKinstry who had recruited them in Coffeeville. McKinstry, an aide to Bragg, had been away at a court martial, had not yet seen battle, and had been ordered to replace the wounded commander, Colonel Harry Maury. McKinstry had served as Bragg's provost marshal, and one of his duties was to supervise discipline, which included overseeing the executions. When the shelling and shooting started, McKinstry began "dodging and jumping about worse than a duck after a june bug," Bell wrote his wife, "and he was the most anxious man to get out of there I ever saw." The company was still under heavy fire, and Bell wrote his wife that she would have laughed had she seen McKinstry "squatting behind a tree." McKinstry, who prosecuted others, escaped court martial for cowardice. As one might predict, he later became a successful Alabama politician.

McKinstry had been called up from his safety in the rear to one of the hottest parts of the battle, as, by the third day of the battle, the 32nd regiment was back under Breckinridge on the right, trying to dislodge Yankees in a patch of woods called The Slaughter Pen, Hell's Half-Acre, and The Round Forest. The Confederates, facing open ground, had to leave their cover in cedars and again move in full view toward the enemy. The single Rebel brigade, one veteran of the 32nd regiment wrote, "contended against four brigades of Yankees and seventeen pieces of artillery." Nevertheless, the Rebels got within fifty yards of their enemy before being ordered to retreat. Had the command not been so timely or the fallback so orderly, the veteran wrote, "none of us would now be left to tell the tale." Of the 280 who approached the guns, only 58 came back. Peter Brown's brother, James W., took sick and was taken to Tullahoma where he died on February 19. His other brother on the battlefield, Sergeant John L. Brown, survived, only to be killed three months later in the fighting in north Georgia, near Chickamauga.

The 24th regiment, what was left of it under Manigault's command, was held in reserve on the second and third days, after having its own equally terrible time on December 31. Though the two or three Rebel brigades in the center drove the enemy's first line from a cedar-lined hill, the brigades became misaligned, and Manigault's men were exposed to cannon and infantry fire from their right that enfiladed—

penetrated from the side—inflicting such damage they were forced to fall back. To the commander whose brigade was adjacent to his, Manigault reported "a failure of complete success." On the second charge toward Sheridan's troops, they stumbled over frozen and bloody ground and pushed the first line of Yankees back, but again their flanks were exposed, and they were enfiladed. Once more the order came to regroup and fall back.

On the third pass over essentially the same ground, Manigault's brigade met resistance from Union artillery, but before the big guns, mounted on a knoll, could be captured, bad luck struck again. A brigade of Yankees came over the hill. It was driven back by another Rebel brigade that took the cannons. Peter Cozzens in *No Better Place To Die* said Manigault's troops were in "some of the bloodiest charges of the battle." Although they were continually denied a full break-through, they could claim to have inflicted one critical casualty. Sheridan's division, commanded by his West Point classmate, General Joshua Sill, was driven back, but Sill rallied the men and himself led the counphrcharge, shouting encouragement. In *Stones* [sic] *River—Bloody Winter in Tennessee*, historian James Lee McDonough writes that Sill was killed instantly by a shot through the head. The carnage on each side was horrendous—nearly 26,000 casualties were reported. Dead men and horses, wrecked wagons, and disabled cannons littered the field. Manigault said his brigade, numbering 2,200 going into the bat-tle, had suffered 530 casualties. Withers's division lost 26 percent of its men on the first day.

One of those casualties was Peter Brown of Mitcham Beat. As he told the story to his grandson, he was crouched behind a cedar stump as a charge faltered. When the fallback was ordered, he broke to run. Sheridan had ordered his infantry to "shoot low," and a minie ball from one of the Yankee rifles shattered the fibula—Peter called it "the little bone"—in his right leg. His brother Elijah was not there to help him; he'd been taken ill and left at a hospital in Knoxville.

The slow-moving .58-caliber bullet did wicked work. No matter if Peter Brown was twenty-five years old and in the prime of physical manhood, no matter if he was loaded with adrenaline, and no matter if the weather was freezing, he lay in agony. Bone, muscle, and vessels were riddled. Somehow he hobbled, crawled, or was carried to the rear, to a Confederate hospital where the leg was amputated below the knee. Though the singing of bone saws and the moans and screams of wounded and dying men filled the hospital, at least the surgeons had chloroform. Peter Brown's first battle was to be his last, and he may have felt a tinge of relief when he awoke. As daylight came the next morning, he may have realized he would never fight in battle again. It was Emancipation Day.

Peter Brown's own freedom was six months away. When Bragg's army pulled out of Murfreesboro on January 3, again without finishing off a crippled Yankee army, even Bell, though a captain, did not know the Rebels were retreating. Many Southern soldiers thought they'd won. Later assessments, however, would put the Battle of Murfreesboro in the same category as the fight at Perryville—a tactical victory and a strategic loss. Field commanders and many later historians laid the blame on Bragg. The ambiguous outcome convinced the British not to side with the South, making that battle, in retrospect, as much a turning point as Gettysburg.

As the Army of Tennessee moved southeast, leaving some of the wounded behind in houses that had been converted to hospitals, the ground had thawed, and the mud was from ankle to knee deep. Captain Bell of Mitcham Beat reported to his wife that he left a shoe buried deep beneath the surface but eventually found a replacement to put on his lacerated foot. The next morning he found "an old pair of boots" by the road and marched on. I have little doubt that the soldier whose boots Bell found was past being in need of them.

By January 5, when the Yankees discovered that the Rebels were gone, they moved into Murfreesboro, and Peter Brown became a Yankee prisoner. He spent the following four months under conditions that had to have been safer than those he'd have suffered in the field. On April 22, he was sent to Nashville, and from there to Louisville, and, on May 6, he arrived at Fort McHenry near Baltimore, where "The Star Spangled Banner" poem had been written. Later that month, with 428 others, he was exchanged. A one-legged prisoner of war was, after all, of some use to Yankees on that front. Peter was moved from Federal custody to the Episcopal Hospital in Williamsburg and then, consistent with his regiment, to the South Carolina Confederate Hospital in Petersburg. On June 16, he was permanently furloughed. A medical report said that Brown's condition was good, though he had suffered "vulnus scolepticum," an oft-used medical term of that war, sometimes abbreviated "V.S." It means "gunshot wound."

My grandfather said, "Pa never spoke ill of Yankees," and now I can make a good guess why. As his son Lee Brown said, many times over, "When he thought all was lost, they saved his life and set him free." It was while he was being guarded as a prisoner that both of his older brothers, with thousands of others, died. J. W. Brown's body was taken from Tullahoma to Chattanooga and buried in a Confederate cemetery there. John L. Brown died March 29, 1863, at nearby Dalton, Georgia, where he had been hospitalized for wounds from "cannon," the records say.

John L. (probably "Louis," for a Dale County uncle) was attended during his dying days by John Wesley Truett, a brother of his wife Charity Truett, and of Peter's wife-to-be, Winnie Truett Johnson. Sergeant Brown's personal effects were listed as "$20 and sundry items." His death was reported in *The Clarke County Journal*, which said, "The deceased, though humble & unassuming, was a true patriot, a good citizen—'pious, just, humane, temperate & sincere.' As a soldier he had few superiors—always performing his duties promptly & cheerfully." His captain, John W. Bell, who probably penned that formal farewell, died about a year later, also in the cold mountains of north Georgia, and the captain's body was brought back in a lead coffin with a rubber gasket and buried in the Bell-Brewer Cemetery in Mitcham Beat. John L. Brown's name does not show up in a search of Confederate cemeteries. His remains may also have been returned; if so, they are lying in an unmarked grave, probably in Oak Grove cemetery.

Peter Brown had the further good fortune of not having to serve under a general totally different from Bragg but equally feckless, John B. Hood of Texas. While Bragg tended to choke, Hood crazily charged; General Lee referred to him as "all lion and no fox." Elijah Brown and Jack Mott were not so lucky; they fought under both Bragg and Hood, with a brief interlude under a far more competent commander, Joseph E. Johnston. Elijah Brown survived the war with only a thigh wound, while Jack Mott was shot in the head at the Battle of New Hope Church in 1864. The record of his examination for a pension says the right parietal bone, at the temple, was shot away; a silver plate was put over the wound, and he was returned to the ranks. He went on to serve in Holtzclaw's brigade, which guarded the Rebel's retreat from the Battle of Nashville and saved the remnants of Hood's army.

After Hood was relieved, Mott's unit came under the command of General Richard Taylor, son of former general and president, Zachary

Taylor, "Old Rough 'n' Ready," who led his troops to Mobile Bay, with Yankee soldiers advancing by land and Farragut's navy by sea. Soon, complete defeat was imminent. A strong leader in his own right, Taylor held his men together to prevent total annihilation and to secure paroles; some surrendered at Citronelle, Alabama, about fifty airline miles from Mitcham Beat, and others at Demopolis, in the county above Mitcham Beat. The final formal surrender of Taylor's army was made at Meridian, Mississippi, to General E. R. S. Canby, a Kentuckian, on May 6, 1865. The veterans of the 32nd Alabama Infantry, Company H, Mott's unit, in a brigade which by war's end included shards of the original 32nd and 58th straggled back to Mitcham. My father said that when Grandpa Mott got home, after being wounded again, in the foot, at Spanish Fort, he was so covered with body lice that he had to strip in the yard, throw his clothes in a boiling washpot, and bathe with lye soap before he could step over his own threshold. Those from the 24th—the original Dickinson Guards, Elijah Brown among them—came home from North Carolina where their final commander, General Joseph E. Johnston, had surrendered to General William Tecumseh Sherman on April 26.

Except for sufferings magnified by the unusual harshness of Braxton Bragg and the madness of Hood, the experience of the Mitcham soldiers differs little from that of others in the Confederate army, especially their cousins from Dale County. As fate would have it, six Brown first cousins were on the battlefield at Stone's River. The Clarke County Brown brothers had at least three Brown cousins in Company B of the Alabama 33rd Infantry, "The Daleville Grays," a company that first fought under Stonewall Jackson in Virginia before their regiment was, unfortunately, transferred to Braxton Bragg's command. Another first cousin, David Brown, was wounded and captured at Perryville and died a Yankee prisoner. One first cousin, also named Peter Brown, who was promoted to sergeant, was killed in the Battle of Franklin. Louis Brown, who had come to Clarke County in the 1850s and later returned to Dale, suffered a mangled hand, but like the Peter Brown of Mitcham, he survived and lived to sire a large family. It's possible the Clarke Countians had another cousin, J. T. Ansley, of the right age to be a nephew, cousin or younger brother of their mother, Eula Ann Ansley Brown. A private in the "The Beauregards," or Company E of the Alabama 15th, also from Dale County, Ansley died in a Confederate hospital in Charlottesville, Virginia, on February 16, 1863, less than six months before his regiment failed in the fighting now considered the turning point of the war, on Little Round Top at Gettysburg.

If the returning veterans' physical hardships and lingering wounds are well documented, any mental scars are shrouded. Apparently, like soldiers from other wars, few talked at length about their experiences. The old soldiers and their wives did not reflect and revel. What they all had endured was too terrible, too painful, and too insulting to dwell upon. The fragments of memory passed down to their descendants stress the struggles to survive; obviously, these veterans knew no more than almost all foot soldiers and officers, in thick of battle, about the panorama. Jack Mott carried a lifetime of regret over stealing a widow's hog. (Sam Watkins wrote about an incident so similar one wonders if the two were together, and he explains how the soldiers returned later to apologize to the woman.) It was the next generation that began to glorify The Lost Cause.

The information my father, who was born in 1897, gathered came from many veterans of the Civil War, who were old men when he came of age to remember. He also heard stories from the women, who bore the heavy burden of caring for families and farms. His grandmother

Harriet Hutto Mott said that when word of their plight got back to Dale County, relatives sent over hams, lard, and other foodstuffs, but all of it was stolen by conscript officers or guerillas—or whatever she called thieves. John Bell was anxious about his family back in Mitcham Beat, and for fatherly reasons. He had had one furlough, and when he arrived home he had changed so much his children thought he was a stranger and ran from him. He wrote often, mostly long letters describing the actions, many expressing concerns for the children's education, even the spelling books they might find. In a letter dated February 8, after the 32nd and 58th regiments had been combined, he wrote his wife, his "beloved Nannie," the following:

> You had better pay the produce tax in money if you can as you will probably need all the corn you have. The affect of $11.33 against the note given to Mixon is perfectly good and Mr. York can only collect the balance after deducting that amount. Therefore if you pay him you will deduct that amount. Present my regards to your Ma, my love to the children and believe me to be sincerely and affectionately yours. Jno W. Bell

It was to be Captain Bell's last letter. He died of illness eight days later.

Like surviving dog soldiers of other wars, married men returned to their families and single men went looking for women; after marrying, usually in jig time, they went to work raising families. They knew little about the larger movements and motives that figured in the national conflict. In our family, closer matters had to be dealt with, and one of them was domestic. The woman Peter Brown married believed she was a widow; she was a sister of the wife of his dead brother, John L. Brown.

Winnie Truett had first married Joshua Johnson and had a son by him named Lafayette or Fate. A Joshua Johnson was reported killed in 1862, at the first battle of Cold Harbor. Some time, well after the surrender, Johnson suddenly appeared in Mitcham. Winnie faced a choice, and she chose Peter Brown. (This story was often told.) When both parties agreed and no property contested, divorce was de facto; that was the frontier way of dealing with such private, dangerous, domestic matters. (Even marriages were not considered state business until 1911 in South Carolina, when licenses to wed became required by law.) Johnson disappeared, and Winnie and Peter raised his son Fate with their other children. Searching national censuses and various family records, I find no Joshua Johnson who matches the first husband of Winnie Truett and the father of Fate. He seems to have vanished.

The larger issue for all families was survival and, following that, recovery. The hopes for prosperity and peace that brought them to Clarke County had been dashed, and it would take many decades and more positive turnings for the family to prosper. But survive they did in those early days; they knew how to subsist. And by the 1890s, many held their original land, and some had acquired more. As veterans and freeholders, these elders would have seen the risk of getting mixed up with Hell-at-the-Breech. As men who had been tested in the greatest conflict in modern history, they had status in Mitcham, if nowhere else. It was clear from my grandfather's stories that our set had distanced itself from the more violent elements of Hell-at-the Breech. They may have thought such separation would further protect them. To be separated both within a community and from a county government only compounded the trouble to come.

The few wiser heads, especially those who were under Bragg, would also have known that terror makes a sorry leader. They would have agreed with the assessment of Bragg by Sam Watkins, who called Bragg a "merciless tyrant" who "loved to crush the spirit of his men." They feared him, but they had learned from him the art of execution.

Of the stories handed down in our family, none is more significant in a look at the Pink episode than one Peter Brown told about being chosen for a firing squad. A deserter had been caught, and the ritual was set in military procedure: Troops were assembled to observe what happened to such traitors. A firing squad was chosen, and rifles were handed to them. At least one had no bullet, so no man could know for a certainty that he'd fired a killing shot. The condemned man, dressed in plain clothes, was sitting on or standing in front of his coffin, some- times with the open grave behind him. If a member of the squad was too cowardly to fire, he too was subject to execution. As Peter Brown told the story, he was selected for a firing squad, and the deserter was sitting on his coffin. When the order to fire was issued, he pulled his trigger, but his gun didn't fire. A malicious or self-serving observer from the crowd came forward and told the officer, "Brown did not shoot." His rifle was examined, and, sure enough, it hadn't gone off.

Peter Brown thought he was to be executed next, for insubordina- tion. The fright must have exceeded any he felt on the battlefield. Shame in duty is worse than fear in conflict—that old truth seems to underpin this memory. The firing-squad scene was the incident most often told about over the years of my youth. Again, a crisis was avert- ed: Another soldier stepped up and said, "I saw Brown's hammer fall." The officer in command determined that the hammer of Brown's gun had in fact come to rest on the percussion cap. Perhaps the officer had had enough of Bragg justice, and he returned Brown to his regiment. Perhaps Brown didn't fire. No perhaps about one matter: Peter Brown had learned the power one friend can have in a crisis.

As students of the Civil War know, Braxton Bragg has been a handy whipping boy now for nearly 150 years, and the imprint of his tyranny may seem magnified in light of the events of the early 1890s in Mitcham Beat. Bragg may have had no influence on the mindset of veterans involved in the Mitcham War, but the Mitcham soldiers had never known a leader of his rank or his cruelty. He lacked the stature afforded other leading generals. No boy babies in Mitcham were named Braxton, so far as I know; Peter Brown named one of his sons Lee, for the commander he wished he'd had.

Some of the Civil War veterans in Mitcham in the 1890s also would have known Simeon T. Woodward (sometimes Woodard), who assembled the initial band of vigilantes in the Jackson area. Some had served in his company. D. C. Mathews says Woodward was the man who rode into his family's yard when he was a boy, seeking to recruit his father for the mob. Considered by the county's earlier historian, Timothy Ball, to be precocious and promising as a young man, Woodward rose from sergeant to captain of the Alabama 5th Infantry, Company I, called The Grove Hill Guards. In that company were several Mitcham men, among them J. D. Huggins, J. C. Mott, W. M. Knight, and others with familiar names—Howze, Wiggins, and, most notably in a consideration of the Pink episode, T. J. Gilmore and W. H. Mauldin.

Woodward was wounded at least three times and captured at least three times during the victorious battles at Fredericksburg and Chancellorsville and finally during the fighting around Petersburg. He was also hospitalized several times for wounds and once for disease. The man who would be described as among Clarke County's "finest and best citizens" as he helped lead the mob in Mitcham Beat was hospitalized at the CSA General Hospital in Charlottesville on August 7,1863, and returned to duty two months later. The official report lists the cause for hospitalization as "gonorrhoea." On April 9, when what remained of his regiment assembled at Appomattox Courthouse, Woodward was at Johnson Island prison, near Sandusky, Ohio. After taking the oath of allegiance in June, he returned to Clarke County and eventually was elected a commissioner, but by the time of the Mitcham War his political career was waning. He had operated a dry goods business for a while, served as a county commissioner, and was twice widowed. (His first wife was the daughter of Isaac Grant, the *Democrat* editor.) When McCorquodale was murdered, Simeon Woodward was living alone with a son on a farm in the southern part of the county. When the Burkes slipped out of the mob's trap, Woodward lost what may have been his last chance for a major victory. After the vigilantes disbanded, the former Confederate captain ran for the legislature and was defeated. He later served as mayor of Jackson and as a teller in the first bank.

It is not likely that men who had served under Bragg, or Manigault, would have been intimidated by Woodward, however powerful he considered himself. They had gone through a harrowing, hellish rite of passage, and they would have recognized his type, gallivanting military fashion on a fine horse over those country lanes, leading looters and killers who roughed up country farmers and threatened women and children. Nor would they have lain low if they'd been trifled with by any under his command. Experienced as soldiers, they knew the lay of that Mitcham land, and fighting against superior numbers was hardly alien to them. With their sons and grandsons, they could have picked off enough vigilantes to send the rest of the cowards back to town. Harassing the vigilantes would have frightened individual men whose courage was not drawn from a mob mentality.

Mature men would not have been so rash, collectively, as to take such action at the outset. Anyone could see the outcome of such an endgame—that was another lesson brought home from the war. Hot-headed actions against a superior force had resulted in overwhelming loss. Other means would have been tried first. Additional appeals to authorities outside the county, even the governor of Alabama, would have been made in conjunction with calls to comrades in the county, because the Mitcham men probably had as many, or more, old-vet friends as Woodward, though fewer in the ruling clique. Moreover, some traded in Mobile and had connections there.

Complicating the role of the older residents, men and women, was their knowledge of what Hell-at-the-Breech had done to bring havoc to their community. Though angry and afraid, they were not entirely helpless, at least not all of them. Moreover, judging from the various land purchases and by what happened in court later, not all were impoverished or illiterate. The Civil War veterans certainly understood how tyranny, operating with the blessings of a government, breaks men's spirits. That was the legacy of Braxton Bragg, and, by extension, of the entire Civil War experience. Without ever having read *The Federalist Papers*, they'd have agreed to a man with James Madison's contention that it is easier to tyrannize a small number of citizens in a political body than a large population.

The experience of the Civil War was too horrific not to contribute to the mind-set of the veterans who were living in Mitcham Beat in the 1890s: These veterans knew in their bones that when appeals for official justice fail, residents who want to live in a civil community must act to protect it.

COWS VS. CORN:
A CASE AT MITCHAM COMMON LAW

*And what is of the greatest Importance of all is that there is an
entire Liberty of Conscience and Commerce for all that come thither,
without paying any thing for it; Justice is duly administred [sic]
to all; and every body can say that what he possesses
lawfully belongs to him.*

—

From a 1731 recruitment letter for South Carolina, circulated in Switzerland

A long-simmering tension between the two Mitcham
neighbors rose to a boil when one's cows broke into the other's corn, the
stand just shy of tasseling. The conflict was complicated. It so happened
that the man who owned the cows was also the brother of two men
married to the corn party's two sisters. Moreover, the wives of the two
men at odds with each other were friends, and their children played
together. The two men had grown up together and attended the same
country school, and they had never liked each other.

The powerful confluence of blood, history, and community ruled out the offended party's killing the cows, or roughing up their owner, or otherwise seeking satisfaction. The cow party did not consider himself in the wrong, because the neighbor's fences weren't kept up properly. Hell, it was not his cows' fault. In those days, cattle were free to range through the reed cane flats and open woods, regardless of property lines, and it was a farmer's duty to fence them out, not in. Other folks' cows might also have gotten into that corn. But identification of offending bovines was not an issue.

In Mitcham, the branding of livestock—cows, sheep, and hogs—was done by distinctive cuts on the animals' ears—literally "ear marks," the source of the term of current use. Even in the 1950s, cows were brought to the Clarke County Stockyard with marked ears. One might be a swallow fork *V* cut in the right ear, and a half-moon knifed from the bottom of the left. The farmers all had their peculiar marks; they are still on file at the courthouse in an old book called *Marks and Brands*. (One man, who was infamous as a cattle thief, reportedly had a mark that trumped all others: His cows had no ears at all.) So, as this dispute progressed, the man whose distinctly marked cows got into his neighbor's corn did not deny ownership of the foraging cattle. As the matter stood, the two stubborn, angry men were at a social, legal impasse.

The context was clear: The man whose corn crop had been damaged was not about to take vengeance. Moreover, the man who owned the cows was not going to budge. And neither farmer was about to seek justice in Grove Hill. This episode happened at least thirty years after the Mitcham War, but it's doubtful that even before that episode would such a spat between neighbors in that beat, a quarrel that did not involve personal assaults, have gone to the county court. Besides, hiring lawyers would cost more than cows and corn put together.

Serious crimes sometimes got the officials' attention. The county court archives cite many instances of Mitcham people being charged under criminal statutes, but civil wrongs small in the eyes of the law loomed large to those living in close and closed communities. One could pout and badmouth a neighbor, or lay for him and pay back in kind, in some sneaky or savage way. But that sort of behavior was frowned on in an open community of interdependent people, which are rare political units; the Mitcham Beat people knew such demeanor would only make matters worse in the long run. How then could justice be meted out, so that this conflict could come to a peaceable end?

Fortunately, the man whose corn crop was damaged knew of a way. He went to the owner of the cows and asked if he would agree to arbitration. The stipulation was that each man would choose an advocate, approved by the other. These two men would review the facts and arrive at a sensible, fair settlement, which both parties would be obliged to accept. The scales of justice were to be balanced in that community. The cow owner, who was also in a social bind, agreed. The litigants chose two men, who were not close neighbors and not related to either—a pair of challenges—and who were respected for their character. Under the rules agreed to, neither party, in person, was to accompany the arbiters. They were to walk through the corn field and determine how much it would have been likely to produce had the cows not broken in; and they were to examine the fences to see if the corn party had exercised reasonable and prudent care. And, of course, there was the matter of standing: Which man was of sounder and more dependable character, and, moreover, how would this decision affect the whole community?

In a decision that says much, the arbiters decided that both parties were at fault, more or less. The corn party's fence was not quite as strong as it could have been, and the cow party's stock had shown uncommonly aggressive behavior in breaking through the weak points in said fence. Therefore, the corn party was ordered to repair his fences, and the cow party was ordered to pay or provide in corn a portion of the potential amount likely to come from the stalks his cows had destroyed. The matter ended as amicably as any quarrel between neighbors who did not like each other from the cradle could have.

———•—•—•———

As everybody who's looked at the blood and gore of the Mitcham War knows, not all differences amongst neighbors, and especially those within one extended family, could be settled so civilly. Still and all, this particular incident shows that a way of settling disputes existed long before labor unions and management were using binding arbitration; in fact, this method had been passed down for generations. James Madison used a form of it in a dispute with a relative. This system of remedial justice would have been especially appealing to people who had avoided the law, defied the law, or been ignored or mistreated by those in legal authority.

Working through disputes in small communities, however one defines community, strains the whole social structure. To get along, people had to go along, to a point, especially in small communities. James Madison's contention in the debate over the United States Constitution that small populations are more vulnerable to tyranny was dramatically illustrated by the hold the Hell-at-the-Breech had on Mitcham Beat, by the real threat posed by John R. Pinkerton, and by the rule of the small clique in the county seat. These frontier efforts at resolving lesser differences required, first of all, citizens who valued civility and who were seeking an alternative to violence, other than simmering or simply moving on. Second, it required an appreciation of tradition and the value of precedence, mudsills of the common law.

The original settlers of Mitcham brought general frontier customs with them, but their attitude about government came from a particular society that developed and flourished in colonial South Carolina. In the 1880 census of the beat, ninety percent of those over the age of fifty-five listed that state as place of birth, and most of those younger had been born in southeast Alabama to immigrants from the state. And not simply South Carolina at large but from the backcountry, away from Charlestown. Many of the original Mitcham Beat immigrants had settled around Orangeburgh, along the Edisto or the Pee Dee rivers, in the old Edgefield and Darlington districts, and in the Waxhaw region along the North Carolina line.

The independent spirit traceable to early South Carolina may appear similar to that developed in other colonies, but it was distinct in origin and attitude. South Carolina was begun as a proprietary colony. Its owners were Englishmen favored by the crown, not Puritans seeking freedom to practice their own religion and to persecute those who didn't. Those Carolina proprietors wanted to make money. Most were absentee owners, living in England and visiting their holdings only occasionally. By 1800, the line between backcountry or upcountry South Carolina and the Charlestown set had long been established, and so had the tradition of self-governance.

The policy made practical sense. Conflict amongst the colonists or between the colonists and the crown would diminish the properietors'profits. Besides, owners living overseas or only occasionally visiting their holdings lacked the power to govern. Consequently, independence came to be regarded as a personal right, granted by the owners and not by the Puritans' God, though, in fact, many South Carolina settlers were also Calvinists, organized in Presbyterian, Swiss Reformed, and Lutheran sects, early-day saints of the Methodist and

Baptist congregations that later became dominant. To the settlers in the upcountry, freedom of religion was inseparable from the other freedoms later articulated in the Declaration of Independence and in the first ten amendments (also known as the Bill of Rights) to the Constitution. In point of fact, these backcountry folk lived in such remote areas that it was difficult if not impossible for justice to be "duly administred to all" by authorities in Charleston.

The South Carolina concept of justice is associated with independence from a central government—out of necessity as much as pride—and it is evident in the Regulator Movement of the 1760s. In simple, it was a frontier action, born in the backcountry of the Carolinas, out of the need for protection from robbers and murderers that couldn't, or wouldn't, be prosecuted by official courts. A combine of small farmers and plantation owners had to take the law into their own hands. In North Carolina, the Regulator Movement resulted in much conflict between vigilantes and sworn law officers.

In South Carolina, differences between country and city folks were usually resolved effectually. After the Regulators had executed a few miscreants and begun to take on a formal character, officials in Charlestown woke up to political realities. Seeing that a more formal system of jurisprudence was called for, they negotiated with leaders of the Regulators and set up regional courts. Thereafter, scofflaws and outlaws in South Carolina, who might have feared vigilante justice, had over their heads the threat that they could be brought to book in a court of justice that had behind it not merely the desire of communities to protect themselves from predations but also the full weight of the colonial court system. The South Carolina Regulators had made their point and won a victory. And wiser heads in the backcountry must have sensed the danger in thinking that independence is possible in isolation. But that folly never died.

The extent and fervor of the fierce, rebellious South Carolina attitude, symbolized in the gamecock, manifested itself, with variations, throughout the nineteenth and twentieth centuries, and now in the twenty-first. The spirit bred into the descendants of the first settlers, evident in both the Regulator Movement and the American Revolution, led them in the 1820s into falling behind John Calhoun and others in an attempt to nullify tariff laws they considered more favorable to northern manufacturers than to southern farmers. This defiance of federal law and assertion of states' rights formed much of the Deep South mindset.

Resistance and defiance had set the stage for rebellion from the crown, so it is hardly surprising that South Carolina led the movement toward secession. Or that it was Strom Thurmond of South Carolina who led his Dixiecrats out of the Democratic Party in 1948, helping set the stage for the Civil Rights movement, the national appeal of George Wallace, and the ascendancy of the Republican Party (which Thurmond joined). As racial tensions increased in the 1950s, the South Carolina gamecock mutated into the white rooster, a symbol of Caucasian supremacy. As Southern Democrats began to change parties, that common yard fowl flew with them to the Republicans' roost, and, as this book goes to press, it crows over a Tea Party. I'd be tickled to see this tough old bird in history's dumpling pot.

South Carolina set the standard for political leaders who favored action over thought and passion over reason. The subtleties and ambiguities acknowledged in the clear thinking of James Madison regarding the principles of the Constitution and the necessary, if limited, role of the federal government did not appeal to people who considered themselves full heirs of the American dream but who were too angry and uneducated to sit still for abstract, idealistic notions to appear before them as concrete, political realities.

If they wanted to nullify an abominable tariff, that was their business, not the federal government's. Within their own communities, residents of Mitcham Beat might have used reason to settle civil disputes among neighbors, but when it came to the Enemy Without, they were like others from the South. Fighting is simpler than thinking, and fiery political rhetoric is entertaining. In following the lead of fire-eaters and demagogues, in defying a federal system to promote a provincial interest, the people in South Carolina and later in Alabama set themselves up as useful foils for more powerful national adversaries. Long before Mitcham Beat, or Mitchamite, became "a term of reproach" amongst the town set who saw it as a place of violence, rebellion, and immorality, so was the entire South, to those Northern idealists who saw the land of cotton in virtually the same reproachful light.

Individual communities might live in peace as long as neighbors had accepted means for settling disputes, but when it came to larger conflicts, laced with abstract notions of justice, resolutions didn't happen. The South that was emerging forty years after the American Revolution, when Mitcham Beat was aborning, was a far cry from the bucolic world envisioned by the Founding Fathers. The ideal of an educated agrarian society working in close accord with manufacturers and abiding by the Constitution hit the hard wall of political reality: Even in the twentieth century Alabamians were told they were as "cultured and refined" as anybody in America (which, sadly, may be true), and they cheered when a politician said federal judges were the South's enemy and deserved "barb-wire enemas." Such an image would have been highly appealing to those Hell-at-the-Breech boys as they regarded formal justice unduly administered from Grove Hill.

The conflict between the South Carolina–influenced settlers in Mitcham Beat and the Clarke County establishment was local, in all the worst senses of the word. Hell-at-the-Breech divided the Mitcham Beat people, and when common civility failed, the citizens were not able to form political coalitions within the county proper. The Farmers' Alliance Movement had set them further apart from the ruling Democrats. The troubles brought on by that division exceeded the limits of civil compromise. The people of Mitcham faced a foe greater than any the South Carolina colonists or their descendants for four or five generations had encountered; it was at hand, complicated, and close amongst them. The impending conflict eclipsed two neighbors' spat between cows and corn; it was about politics and power and who had a place at the table.

Of most importance to me, the dispute between the two neighbors demonstrates that Clarke County's "criminal colony" was founded on a concept of civility, an ever-fragile ideal.

———•◦•———

Meanwhile, through many crops of corn and many generations of ear-marked cattle, both the cow and the corn parties lived less than a quarter of a mile apart, never as close friends, but both visited in each other's houses, their wives cooked, canned, quilted, and gossiped together, their children grew up together, and the families were formally courteous, one toward the other. And now the two Mitcham Beat litigants are neighbors in perpetuity, buried three paces apart in Oak Grove Cemetery, which is well fenced.

THE LAST FAMILY

Let not Ambition mock their useful toil,
Their homely joys, and destiny obscure;
Nor Grandeur hear with a disdainful smile
The short and simple annals of the Poor.

—

THOMAS GRAY
"Elegy Written in a Country Churchyard" (1775)

The Seaborn Goodman family lived in a log house near the banks of Wells Creek in Mitcham, about three miles from Bedsole Store, for about 150 years, and old lady Sallie Goodman, a Huggins, was known far and wide because she had six fingers on each hand and six toes on each foot. She would take off her shoes for people. A man named Peter Brewer had been granted a government patent on the place in 1860, and Brewer may have built the house, but the Goodmans had been there as long as anybody knew, so Brewers must not have lived there for long, or at all, after the soldiers returned. When my father was young, Seaborn and Sallie were still living, but they had long been dead when I came along, and I never got to see Mrs. Goodman's fingers or toes. Here was yet another story I had to take as fact, on faith.

Three of their children, two old-maid sisters, Alice and Vernie, and their bachelor brother, Tommie, were living in the log house when I was a boy. A dirt lane, now called the Brunson Road, narrowed in front of their place because a magnificent oak spread its limbs about twenty feet across the road, in front of their gate. Nobody in the old days would think of removing such fine shade.

The yard had a paling fence around it and was swept clean with a brushbroom made from slender young dogwoods bound with cloth strips. There were peach trees and flowerbeds scattered about, and near the porch was what we called a bored well, as opposed to a hand-dug well. It had been drilled with an augur and curbed with fat pine boards into, say, a six-inch square. That heartwood, laden with tar and other resins, would never rot. Later, terracotta pipe was used for curbing. Over the well was a narrow shelter with a slanted roof and a windlass handle on the right side. To the rope was attached a slender bucket, fluted at the top, about three feet long, designed especially for these bored wells. It was about five inches in diameter and fitted with a valve at the bottom. When the bucket struck the water table, which was probably less than twenty feet down, the impact would lift the valve, and the bucket would fill from the bottom up. If you were drawing water, you'd know the bucket was full when you heard it "swallow." If you were too weak to crank up a full bucket, you could begin soon after it struck the water, before the gulp. When the well-bucket bottom cleared the curbing, the water was poured into a pail; then a board was placed over the open curbing to keep trash or cats from falling in.

Cats were always falling into dug wells, which were sheltered but often left uncovered.

One of the old stories, possibly true, was about a jackleg preacher who had a cat go missing and noticed a tang to his well-water. He called in a mischievous neighbor boy named Wat to help him clean out the well. Incidentally, the preacher had a blind mule that he kept a bell on. He and Wat pushed the well shelter over, and the preacher tied a rope around his waist so Wat could lower him into the well and help him back up. While he was down in the dark, knee-deep in water, and trying to find the drownded cat, the mean Wat yelled that he had to step off in the bushes but would be right back. He found the mule, tied it up, and took the bell off. Then he started circling the large open hole, maybe four-by-four feet, ringing the bell. A voice came up, "Wat! O Wat! Ketch the mule!" No answer came back. The bell got closer and closer and closer. The preacher in the well feared what might literally befall him. Finally, as the bell neared the open hole, a voice from the well bellowed up, "Wat! You sorry son of a bitch! Finish your business right this minute and ketch that goddamned mule!"

The Goodmans, with their covered bored well, would face no such crisis, and, moreover, they'd tell no such coarse and profane stories on people, real or apocryphal, preacher or not. They were talkative, though, and Alice and Vernie were bright; Tommie was polite and quiet. In the old parlance, he was "simple." My dad said he got Tommie to go squirrel hunting once, and Tommie took along an old single-barrel shotgun with the bead off. So he stuck a whole kitchen match in the bead hole. With such an innovation, Tommie could shoot high or low depending on what part of the match he was sighting off of.

Another brother, Horace, a crickety fellow with a quaver in his voice, lived across the creek but in his own house, alone and childless.

He'd lost two wives, one to an early death in childbirth, one to an early divorce. An old man in Mitcham said that Horace had come by their house with his first wife, when she was in hard labor; she was writhing in pain, lying on a mattress in the wagon bed. Both she and the baby died before Horace could get them to Dr. Toll Pugh, who lived between Mitcham and Grove Hill. Horace threw the second wife out after two weeks because, it was said, he didn't like the way she made biscuits. When I knew him, he was an old single man, living at what was first the Oscar Gilmore place, then the Vander Ward place, and, after Horace died, the Paul Huggins place. A remodeled version still stands near the junction of Brunson Road and Route 154. Horace Goodman walked the mile or so from there, back to his sisters' table, at least once a day.

Horace was short and wiry, built like his father, Mr. Seeb, my dad said. Tommie was short and thickset. Alice was a skinny stick of a woman, and Vernie was cherubic and stout. The sisters had gone to school with my father, and they kept all their schoolbooks and pictures. Their most influential teacher, later to be our neighbor in Antioch, was Sid Payne, a cousin of Dave Mathews. Mr. Sid taught those children grammar, spelling, and the importance of history, and shortly he was off to France as a member of the Rainbow Division of World War I. When he came to our cane mill each fall, he and my father would talk about those old days in Mitcham. He told me that my dad was one of his best students, and he told me he'd seen a Frenchman drink blood from a freshly slaughtered cow. I marveled at both statements.

By the late 1950s, after most of us had left for Antioch and other communities down toward Jackson, the Goodmans were even more isolated. Aside from occasional visitors, *The Clarke County Democrat*, and a batt'ry radio, they had little contact with the outside world. They became museum pieces, antique reminders of the old days. Folks came out to marvel at them, and a Grove Hill artist made a painting of their rustic cottage. They never appeared bothered by nosy observers. They were gracious to a fault.

When I was up there with my father, we usually stopped by. Their garden, across the road, was neat, hoed clean. They maintained what he claimed was an especially rare, hardy, and fierce strain of chicken called the Bedsole game, developed in and for the people of Mitcham Beat. The biddy hens were known for protecting their brood against blue-darter hawks, rival domestic fowl, dogs and cats, and mean children. The Goodmans also saved seed from an ancient Mitcham strain of collards known as bluestem, which my father declared vastly superior to those plants grown from store-boughten seed or nurseries. My dad used the buying of a hen or getting some collard seed as an excuse to visit. He brought the Goodmans news, and they talked about who'd been heard from, who was now where, who'd died, and this strange weather. They liked to see their old neighbor, Coley Brown, and he loved being with his old schoolmates and neighbors.

One spring a professor of English at Vanderbilt came down to turkey hunt with me. We stayed in the little house where Lee Brown had lain a-corpse. I took him by the Goodmans' home for a visit. It was a chilly morning in late March, and Alice and Vernie invited us to sit by the fire and talk. I got apprehensive about this man's seeing a version of the true stock I had come from. That was foolish, and vain, and I'm ashamed to admit it. I had no reason to think this professor, learned though he was, would dismiss the Goodmans—and, by association, me. He was not that sort of academic. Though he had been educated at Vanderbilt and Yale and had been raised in Montgomery, he was from an old Pike County family, and he could get along with anybody. He was quiet and smart, and so thin that if you took off his horn-rims and

Sunday clothes and put him in brogans and bib overalls, he could have passed for a Goodman.

At the outset, I overspoke. "There is no other place as fine as Mitcham Beat," I sputtered, and Vernie responded in a flash, "Then what compels you to stay away?" Count on an old maid (now a quaint and politically incorrect appellation) to nail you every time. The professor never patronized them. He was, in fact, fascinated. After we left, he noted, in his keenly observant, respectful way, that the Goodmans had all the essentials of life in their fireplace room—an open copy of the King James Version of the Bible on a table, paid-up burial policies hung on nails above each bed, and a shotgun in a rack made from limb forks hanging over the front door. Come what may, they could deal with this world and the next.

The Goodman family from time out of memory had a reputation for keeping to the old ways and resisting modern conveniences. My dad said that when he was young they still cooked over their fireplace, with spider-pans and pots on hooks. Long cuts of wood could be used, and the hot coals moved about from pot to pot. Finally, they too took one small step into the modern world and added a little plank kitchen back of the house. They stopped using just the fireplace for cooking. My dad said he was walking down the road one morning and saw Mr. Seeb coming toward him, pushing a wheelbarrow full of short, finely split wood with his axe on top. He had a long, white beard. As they approached, my dad noticed that Mr. Seeb looked mad and was talking to himself. When they got within good earshot, my dad said, in a loud voice, "Good morning, Mr. Seeb!" Without looking up or breaking stride, Mr. Goodman muttered, "Goddamn the man that invented the cookstove!"

The Goodman "girls," as they were always referred to, eventually caught on to the modern kitchen appliance, and at dinners-on-the-grounds everybody wanted to get some of their apple turnovers—called "tarts" in Mitcham Beat. The girls were especially fond of my brother Henry, who would stop and eat with them when he was going to get the mail, over at the crossroads near Horace's house. Then, my mother said, he would eat another meal at home. Horace was a well-meaning, earnest but fussbudget fellow, always inquiring about everybody's health and expecting to hear dire news. He talked through his nose and had a stylized stammer. Henry, a born mimic, would drive my mother crazy when she asked if he'd seen anybody on the road and heard any news. "Yes," he'd answer, "I ran into Horace Goodman, and he said, 'H-h-henr-ry, h-how's M-m-m-miss Alliene?'"

The Goodmans had at least three other sisters. One married Easter Motes, another Horrie Pugh, and the third Sam Small, son of the Peter Small whose role in the Pink episode is elsewhere detailed. Easter Motes was a bootlegger and proud of it. Somebody asked him one time if he'd taught his boys to make whiskey. "No, sir," Easter said. "I never taught my boys to make whiskey. I taught them to make *good* whiskey." Horrie Pugh and his wife were gentle and quiet people; they lived across the road from Horace and had no children. Horrie rode with us to the cemetery workings and had a good sense of humor. He died singing, "When They Ring Those Golden Bells for You and Me."

Sam Small was always a regular at the dinners-on-the-grounds at New Prospect. He, Papa, and several other old men would never darken the church door. While the preaching and singing were going on, they'd sit out on the tables, shaded by a tin-roofed shed. I and other children who had escaped our mothers' eyes would stay out too and listen to them talk, and, if lucky, we could ease up a cloth on one of the dinner boxes and make off with a piece of fried chicken. Eventually, the deacons got smart, and when the collection was being taken up, they would come outside the church and pass their hats. Old age was no exemption. The men who stayed outside had to pay for the privilege of skipping the service, smoking pipes and chewing tobacco, laughing, remembering old times, and talking politics.

Some subjects were never brought up, not because they were unseemly but because they were stale. Mr. Sam's left arm was gone, and he wore a clean white shirt with the sleeve folded and held with a big safety pin that was displayed like a badge of honor. The arm had been amputated after an incident that occurred during a quarrel with his son, Arvin, who, because of his light hair as a child, was called Cottonpatch. The quarrel started one night when Cottonpatch was a teenager. He had his foot propped up on the fireplace and refused to move it when his daddy told him to. Mr. Sam reached for the poker and brained Cottonpatch with it. In his addled state Cottonpatch grabbed the shotgun from over the mantel and shot his daddy down.

A relative told me that Morgans Creek, between the Smalls' house and the big road, was seven feet out of its banks, and that Cottonpatch, scared nearly to death, had somehow made it through those waters all the way to Ira Pugh's house, near New Prospect. He couldn't swim a lick, and large holes had been blown out by the flood. Mrs. Small was left to tie up the arm, which was all that had been hit, and try to stanch the blood. The next morning, Arvin and Ira somehow got Mr. Sam across that torrent—even the bridge was covered—and put him in Ira's log truck, which had been backed up to the edge of the floodwaters. They took him to Angus Hill's store, and then somebody else got him to the hospital in Jackson where old Dr. McCrary amputated the arm. Mr. Sam seemed perfectly happy when I knew him; like most other men of his generation in Mitcham, he seemed to have been born with cordial, formal manners. From all I could tell, the quarrel was long forgotten, and there were never any hard feelings about the unfortunate episode. The sheriff tried to get Sam Small to testify against Arvin, but he refused, saying the whole business was his fault. He never should have struck the boy with that poker. Tempers will flare in every family, and such things will happen.

Cottonpatch went away and was a fireman in Mobile and Selma, but soon after Mr. Sam died in 1968 he came back to Mitcham. A relative said he returned to take care of the old kinfolks—and he did. He took over maintaining their houses and seeing to their needs and eventually buried them all, except Alice. After Vernie died, Alice went off to Lucedale, Mississippi, to live with a niece or nephew. Arvin made certain his mother was buried with the Goodmans at Oak Grove; Mr. Sam had been buried with the Smalls at New Prospect. His duty done, his debt paid, Cottonpatch left. He said he couldn't stand it there any longer. And he vanished. In his own way, he disassociated himself from Mitcham. A relative wondered whatever happened to Arvin Small after he left Mitcham. After much searching, she and I found that he had died in Montgomery in 2004 at age 77. His death certificate lists no next of kin, no parents, none of the usual personal information. His remains lay unclaimed in the morgue for two or three weeks before he was given a pauper's funeral and buried in an unmarked grave.

Before Cottonpatch came back, Aunt Grace Brunson, my father's younger sister, and Uncle Willard, who never left Mitcham, were the Goodmans' closest neighbors. Aunt Grace was an effusive, free-hearted woman and always good company. Uncle Willard had an understated, dry wit that could cut through big talk. Because the Goodmans had no motorized vehicle, no phone, and no electricity, Aunt Grace and Uncle Willard were their modern-world interlocutors until Cottonpatch Small returned. Aunt Grace and Uncle Willard, and later my uncle, Lenson Brown, who lived amongst his wife's people, the Pughs, over near New Prospect church, would bring the Goodmans their groceries. They outlived the Brunsons, as they had almost everybody else; with Cottonpatch there, and with Uncle Lenson to lend a hand occasionally, they lived out their lives in peaceful solitude.

But, like their father, the Goodmans never made peace with modernity. In the late forties or early fifties, when the local electric co-op wanted to set utility poles on their land, they refused to grant an easement. They did not believe electricity crossing your land or coming down inside your house was good for your health. And they stood their ground. The company could have taken them to court, and won, but instead of using force, they chose another route for the power lines. Fifty years after the Mitcham War, the county leaders thought it wise not to rankle people from that beat, even a family as apparently powerless and old-fashioned as the Goodmans.

Rumors circulated that the Goodmans were rich. After all, they did sell a few cows, and they spent virtually nothing to live. Supposedly, they had their money buried in a churn somewhere back of their house. Stories were told of a Jackson undertaker sneaking around at night with what was called a "money needle"—a mysterious device that surely would be a big Ronco seller today, but I've never laid eyes on one—and digging holes in search of that hidden treasure. If anybody ever found it, they never told, and the Goodmans showed no signs of despair over a lost fortune. The undertaker is now dead.

Never presumptuous, the Goodmans accepted neighborly intercessions with gratitude. Aunt Grace said that she and Uncle Willard had to take Alice to the doctor in Thomasville, and while they were sitting in the waiting room, Alice said she needed a drink of water. "It's out there in the hall," Aunt Grace said. She noticed that Alice was gone a long time, and she got to worrying about her, so she went into the hall and there Alice was, looking at the water fountain. Aunt Grace said, "Alice, this is a water fountain. This is where you get your water." Alice replied, curtly, "Grace, I know what it is, but where do they keep the dipper at?"

A doctor in Grove Hill told Vernie she had a skin cancer but that it was too deep for him to cut out. He referred her to a specialist in Mobile and assured her it was a simple outpatient procedure. It wouldn't take an hour altogether. The long trip, not the operation, was what concerned Vernie, because the Goodmans rarely went to town, usually only when they had cows to sell at the stockyard and could ride with whoever hauled them. They feared being run over by a car. They wore long dresses and sun bonnets and would hold hands and run across the street in Grove Hill. They were regarded by people in town as a spectacle, but they were too scared to care. This going to Mobile for an operation and getting back home, however, was something else altogether. They needed help, and Aunt Grace was up to the task.

She explained to Vernie that Willard would take her to Grove Hill, to the Greyhound stop at the Rebel Coffee Shop, and would help her buy a round-trip ticket. She was to stay on the bus till it pulled into the station in Mobile, there on Government Street, and she should have the money ready for a taxicab. She was to walk outside, and taxi cabs with signs mounted on the top would be all lined up right there. She was to select one, sit in the back seat, and give the driver the doctor's address that she had written down, and he would take her to the clinic up on Springhill Avenue. She was to pay the taxi driver his fee and fifty cents extra, for what they call a tip. After the operation was over, Aunt Grace's son, Willard, Jr. (whose childhood nickname Toog—rhymes with Shug—remained in the family) would come pick her up. Toog was a policeman at the town of Eight Mile, a Mobile suburb. Vernie was to call him when it was over. He would come down and take her back to the bus station and see that she got on the one that was going to Grove Hill, and Uncle Willard would be there to pick her up, back at the Rebel Coffee Shop.

Aunt Grace said she and Vernie worked back and forth over this plan, but Vernie kept sticking on one point. One vital detail was missing from the instructions.

"Now, Grace, after this is all over, I just call Toog?"

"Yes, Vernie, he won't mind it a bit."

"And the place where he lives is Eight Mile?"

"Yes."

"That's right."

"And I am to call him?"

"Yes, Vernie. Don't you worry. He'll be off of work by then. When the doctor has finished, all you have to do is call him."

"Now Grace. If Toog lives eight mile from that office and I call him from that fur away, do you think he could hear me?"

Aunt Grace had dozens of these stories, and she delighted in telling them. She greatly admired those Goodmans, as did we all. Toog, his brother Ford, and their sister, Opal Faye, were always good-hearted and cheerful—the last children on our side to spend all of their growing-up years there, and then, like the rest of us, to leave for good. Uncle Lenson was the last Brown in Mitcham, and he died in 1989. He and Aunt Lola had no children. He was kind and courteous but generally kept with his wife's people. He had been a famous left-handed pitcher in the days when Mitcham teams played others from northwest Clarke County on Saturday afternoons. There are still a few old people who can describe his legendary curve ball and project on what he'd have done if he had made the big leagues. But he didn't, maybe didn't want to, and his death brought the Browns' living connections to Mitcham to an end.

The Goodmans remained their steadfast selves in a changing world, and then they died, one by one. Tommie went first, in 1973, in his eighty-sixth year; next Horace in 1977 in his eighty-first; then Vernie in 1982, in her eighty-eighth year; and, finally, the ever-thin Alice in 1991, in her ninety-fourth year. She proved the truth of the old saying, "It takes a lean dog to run a long race."

The Goodmans are buried in a row in Oak Grove Cemetery. If you'd known them, you'd have to be hard-hearted not to hope that such virtue never dies.

A CONCLUSION

Papa and me, Easter 1957

DUSK-TO-DAWN

For years I had it fixed in my mind that Mitcham Beat died on Friday, April 29, 1960, about an hour before milking time, and not in Mitcham at all but down in McLeod's Beat, exactly eight miles between Jackson and Grove Hill, twenty long, mostly dirt-road miles from The Old Place. It died in a weathered double-pen farmhouse (the hall had been enclosed) on a shelf of sandy soil above Edwards Mill Creek, about a half-mile off the blacktop, below Antioch Church. Lee Brown had been there since he came back from the hospital after getting a pin in his hip after him falling and breaking it, or it breaking and then him falling.

It happened January 15, 1960, the last day of squirrel season. My dad and my older, married brothers—I forget how many of the five,

Elmore, Tollie, Roy, Henry, or Bobby—were going back to Mitcham for the ritual final hunt, but I was not allowed to stay out of school and go too. Not me. This hunt was for grown men, and I was just fourteen. To hell with them.

My brothers loved to nettle. By then, I had the theme of their stories down pat: They were the heroes of the golden age. All had been raised in Mitcham; two of them, with many first cousins, had made it through World War II, uninjured. I could never measure up. They told tales of elaborate practical jokes, of standing down bullies and spiteful schoolteachers, of surviving floods, tornadoes, and harycanes, of no electricity or telephone, of kerosene lamps and lighterd knot torches and carbide lights you had to piss into, of squalling coons out of trees, and of following famous dogs that could catch and hold a wild hog and tree four squirrels and a wildcat up one tree at the same time. Yessir, that was some fun. But then there were those hard times. . . .

Stories that did not make them out to be hell-raisers cast them as hardy pioneers, tougher than I could ever be. I was a suck-bottle mama's boy spoiled by modern conveniences and lax discipline. Why, they'd picked a hundred pounds of cotton a day and had been whipped twice a day, for no good reason. If only I had been around during the olden days, what a man I might have had a chance to become.

Down in the civilized world, towards Jackson, I was trying to compete with the town boys, who went to Little League, or the soda fountain, or wherever, after school. I thought I had it plenty rough, being stuck out there with the old people, but to my brothers I was an afterthought who faced no hardships whatsoever. No, I was doomed to a duller, emptier life. And the worst part is, I believed them.

None of my town classmates knew about Mitcham, or, for that matter, much about Antioch, but I was still identified with the country set—and, to be fair, also identified myself with the school-bus bunch. All of us country-road children were outsiders, most of us with the customary blend of pride and that then-rampant inferiority complex.

On an ordinary afternoon after school, I had to milk two cows, strain the milk, separate the cows and their calves, slop the hogs, feed and stall a malevolent mule, gather in firewood and kindling, draw water, close up the chickens to fend off varmints, and, after supper and washing the dishes, go over the linoleum kitchen floor with a string mop and then do my homework. All this I did by myself, after the sister four years older ran away to get married. I had the Truetone radio for company. By dark, WSM and WLAC from Nashville and WWL in New Orleans—from the Blue Room of the Roosevelt Hotel—came in clearly. My mother usually was in bed with a sick headache or some minor malady when no company was around or no trouble was afoot. Given the number of children she had birthed and the farm work she did, she had a multitude of maladies, but she was an absolute dynamo, socially charming, imperious, and with more energy than anybody I've known. She lived to a very old age and kept her incisive wit to the very end. As she was losing consciousness, her last words were, "Tell Tollie to bring in the cows."

By the time I was twelve, all eight of my older sisters and all five brothers had left home. I was by myself, virtually an only child, though the youngest of fourteen. After supper, my father sat on the front porch, alone. He'd roll up his overalls britches and bathe his feet and shanks and hurl the washpan of dirty water into the yard. I knew what he was doing thereafter—deep in thought, watching the sun go down. If he had anything to say at all it was about our past and about our present prospects. In those dark ruminations, he saw glory in the past and gloom in the future. When the weather was warm, April till October, and I had to get up in the night, I'd often jump when I found him out on the porch, rocking in the shadows, surrounded by the loud chorus of katydids, frogs, owls, and whippoorwills. "Woke up and could not get back to sleep," he'd say.

A home that had once been boiling with children was down to my parents, me, and Papa, unless he was making rounds of his other children's homes. When he was with us, which was most of the time after January 1956, he would sit on the porch with my dad in hot weather or by the fire in cold.

That January day in 1960 my usually boisterous brothers returned somber and my dad not with them. The story they told was this: Papa had been up there in Mitcham at the home of one of his two daughters, my father's younger sister, Aunt Grace Brunson, and her husband, Uncle Willard. After Grandma died, he'd sold their old barny house near Highway 84, between Coffeeville and Grove Hill, and had bought the little house in Mitcham where my dad's older sister, Aunt Vadie Brunson (she and Grace married brothers) had lived before she and Uncle Clint moved to Grove Hill, to a painted house on the main street. For years the two sisters lived a hundred yards apart, and their children, double first cousins, grew up like brothers and sisters.

Papa was in Aunt Grace's living room and wanted to poke the fire. Aunt Grace had told him not to be getting up without her in there with him, but he was never one to mind. He was tall for the times, maybe six feet, and thin, and, as he was at the age of eighty-eight, his bones were brittle. He walked with a cane but carried it, we all thought, as much for style as for support. He'd fallen at our house a time or two and scared everybody. Aunt Grace heard him huff and groan and found him on the floor. He couldn't get up, so she hollered and got help. Don't ask me how. The men came in from the woods. Nobody blamed Aunt Grace, for they knew what pride and temper Papa had.

Dr. Jack Dozier from Fulton was sent for, and he said they had to get Papa straight to Mobile. There the surgeons inserted a pin in his hip. He'd never been a hospital patient before, and after he came to from the operation they put him in a double room. He was alert and keen on what was happening around him, my dad said. When the nurse came in to record vital signs, he watched her turn the old fellow in the other bed over and take his temperature, from the rear end. Papa watched closely, but he didn't see that when the procedure was finished the nurse had put the soiled thermometer in the lower shelf of her trolley and had taken out a sterile one from the upper. When she approached, shaking down the thermometer, she said, "Now, Mr. Brown, open up your mouth." Papa replied with all the force he had left: "I am an old man, young lady, and I've done many things in my life, but I am not opening my mouth!"

In those days, they didn't get the patients up right after surgery, and by the time he was dismissed from the Mobile Infirmary and brought to our house, he was fighting pneumonia, and that keenness he was famous for was fading. He could be placed in a chair but couldn't walk. A hospital bed was set up in a big bedroom off the hall, across from the fireplace room. It became a sort of lounge, with a vinyl sofa moved in and the new TV in there, and lots of straight chairs and rockers, and a butane heater against the wall, with its orange ceramic teeth aglow and a Maxwell House coffee can on it to serve as humidifier and spitcup.

Nights and weekends it was a throng, people coming and going, cousins, neighbors, old friends, laughing and talking, over the television blasting Jackie Gleason or Gunsmoke, and most of the men chewing tobacco or smoking. The womenfolks were all back in the kitchen, though they would look in on the men, in disgust at their coarse humor. When his oldest friends came by, Papa would cheer up. He and Mr. Lacey McLean from Hebron laughed hard about a black woman in the

Clarke County jail who had yelled at them through the bars one Saturday, begging them to bail her out. "I'll cook for you! I'll hoe for you!" she hollered. "And I'll plow yo mule till he fart the wing-wang blues!"

The scent of cigarette smoke and oil of pine carried all over. My mother stayed on me about keeping the place reasonably decent. I told my uncle Pete, who'd come in from Texas where he operated a service station, that I wished I had five cents for every cigarette butt I'd hauled out in the overflowing ashtrays. He ran his hand in his pocket and came up with a nickel. As he gave it to me, he said, "That's for *every* butt you've toted out. If you'd said *each* butt you'd now be a rich boy." That damned word gene had struck again.

For a while Lee Brown was in his right mind, but then he began to come in and out of delirium. He lost control of his bowels and bladder, and it fell to my father, the oldest child, to supervise his care. My father was then sixty-two years old, and all his life he'd lived as reflection and shadow of his father. His moods ranged from despair to stoicism. He sat by that bed, doing his duty, typically ruminant, keeping vigil in a kind of daze. He rarely joined the long, often crazy and convoluted conversations going on around him. His brothers and sisters spelled him, and everybody brought food. Florine Harrell, a registered nurse and good neighbor, would come by to give Papa a penicillin shot about once a week. I'd have the needles boiled and waiting for her. She'd hold up the vial of yellow medicine at eye level and draw the syringe full and press the plunger down to expel the bubbles. No matter who else helped, family or friend, my father was in charge of the worst chores. He cleaned Papa with soap and water after he'd fouled the bed, and he rolled Papa over while my mother worked a fresh gown on him and changed the sheets. The pine oil used to mop around the bed and the Air-Wick on a window sill could not mask the stench of mortality.

Late at night, after everybody else had gone to bed, I would often wake up to Papa's voice calling me, drawing out my name, waiting. I'd roll out, my bare feet hitting that glacial linoleum, and go in there to be with him. He usually wanted me to rub salve on the black bedsores that had developed on his heels. Sometimes, I would bring him a bowl of vanilla ice cream, which was about all he would eat, and spoon it to him. He'd always had a sweet tooth. We talked then. Occasionally it was like old times, like the many nights we had slept together over the four years after Grandma died.

In those earlier days, he would dress in a nightshirt, with a nightcap in winter, and take a long leak in the slop jar, which he called a "chamber." He took some kind of medicine that made his pee blue-green. When we'd crawled into the sack, he would tease me and ask me if I could spell *asaphoetida*, which he took to be the sign of a sound education. Then he would ask me if I had swallowed a lump of it, which he took to mean I would break wind during the night. We laughed and laughed.

I loved his cheerful fatalism, forthright manner, and old-fashioned humor. When he saw a child misbehaving, he would say, with a hearty laugh, "Now that one will wind up in the penitentiary." And of an uncommonly bright child, he'd say, "They'll never raise that one," meaning that the good die young. If he approached a gathering of people he didn't know, he'd pick out one man and walk straight up to him and extend his hand and say, "My name's Brown. What's yours?"

There was one old joke, probably old before he was born, that he loved to tell: A man who lived up around Tallahatta Springs, north of Mitcham, back in the olden days, was reviled and set apart because he was the meanest man anybody ever knew. One day that man died. Now, in keeping with the custom of that time and place, folks up there could not be buried unless something good could be said about them. They laid him out, put him in the long box, and dug his grave. But when it came time for the formal parting of this dead farmer, nobody could think of a good word to utter. So they stood around and tried to think of one. And they waited. Time rocked on. Dinnertime came and went. They sat down and kept trying. The sun was getting low, and they all had to get back home to feed their stock and do the milking. Finally, one man jumped straight up and said, "Well, I'll say this for him! He was not as bad all of the time as he was some of the time!" And they buried him properly and got away from there.

My grandfather loved to repeat those old stories; he enjoyed the telling, the roll of the words, and his blue eyes twinkled. I looked forward to the jokes and could guess from a scene or a word what was coming. One ritual happened when we'd be driving past a bony old nag standing drowsy and dopey in the middle of a hardbitten pasture. He would say, as if for the first time, "Appears to me somebody is planning to build a horse." And I would play straight man. "Why is that, Papa?" And he'd come back with the snapper, "Because they've already put the frame up!" And we would laugh, as if we'd never heard that one before.

One of my older brothers told about an exchange that carries many messages. In the early spring when he was twelve or thirteen, he and our grandpa were walking towards the Campbell community, where a lot of the old people lived. A man had sent word that he had plenty of sweet potato draws—or slips, as they are also called—and Papa could come get as many as he needed. Way up there above our settlement, they came to a churchyard where a burial was going on. Folks were gathered around an open grave with a pine box beside it. Papa was not close to those people, but he told his grandson that it wouldn't do for them to walk on by. To show their respects, they fell in back of the crowd. There was a preacher at the head of the grave, and an old man sitting by it. He was burying his wife. And he was wailing. "O Lord! We were married for fifty years! And between us there never passed a cross word!" My brother said Papa leaned down and whispered, "Now that's a damned lie!"

Some nights, after Papa and I had gone to bed, he got in a mood to talk about the Mitcham War, of the Burkes being under the Morgans Creek bridge as the mob thundered over on its way to kill Tooch Bedsole. I had a notion he had ridden, if at all, with some group of his own, not the "mob," a term he never used. He did not speak favorably of the Burkes. He also rambled regularly, as if he was talking to himself, about riding in a wagon, somebody handing him a cocked gun and telling him to shoot somebody. He'd get indignant, as I recall, but then he'd wander off into an aside on the .38 Winchester lever-action rifle. The nonsequiturs were too much for me. I'd heard these stories before and seen most of them at Locke Bolen's theater in Jackson. Posses hot after outlaws who hid under bridges while pursuers rode over them was a stale scene from a stock plot. Besides, as I passed age thirteen, my night thoughts were elsewhere. After Papa came back from the hospital and lay in that bed, his lucid moments were becoming fewer and fewer, and the old stories had ceased.

It was almost better when he was delirious. When he was in his right mind, he'd look at the flaccid flesh of his biceps and tears would well up in the corners of his eyes and he'd say in a whispery voice, "I was a man once." That was as close as he came to self-pity.

I had seen him weeping only once, to that time. Before lawns and mowers came to Mitcham, the cemeteries were kept as clean as the front yards used to be. Every blade of grass, the farmer's foe, was hoed up, swept up, and hauled out. The graves were mounded with the soft soil, like rows in a field. Come the Resurrection, those rows would open up, like beds of potatoes or banked sugar cane, and the dead would rise and flourish.

Papa, my father, and I were up at Oak Grove once, and I watched him hobble to my grandmother's grave, put down his cane, and kneel at the head. I was standing behind him. He began to smooth out the soil above where her face would be. He was sculpting it with his hands, caressing it. I saw that he was crying, and then I heard him say, "Mattie, Mattie, I don't know how to live without you!"

He was affectionate but not sentimental. Grandma was neither. She seemed stoic and stingy, never taking children up on her lap and kissing them as our grandmother Etheredge did, always hoarding money, rarely smiling. She had lived through wars, depressions, bank closings, and rationing, and she and Papa kept their money separate. When my uncle Hallie, a well-off truck farmer in Baldwin County, took them on long trips to the West and North, Papa said, "Mattie always has to have a new dress, and she makes me buy it out of my money." In one photograph of her as a woman in her late forties, she is much more fashionably dressed than her sister Edna; she strikes me as the kind of woman who would be a smashing success in today's culture—she was a good mother, had dealt with a spirited husband, and had kept a family stable. She dealt sternly and rationally with everybody, even her husband and eldest son. The only exceptions were named Mott.

She understood money. After Mattie Mott Brown died, my mother helped my father's two sisters, Vadie and Grace, go through her trunks. Under the old clothes and quilts they found books of WW II ration coupons, and sacks of coins, separated by all denominations—pennies, nickels, dimes, quarters, fifty-cent pieces, silver dollars. Mama said they moved the trunk and spied a knothole with something in it and drew out yet another sack of coins. Grandma was stolid—pure old Mott my dad claimed, tight as treebark, much like him—but she was also prudent, and she meant to do her part to keep that family provided for, come what may.

When I was little my dad would drop me off at their house while he took the shelled corn down the road, to Angus Hill's gristmill, in a shed by his store where an ancient black man named Vander Todd, the best miller in the county my father said, ground it into fine meal. In the winters, I sat by the fire with my father's parents and went through the old sepia or black-and-white photographs Grandma kept in a dresser drawer. I asked her who the people were, and she explained convoluted connections, most now forgotten.

When I was very small, I'd sit in Papa's lap when he churned in the crock that was set by the fireplace and turned when the fire was hot. When the cream had clabbered and was ready, he would sing a little dittie in rhythm with the up-and-down of the dasher: "Churn, churn, come butter, come butter. . . . Two little babies, one loves milk and the other butter." He also rocked toddlers not afraid of his moustache, and he would sing, "Bye-o baby bunting, thy father's gone a huntin', to catch a little rabbit skin to wrap his baby up in." If older grandchildren were around, he'd stop the rolling store and buy us hoop cheese and cinnamon rolls—or, as he called them, "gentleman rolls."

We'd hear him humming, something tuneless, when he was rocking by himself; it usually meant he was in deep thought. My mother said he didn't know he was humming. I think he did. Maybe it was just that the vibrations in his throat and chest were soothing. Sometimes he would come out of the reverie and utter something, to nobody in particular, that had arisen from his encyclopedic, circling memory. Once he said, "I see only two items in stores nowadays that I remember from a boy, Arm & Hammer baking soda and Coats & Clark thread." And then he would go back to humming and rocking.

As I grew older, I meddled all over my grandparents' house. In the back bedroom, used for company, Grandma's spinning wheel was mounted on the wall. She also had her carding boards, with sharp little teeth that made them perfect for sneaking up behind somebody and giving them a good scratch. She said she would take down the wheel and set it up and show us how to spin, but she never did. The room had a musty, unused smell. There was a slogan nailed to one wall; it was blue with glittering Old English type that said, "Blessed Are the Pure In Heart/ For They Shall See God." I was crawling under the bed once and found a bottle of clear liquid. I knew it had been hidden, and I brought it out, opened it, and touched it to my tongue. It was awful stuff. Why would anybody want to drink something that tastes like pine straw? I put it back exactly where I'd found it. Years after the house had been razed and the pine trees tall, one of my brothers and I were wandering back through the woods behind the old place and found our grandparents' trash dump in a swale. Amongst the rusted cans were Gordon's gin bottles.

During those gray, clammy cold winter afternoons, the two sat in their rocking chairs and rarely talked. The chairs creaked, the mantel clock ticked. When they did speak, it was usually to quarrel, in snappish bursts, about anything. They were always irritable with each other, and they especially liked sparring over who would die first. She would say, "When I die, I want you to see that Vadie gets the chiffarobe." And he would say, "Oh, I'll die long before you. Motts live forever." She would sull and begin to twiddle her thumbs or take up pleats in her apron, pull them out, and start over. The fire would sizzle, and he would sigh dramatically. Like other old, long-married couples, they had become mirrors of one another's mortality. Eventually, he would stalk out of the house and go find some work, any work, to do.

Left alone with her, and her not talking, I would look out the window, past the pomegranate bushes, at the cornfield beyond in the paling fence, the stripped brown stalks tilted in crazy angles. In the middle of the field was an abandoned open well, with a fence around it and weeds and bushes growing inside. Children were warned not to go near that fence because of Old Redhead-and-Bloody Bones. That creature lived in the old well, and he would jump out, snatch little children, take them back down into the dark depths, and eat them up.

I suppose it was during these moments when Papa was working off his cabin-fever ill humor that he went all over his place pruning pine trees as far as he could reach with an axe. He probably turned that domestic wrath into other good works as well, for his sheds and cribs were always orderly, the plows, tools, and harness neatly placed. He kept seven or eight head of Red Poll cows, an old dual purpose (meat and milk) breed that I never saw since. They were skittish and mean and able to outrun a stripling boy. Papa quit plowing at age eighty-four, they said, on account of his mule had died.

Grandma slept late in the mornings—another habit my dad attributed to the Motts—and Papa would get up and fix breakfast and then have to call her two or three times. At some time during their nearly sixty years of marriage, it had become the morning ritual. On January 23, 1956, he called her with his usual impatience—"Ay God, Mattie, I said get up!" When she didn't respond, he went into the bedroom and found her dead. They had no telephone, so he had to go a quarter mile to Ab Wilson's house. He must have forgotten his walking stick because he fell in the road, and Ab said he'd crawled much of the way. If he had any crying to do, he did it privately before the funeral.

Four years later, as he lay in that railed and canted hospital bed at our house in Antioch, after his fall, he was oblivious of the prayers muttered over him by various preachers, even when he was in his right mind. He was not, like his eldest son, formally religious. He had many superstitions, and I've forgotten many of them. He didn't like to see people walking around with just one sock on; and using two brooms at once on the same floor was also bad luck. I heard him scold Uncle Lenson about sharpening his pocket knife on a Sunday. "You'll see more blood than you want to before this week is out," he said.

Though his memory was copious, he lived much in the present. He liked action. If he was at our house after Grandma died, and he wanted to get back to his little house in Mitcham and the conversation was too silly or trivial to suit him, or he could not hold the floor, he'd take up his stick and say, "Well, I'll be walking on. You all can pick me up by the way." The talking would abruptly stop, and somebody would drive him home.

After World War II—he was nearly seventy-four when it ended— my brothers bought late-model cars and tried to scare him by floorboarding the gas pedal. When they got up to about eighty, he'd say, "Is that all this thing will do?" When the driver stopped at a red light and no cars were around he'd say, "Go on!" One morning after he'd been bedridden for a while, when only he and I were in the room, he told me, "I am getting up from this bed, Jerry, and you and me are going to fish the Columbia River."

When he was out of his head, he thought my mother was his aunt, Caroline, the wife of John Wesley Truett. As I've noted, Uncle John Truett was the brother of Papa's mother, Winnie Truett, and the one who cared for his brother-in-law, Papa's uncle on the Brown side, John L., as he died near Chickamauga in 1863, after being hit by cannon fire. I gathered Papa had stayed with the family of John and Caroline Ward Truett often when he was boy, and he'd fixated on his uncle John's wife as a nurturing woman. As Papa lay addled, he referred to my mother by that name so often that after a while I got to calling Mama "Aunt Caroline." When she was taking a pan of biscuits out of the oven, I'd say, "Them are some fine looking catheads, Aunt Caroline." She'd tell me to hush, but then she would get tickled. Anything to dispel that dread.

———•·•———

March, the time to begin putting in the crop, rolled around, but my dad couldn't leave Papa. So I hitched up our lean, mean, snuff-brown mule, Ida, and eventually laid off and planted the big field across the road, about twenty acres. For about two years I had done some plowing and knew gee from haw, but the rows usually were crooked or not contoured just to suit my dad. He was particular and prickly. I had trouble making the mule walk where I wanted her to. She went at a fast clip—my dad said she was out of a buggy mare—and even with a muzzle on she tried to nip at the sassafras bushes at the row end. When the plow ran too close to them at the turn, it would often rip out a root, and the fragrance would fill the air.

By the spring of '60, I was becoming a steadier hand. Getting ready to plow was easy, after I caught that damned mule. If I didn't bridle her in the stall, she'd bolt past me and run from one end of the calf pasture to the other, playing her hateful game until she was cornered. That done, I enjoyed the ritual of the harnessing.

First, I ran the currycomb over her old back and dobbed her fetlocks and flanks with tar-and-lard on a corncob to fend off horse flies. Then came putting on the collar, the hames, and the backband, setting the loggerheads, running the traces back to the bulkhead of the plow where the singletree was attached, and finally leading the cotton-rope plowlines back to the waiting stock. Then I'd take hold of the handles and say, *Humupah!*, just as my dad did, and off we'd go to the field, the plow hopping and skittering.

All through spring break—Alabama Education Association or AEA holidays, we called them—I followed from good daylight to near dark a cultivation ritual only slightly modified from the days when plows first broke ground in Mitcham Beat. With a turning plow, a steel-beamed moldboard turning plow we called an Oliver stock, I plowed one round, back and to, throwing up a bed or mound of the loamy soil. Between each bed was left an unplowed sliver of earth that we called the balk. After that was done throughout, I hitched Ida to a fertilizer distributor we called a knocker. It was a basic wooden Georgia stock with a shovelplow in front and a short heelsweep behind it. The plows would take out the balk and open a furrow for whatever nitrogen-phosphorus-potash analysis we were using—6-8-4 or 4-12-12, I forget. Cleats on the wheel shook the hopper, making that racket, keeping the fertilizer from clumping and making it flow evenly through the nozzle into the furrow.

When that was done, the third pass was with a spring-tooth, four-pronged harrow called a "gee-whiz" that would pull soil down from the edge of each bed. That plowing created the soft, moist, feminine seedbed in the furrow. Over it was run the planter, with a metal canister on top, underneath which was a changeable plate, notched and calibrated and geared to the revolutions of the planter wheel, so seed dropped at the distance set on that particular plate—for us, eighteen inches for corn, twelve for peas. The planter had a two-blade runner, shaped into a prow, in front that opened the ground and two beveled wheels behind that clamped over the seed that had fallen through the notches in the plate. When the planter had passed, behind us in the furrow were the mule's hoofprints, my tracks, and a neatly sealed triangle of mother earth. Beneath was the seed, waiting to spring.

The corn came first. I would plant two rows of Coker's 8-11 (we had switched from the old shoepeg of our ancestors to one of the new hybrids by 1960), and then I would skip a furrow. When the corn planting was done, I would put on another plate and pour purple-hull peas into the canister and plant the row left between the corn. Two rows of corn to one of peas, that was my dad's system. The legumes would add nitrogen to the soil, and they were also one of our major crops, because, by that time, my dad had turned almost exclusively to truck farming. Our cotton allotment was in pastureland, as the Soil Bank dictated. We still had a big patch of sugarcane for syrup to sop and sell. The field corn was for our meal barrel and to feed the stock. In patches and gardens scattered about we raised turnip greens, collards, sweet potatoes, tomatoes, watermelons, okra, sweetcorn, cantaloupes, butterbeans, snap beans, eggplants, and lady peas. My dad would sell anything to anybody—and he loved to peddle and haggle—but his main customers were grocery stores and greasy-spoon, meat-and-three cafes.

When World War II ended and so many people left the country and went into what my dad scorned as "public work," the market for vegetables in the towns increased. He seized the moment, and the flow of folding money also increased. Old man Steve Gordon, who ran a dry goods store in Grove Hill, his palsied head atremble, liked to tell my dad he was the only country fellow he knew who left town with more money than he'd brought in. It was during this period that we took prodigious leaps in our standard of living: We got a pump for the well, a deep freezer that resulted in the tearing down of the smoke house, a gas stove that replaced the old Home Comfort, and a television set. And all of that without my dad's borrowing from banks or submitting to bosses in the public workplace.

Throughout that planting time, when I was going on fifteen, I would come in from the fields near sundown, stall and feed the mule, after she'd wallowed in a bed of dust by the crib. Then I'd milk the two cows and come in to find my father, musing by Papa's bedside, with his finger moving slowly under his nose. He would look up at me, sad and worried, and ask me how the day had gone. It was the first time in his working life that he himself had never played a role in the spring planting. When I told him all was well between me and ole Ida, he would thank me, and a great feeling of manhood would flood my chest. With Papa in the bed, my dad in a chair, and me standing by him, we made a tableau of three generations of South Alabama dirt farmers.

My mother always had a big supper laid out, after her fashion at every meal. My dad said she always cooked enough to feed a log rolling, even if we didn't have company. For supper, there would be fried corn-cakes and buttermilk and God knows how many vegetables and meats and desserts. Whoever was there ate with us, with at least one person left by the bed. Papa and I would probably have our moment, later in the night. Our ritual had become so familiar I was too young or tired or exhilarated to dwell on what was coming.

———•◦•———

When the school bus let me off that last Friday of April, there were only a few cars in front of the house, not enough to trigger an alarm. My mother was taking clothes off the line by the chicken yard. She had her washday apron on, its pockets bulging with pins. She was folding sheets and putting them into a wicker basket. She called me over, and her demeanor was stern. I knew what that meant. When nothing was wrong, she could be high-strung. But in a crisis, she was cool, crisp, and commanding. "He's going to die this afternoon," she said, "and there's nobody in that room with him but your daddy and the family. You go get somebody else in here."

I got in our '54 Chevrolet pickup—the key must have been in the switch—and set out. I'd driven over our field roads and on the dirt roads from Antioch to Hebron but never on the blacktop; I didn't even have a learner's permit. Everywhere I stopped there were complications: Mr. Moore was not home from work. Mr. Purvis couldn't drive but said somebody would get him there soon—which meant he had sense enough not to ride with me behind the wheel. Henley Harrell was off somewhere. When I got back, the same two or three cars, my aunts' and one uncle's, were there. I don't even remember which uncle it was, probably Uncle Hallie or Uncle Lenson. Uncle Dewey ran a service station in Theodore, down near Mobile, and Uncle Pete ran one in Port Arthur, Texas. They came when they could.

I stood outside the window of the room where Papa lay, watching a buzzard wheel high in the sky, hardly a forgettable image, even after these fifty years. My mother had stayed in the back of the house. All was quiet for a while. Then I heard the scream. It pierced my ears like an icepick. "O Papa! Don't go! Wake up!" I don't remember which aunt it was. And then my dad's voice, "Papa! Papa!" I knew he was weeping. Then one of my aunts started to preach: "O Jesus! If every sinner could be with us now! O Father, they would repent them of their sins!" How long this keening went on I cannot remember, but it rose into a chorus of wailing. I got away from there and went to the cow lot.

Soon people began to arrive. My mother had made it to the phone and gotten my brother Bobby, a Baptist preacher, and his sensible wife, Dorothy, a Harrison from Chilton, in upper Mitcham Beat. They took over. Dorothy went in and closed Papa's eyes and pulled the sheet over his face, and Bobby called Red Woodson, the undertaker in Jackson. By the time I had the guts to go back in the house, the hearse had come, and Red's men had taken Papa away. In the hall, I bumped into one of the aunts who'd been raving, expecting I'd have to mutter some comforting words, but she was as steady as a stone. The Browns were never a maudlin people, and they disdained anything but formal expressions of emotion in public. When the old folks saw someone taking on dramatically and hysterically at a funeral, to attract attention, they were known to say, "Ashes to ashes, dust to dust, one fried chicken would hush that fuss." Somebody stopped the mantel clock, and everybody left but the three of us.

I finished my chores, and Mama put supper on the table. Afterwards, my dad went out on the front porch and started to rock. Soon his old friend and hunting partner Clarence Snell drove up in his battered Jeep station wagon, and they talked far into the night, about mundane things, crops and weather and world news, with no mention of what had happened that afternoon. Mr. Clarence knew about death and suffering. He'd been in the Rainbow Division in World War I, and he'd caught a piece of shrapnel under one eye that left a permanent hole in his cheekbone. Eventually it worked its way out, and he carried the fragment in his britches pocket. He was raised in that house—it was still called the Snell Place—before the family sold it to us in 1946. The Snells had also come over from Dale County, and the two old friends probably knew the families had intermarried over there in southeast Alabama. They were more like brothers or cousins than neighbors. I was worried about my dad and hid out in the privet hedges, listening. Given the even, unemotional tone of his voice, I hoped that whatever the public ceremony entailed, the worst was over.

That Saturday, I was in Grove Hill, at Peerless Drugs, when Mr. Dave Mathews, the man who had been a country teacher, a high school principal, a legislator, and the county school superintendent for several terms, came down the sidewalk. He later became known as the county historian and the only person of standing who took up for Mitcham Beat people. He was an important person, a big man physically, proud and authoritarian, with a reared-back walking style, and I, a country boy, was surprised when it appeared he knew who I was. Maybe it was a cast in the eyes or a set of the ears, family marks he'd have recognized right off, without knowing my name. "A great old man died yesterday," he said, and kept walking. I think that was the first inkling I had that my grandfather had had something of a public, political life.

The plans for the funeral had been made long before Papa died, though I didn't know it. That was like my dad. He had gathered his brothers and sisters together and talked it over: Papa would lie a-corpse in his little house, up there below Aunt Grace's, and, of course, he would be buried beside Grandma, in Oak Grove Cemetery on Sunday afternoon, at two o'clock, after folks had gone to church and eaten their dinner.

With one of my brothers-in-law I got to Mitcham that Saturday about sundown. Cars lined the road on both sides. I dreaded that moment, scared to see my father. I found him in the yard, talking amiably with men I didn't recognize. We spoke, and I saw that he was all right, and I went into the house, filled with people. The death smell of the mums hit me at the door. I walked into the fireplace room, and there was the gray coffin, against the wall, on a silvery stand, the lid open. Papa lay with his head propped on a silk pillow, his moustache neatly trimmed, as he would have liked, and looking, all in all, dapper in a dark suit and necktie. I thought, "You do enjoy having the women make over you." My cousin Roger Truett, two years younger than I, and the great grandson of Uncle John and Aunt Caroline, told me years later that he saw Papa in his coffin and remembered that he looked "perfectly at peace."

Lee Brown's vanity, if nothing else, set him apart. Unlike other farmers, he never wore bib overalls. No one can remember seeing him in a pair. Always he was in britches and galluses. No one recalls seeing him without the top button of shirt buttoned, and never in a short-sleeved shirt, even in summer. In one old photograph I have studied many times over, taken in his sixties when he and Grandma were keeping a horde of the grandchildren, she is in a frumpy everyday dress, with the youngsters gathered round in dirty playclothes, and there he stands, in a necktie, with his moustache obviously dyed with blacking. I have his last overcoat, which must have cost him a fortune; it is fine wool, herringbone, and I guess it weighs five pounds.

As I stood by the open coffin, studying his body, the strong old face, with the high chiseled cheekbones and the deep septum of his nostrils, and the right hand folded across his heart with the bone felon on his index knuckle prominent, it was hard for me to take in that he was dead. Uncle Hallie must have felt the same way. He came up behind me and said, "He looks like he wants you to feed him another bowl of ice cream."

The crowd at his funeral might not have been so large had he not been buried on a Sunday, but that was his way. He always had good timing, and he enjoyed funerals, the bigger the better. They always seemed to make him merry, even if he didn't go into the sanctuary. That service was the second time I'd seen him inside a church; the other was when Grandma was in the coffin. He always stayed outside, sitting on the dinner tables and talking with other old men.

I don't remember what the preacher, Dr. H. Grady Ketchum, said over him at the funeral, but I do recall our singing the old standards, "Amazing Grace," "Rock of Ages," and, my favorite, "In the Sweet By and By." We'd sung the same hymns at Grandma's funeral. I was not even thinking of crying until I saw my dad pull out his handkerchief, and then it all broke loose. I too began to cry, deep heaving, uncontrollable, for a good man gone, for the spirit that hallowed our days. In those days before cremations, memorial services, and clever eulogies became the fashion, and photographs of the dead replaced mortal remains brought into the sanctuary, we grieved over the body lying before us. We grieved, as the procession of mourners filed by the open coffin for a final viewing. The deepest of that grief came when Red Woodson and his man folded the silks over the face, closed the lid, and turned the final, symbolic key. Then it was truly over: Papa had disclosed no secrets, expressed no regrets, claimed no credit, uttered no deathbed confession.

When the graveside ceremony was done, the crowd began to break up and move away, but I stood by the hole and watched a man nailing boards on top of the pine box and heard the first shovelfuls of yellow dirt thump hollow on the raw wood. We drove home in silence, and I went in the house and changed clothes. I had no thought then of what true story my grandfather had carried to his grave, or what memories lay buried under the other tombstones in that lonely cemetery. I'd be an old man myself before the telling details began to emerge.

The sun was going down, and I had the milking to do.

———•◦•———

FAMILY PHOTOS

Peter Irvine Brown (1837-1907)

(The following is a genealogical family group record form, printed sideways on the page.)

HUSBAND'S Name (in full)

TEMPLE ONE

(2nd) Peter Irvine Brown .... Place ....
abt. 1840
3 March 1907 .... Place .... Mc Intyre, Henson Co., Alabama
1863 .... Place .... Oak Grove, Mobile, Alabama
John Andrew Jackson Brown .... Mother (Maiden Name) .... Eula Ann Mulkey
.... Place .... Mc Intyre, Henson, Alabama

HUSBAND:
Baptized
Endowed
Heir
Relationship of Heir

WIFE:
Winnie Truett .... Place .... Ozark, Dale Co., Alabama
abt 1842
1900 .... Place .... Oak Grove, Mobile, Alabama
William Truett .... Mother (Maiden Name) .... Aley Wiggins
(List) Joshua Johnson

Baptized
Endowed
Sealed to Husband
Heir
Relationship of Heir

Where was information shown on this family record obtained? **Family records**

Name and address of person submitting this sheet:
James Joseph Zackariah Geiger
36 N. Gilbert St.
Mesa, Arizona
State .... Marriage
Ward .... Mesa First

CHILDREN (Give names in full in order of birth)	WHEN BORN Day Mo. Yr.	Town	WHERE BORN County	State or Country	DIED Mo. Yr. Day	MARRIED	BAPTIZED	END
Eula Ann Brown	1865	Mc Intyre	Choctaw	Ala	Silas Oct 19...	John Butto	24 June 1944	29 Ju
John Brown	1866	Mc Intyre	Henson	Ala	Oak Grove, Clarke Co. Ala 1887		24 June 1944	29 Ju
Fernie Brown	1868	Mc Intyre	Henson	Ala	Oak Grove, Clarke Co. Ala 1898		24 June 1944	28 Ju
Lee or Leroy Brown	14 Sept 1871	Mc Intyre	Choctaw	Ala		Martha Ann Witt		
Mattie Brown	1873	Mc Intyre	Henson	Ala	Escambia Co. Ala Jan 1941	Allen Tyree	24 June 1944	29 Ju
Mary Brown	1873	Mc Intyre	Henson	Ala		Henry Hutchinson		
Ellie Brown William W.	1875	Mc Intyre	Clarke	Ala		Addie Bennett		
Della Brown	1877	Mc Intyre	Henson	Ala		William Lewis		
Elijah Brown	1879	Mc Intyre	Henson	Ala		Delia Pugh		

1941. Joseph Fielding Smith, Church Recorder. Printed in U.S.A.

Indicate which child is the direct ancestor of the heir by placing an "X" in front of name.

The left portion of the Peter and Winnie Brown family records in the oblong pedigree compiled by Zack Geiger. Several family groupings are included in the binder. Peter was Winnie's second husband, as Geiger noted, and Joshua Johnson her first. Peter Brown's middle is spelled exactly like the valley and town in southern Scotland, suggesting ties to that country. Spouses of the siblings and Mormon data complete the page.

Andrew Jackson Mott (1840-1917) and Harriett Ann Hutto Mott (1845-1932)

Ferdinand (Ferdie) and Lee Brown, c. 1890
Their mother spun the yarn and wove the cloth for the jackets, which she made.

Lee and Mattie Mott Brown stand solidly and independently in front of their house near Angus Hill's store. The paling fence was typical. The lean-to roof over Grandma's left shoulder covered an extension of the porch and a dug well, conveniently located. Passersby could stop for a cool drink of water and rest under the shade of the big live oak.

Lee and Mattie pose with grandchildren. On the right is a neighbor, Lucy Brunson.
Typically, Lee Brown is wearing a necktie and his moustache has been blackened.

Mattie Mott Brown, left, with her mother, Harriet Ann Hutto Mott and her sister Edna Powers. Photo taken at a family reunion, probably in the late 1920s. Grandma Mott, a native of Dale County, died in 1932, at age 85.

This photo of Elijah Brown, c. 1918, was used by forensics experts at the University of Montana and the Missoula Police Department, to identify the cover photograph. The women on either side are probably a granddaughter and her mother.

Taken probably by a traveling photographer about 1904, this well-composed photo depicts a merry Peter Brown with his second wife and two youngest sons, Billy and Elijah, who are dressed in matching hunting garb. The canvas leggings are to protect from briers. The house is board-and-batten with the open hall visible to the left and the cypress shingling evident.

Lee Brown, my parents and me, Easter 1957

John Coley and Alliene Etheredge Brown at their home in McVay, about 1968.

Howell Hutto in 1980 at a dinner-on-the-grounds at Oak Grove Church. He died in 1983, in his 99th year. A cousin of Mattie Brown, he was an eight-year-old when Tooch Bedsole was killed by the mob, and he counted six bullet holes in the tobacco plug Bedsole had in his left shirt pocket.

W.E.T "Babe" Burke and his wife, the former Sally Hare, c. 1890

Called the Black House School, because the original had burned, this one-room structure was located on what is now called Brunson Road. This photograph was taken about 1912. At far left, front row, in knickers is John Coley Brown. Beside him is his brother, Connie. Sixth and seventh in the row are brothers Hallie and Pete. Their sister Vadie is in the striped dress. Vernie and Alice Goodman are on the back row, between the big girl and the big boy. In the bowtie is teacher Sid Payne. He was in France in World I and later was the Browns' neighbor in the Antioch community.

Lenson Brown, center, was not only the star southpaw pitcher for the Mitcham baseball team, he apparently could dress in his white courting clothes after the victory and serenade the team. At far right, in chest protector with his catcher's mitt under his arm, is Lee and Mattie's youngest son, Dewey. Displaying a range of get-up, from cleats and uniform britches to bib overalls are, from left, Vidman Small, Bill Huggins, and Vollie Small.

The shattered tombstone of John Robert Pinkerton in New Prospect Cemetery. Efforts to mend the marker, which may have been shattered by rifle shots, failed. The date of his death is still visible.

ACKNOWLEDGMENTS

The flaws, errors in fact, lapses in logic, digressions, switchbacks, repetitions, and twisted sentences in this book are the sole property of the author. The property, like most of what was Mitcham Beat, is posted. However, merely for the price of this book, I offer permission for readers to rove the old lands.

I have pointed out, now and again, that this book is not an exercise in scholarship. I have eschewed, to my delight, footnotes and bibliography. I call this a work of journalism, a term that is stretched so wide these days that it refers to any ephemeral communication or televised bombast. But I am using it in a typically antique sense—verifiable facts from a transparently subjective source.

In the midst of many muddles, I have had much help over the years, so these acknowledgments must, of necessity, be longer than normal.

I offer the following, earnest expressions of gratitude:

Of all those whose assistance I acknowledge, none stands higher than Fred Huggins. He is the grandson of William Wrighty Brown, Lee Brown's brother, and of Beatrice Bennett, a member of a highly respected

Mitcham family. On his father's side, he is also related to the Bedsole family. Fred was eleven when Uncle Billy, Aunt Attie, and his parents left the old place, joining the Mitcham diaspora. Fred knows that community better than I ever will, and to that knowledge is added the even more expansive knowledge of his late mother, Cousin Nora. She was a natural historian, a careful story teller, and a repository of wisdom. Moreover, she was blessed with those warm and welcoming country manners I admire so much. Fred was the first descendant of Peter and Winnie Brown to be elected to county office, illustrating one of the main points in this book. Though the stigma of Mitcham Beat sent him into a runoff for his first six-year term as probate judge, he was elected outright for two more. He was probate judge for as long as John Marshall Wilson. Later, others in our family would rise to county offices, one sign that Mitcham people came to value public engagement.

I have shamelessly leaned on Judge Huggins as this manuscript has evolved. Not only is he a master of public records, he is also an excellent writer and editor—which is no surprise considering he was a newspaperman before being elected probate judge. His wife, Gloria, has provided a more objective view as she has followed our discussions, deliberations, and debatings with amusement and bafflement—natural reactions amongst those who were not raised around the quaint, often eccentric ways of that community.

I owe Fred an additional debt: One of his Huggins cousins, Kathy Abel, gathered and organized Clarke County archival records and helped me locate key documents. Clarke County is one of the few in Alabama where the courthouse has never burned. Records in the vault go back to February 1813. Those holdings are a treasure.

Fred is writing his own book, and it will include moving and often funny stories. He has read several drafts of this exercise, and I have heeded his advice in all matters except his efforts to divert the compliments in these acknowledgments.

The faithful work of two other cousins is also reflected in these pages. Wayne Harrison was the first to discover the old documents in the courthouse, and Roy L. Mott, Sr., a pioneer genealogist and early master of computer technology, is the authority on Mott family history.

I have often given formal credit to Hardy Jackson, Joyce Burrage, Jim Cox, but that's hardly enough. Without the work of these three, I would not have had the footing necessary to begin. Each has read portions of the manuscript in earlier drafts, offered valuable comments, and granted me permission to apply their good work. Moreover, Hardy provided me with the research by Joyce Fuller and others which was drawn on for their history of the Mitcham War. As a final favor, he put me in touch with Jane Powers Weldon, who copyedited this manuscript and won my lasting respect for her wordsmithing. Clarke Countian Tommy Franklin's novel, *Hell-at-the-Breech*, offers a perspective different from mine, and characters not consistent with those in my memory, but it stands on its own as an imaginative exercise in prose fiction.

Others have helped more than they can know. David Vest, a poet, musician, scholar, humorist, and genuine genius, is the Alabamian who prodded me into writing about Mitcham Beat. Whether my old Vanderbilt friend regrets doing so, after reading this book, is a matter for his own conscience. In prompting a less talented writer, he has only himself to blame.

One of my nieces, Stephanie Oliver Hutchinson, assembled the large digital file of family photographs from which most of the images in this book were taken. Our family owes much to her service, skill, and good spirit. One of my nephews, Daniel Glen Overton, head of Clarke County's engineering division, has provided maps and knowledge of topography that have been invaluable as I have tried to envision the environs of Mitcham Beat in the time span covered in this book. Another nephew, Don Daugherty, a Vanderbilt-educated lawyer, offered sound suggestions about the writing and spent a day with me in the courthouse, poring over records and explaining arcane legal procedures—and he did this even as he was dying of cancer.

Historian Jean Till Styles, whose forebears and mine came together, in the same ship, from Switzerland to South Carolina in 1735, has written an invaluable essay on the general circumstances and the particular recruitment of those German-Swiss pioneers. Those who trace their lineage to the Orangeburgh families and the South Carolina mindset will benefit much from Jean's scholarship, as indeed I have.

My friend and former colleague Leah Atkins, whose history of Alabama Power Company, is a masterwork, set me straight about the career of Massey Wilson, a man who deserves his own biography. My sometime North Carolina neighbor Edwin Bridges, director of the Alabama Department of Archives and History, has not only assisted me personally, but he has directed me to a scholar on his staff, Norwood Kerr, and the researcher Ken Barr, who tracked down many of the newspaper accounts.

Sheila Sprague, a descendant of the distinguished Bell family, provided me with the letters Captain John W. Bell wrote to his wife from Civil War battlefields, and her cousin, Johnny Doggett, sent me copies of the ledger of the captain's son, John R. Bell, the Mitcham Beat merchant who plays a key role in this account. The Bell and Brown families have now been related by vicinity and respect for 150 years.

Alan Pitts is the most knowledgeable person about Alabama Civil War records I've encountered, and his on-line service to the inquiring public deserves an award. Together with his advice and my own searches through ancestry.com and footnote.com, I have been able to track the careers of many of the veterans who shaped the society of Mitcham Beat and to avoid many mistakes. James Staub, late the associate provost of the University of Montana and a student of firearms, explained to me how those .38-caliber Winchesters operated and identified the rifles in the hands of my great uncles.

Pierre Manigault, a descendant of the commander of the Alabama 24th Regiment, sent me General Manigault's memoirs, *A Carolinian Goes to War*, which offers an objective, inside view of the realities of that ordeal. My great and good friend, the late Dr. Ed Dyas, an orthopedic surgeon in Mobile and honorary member of the Brown family, explained to me in detail what a .58-caliber bullet would do in the lower leg of a young man shot down in the chill of the Stone's River battlefield and how Civil War surgery was done.

For the information related to Dale County, I am happy to thank Manonia Snell, who prepared a comprehensive, invaluable genealogy of Browns and other families who came from South Carolina. Her husband, Jesse, is a descendant of Louis Brown, brother of Jack Brown. Jesse's grandfather was Louis Brown, Jr., who came to Clarke County with the migration but returned to Dale County after the war.

My long-time friend, Judge Val L. McGee, the historian of Dale County, researched land records, offered insights, sent maps, and even provided me with a soil survey revealing how poor the land was in the Choctawhatchie valley. He spent hours helping me, even as he was completing *Selma: A Novel of the Civil War*. No work better describes the subtle legal aspects of slavery or the folly of heeding demagogues.

Margaret Pinkerton Cox of Choctaw County proved to be a key source for information on her family, within which John Robert Pinkerton was an exception, a fact all of us from extended families can relate to. I hope she writes about the adventures of the many entrepreneurial and honorable Pinkertons.

Michael Strong, a scholar, editor, and literary agent, read early and late drafts and offered some realistic advice about the commerce of publishing a book that hews to no genre and appeals to a limited audience. Surely, he is right, and, like the rest of us, he has a living to make.

Sam Hodges, a reporter, novelist, historian, and a writer of immense skill and incisive wit—and, I must add, a heart inclined to charity—has served as coach, sounding-board, and inspiration. This assessment of Sam's character and competence is far from original.

My friend and very distant cousin Nelle Harper Lee, maybe the most beloved writer in America and a frank, funny, and wonderfully kind person, read the manuscript and wouldn't let me stop fiddling with it. A heartening, stern word from her is worth a thousand from strangers.

My colleagues at the University of Montana School of Journalism have listened with patience to some of these rambling anecdotes, though their eyes were often fixed on the middle distance. To Carol Van Valkenburg, Dennis Swibold, Jeff Hull, Clem Work, Kathleen Whetzel, Keith Graham, and Nadia White, and other supportive colleagues in that exceptional school for writers and thinkers and supporters of the First Amendment, I express my respect and gratitude.

I have been fortunate to have received an education and to have had opportunities not available to my ancestors. I list the following six teachers with homage and lasting appreciation of their dedication, intelligence, and influence: Fannie Ruth White, Alice Williams, Zell Chunn, Lucy McVay, Kathleen Davis, and, especially, Lily G. Lawlis—my teachers from first to sixth grade. Without the democratic example they set, inspired by such leaders as Dave Mathews and Sid Payne, few of us from the dirt roads would have seen that open American avenue before us.

At Auburn, my journalism teachers were two immensely intelligent men of exemplary integrity, Paul Burnett and Mickey Logue. Their red marks throughout this manuscript would send me straight back to the pea patch. They did the best anybody could to confirm that journalism is essential to democracy, and that it begins with accurate facts and clear writing and requires readers who value the same.

But other good teachers, in and out of the formal classroom, left their marks: Neil Davis, Jack D. Smith, Charlie Rose, Sara Hudson, Frank Barbaree, Donald R. Smith, Bob McGiffert, Taylor Littleton, Bob Sanders, John Dunkelberger, Joe Hood, John Fletcher, Max Bass, Allen Pearson, Caine Campbell, Malcolm McMillan, Budge Breyer, Bob Mount, Husky Kirkwood, Tom Lenard, and Lowell Wilson. This panegyrical paragraph would not be complete without due tribute to administrator-leaders: E.V. Smith, Harry Philpott, Ed Hobbs, Paul Parks, William Muse, Jack Simms—all protective of the promise and prospect of a land-grant school too often identified with football and political tomfoolery.

In graduate school at Hollins College I benefited from association with Malcolm Cowley, George Garrett, Richard Dillard, Lee Smith, Julia Sawyer, and Shelby Foote. At Vanderbilt, I found instruction and inspiration in Thomas Daniel Young, H.L. Weatherby, Rob Roy Purdy, John V. Glass, Jim Colquitt, Edgar Hill Duncan, Robert Hunter, and Walter Sullivan—great men, all.

Two of my teachers deserve special thanks, Ward Allen of Auburn University, the noted *Authorized Version* (KJV) scholar, the most faithful of correspondents and the wisest of men, and, finally and forever, James Melville Cox of Dartmouth College, the famous Mark Twain scholar and the single most brilliant and inspiring human being I ever met.

And, then, within my own family, there are those whose presence permeates every page. They are Elmore, Tollie, Roy, Pauline, Dot, Henry, Bobby, Christine, Lucille, Eloise, Georgia, Alice, and Marie— my thirteen siblings. Though the boys are gone on, I think of all of my brothers and sisters as living, vibrant, and various—and generally far too kind to an often mean, always inquisitive little brother. And their mates were equally tolerant, even indulgent. When I think of their many acts of kindness, their instruction, and their patient forbearance, I feel both damned lucky and, uncharacteristically, humble.

My old friend Dick Parker, who heads Looking Glass Books, a talented writer as well as successful publisher, was brave and cordial enough to take on this project and to put my ragged manuscript into the hands of designer Burtch Hunter, whose skills are evident from cover to cover. Without their help, this book would not have become a reality.

My wife, Libby, a Nashvillian, has listened with patience to these maunderings and consistently offered sensible advice and the strength of her own character and lovely grace. Our daughters, Brooks and Lindsay, are smart readers and sharp editors, with thoroughly wicked senses of humor, though for the life of me I don't know how they could be so compulsively critical and effusively argumentative. Surely they take after their mother's people.

J E B